MAP OF WESTERN EUROPE

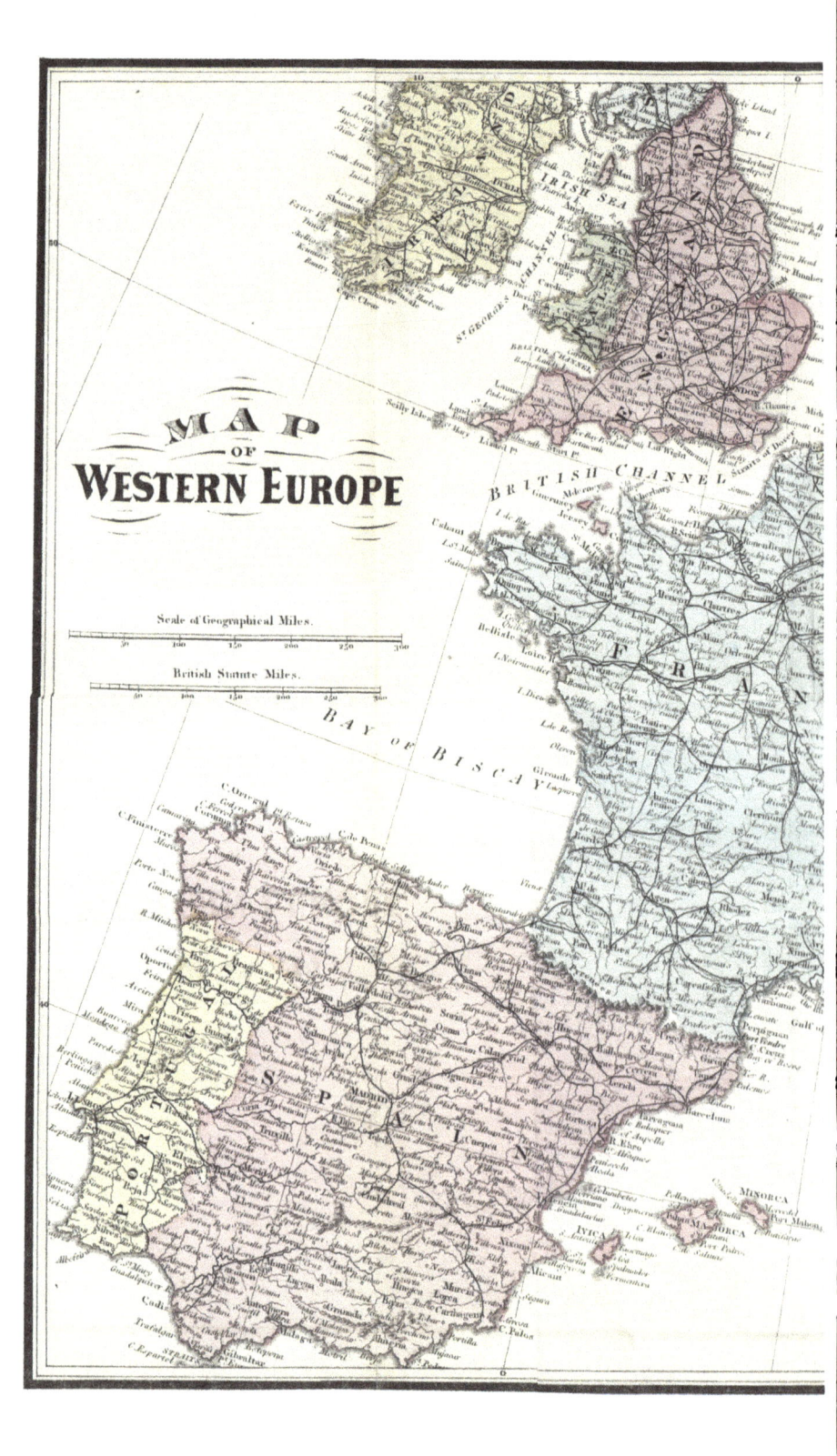

Scale of Geographical Miles.

British Statute Miles.

DENMARK
BALTIC
COPENHAGEN
HOLLAND
GERMANY
PRUSSIA
BERLIN
POLAND
WARSAW
AUSTRIAN EMPIRE
VIENNA
HUNGARY
SWISS
PIEDMONT
TUSCANY
ITALY
ROME
NAPLES
CORSICA
SARDINIA
GULF OF VENICE OR ADRIATIC SEA
DALMATIA
CORFU
CEFALONIA

THE YEAR OF BATTLES:

OR THE

FRANCO-GERMAN WAR OF 1870-'71.

COMPRISING A HISTORY OF ITS ORIGIN AND CAUSES, THE BIOGRAPHIES OF THE KING OF PRUSSIA, THE EX-EMPEROR OF FRANCE, AND THE STATESMEN AND GENERALS OF THE TWO COUNTRIES; THE FINANCIAL, SOCIAL, AND MILITARY CONDITION OF EACH, THE WEAPONS IN USE, AND AN ACCURATE HISTORY OF ALL THE MILITARY MOVEMENTS AND BATTLES OF THE WAR, THE REVOLUTION IN FRANCE, THE SURRENDER OF PARIS; THE CONCLUSION OF THE WAR, THE TREATY OF PEACE, AND THE ORGANIZATION OF A PROVISIONAL GOVERNMENT.

BY

L. P. BROCKETT, M.D.,

AUTHOR OF "HISTORY OF THE CIVIL WAR," "CAMP, BATTLE-FIELD AND HOSPITAL," "WOMAN'S WORK IN THE CIVIL WAR," "OUR GREAT CAPTAINS," ETC., ETC.

WITH MAPS, PLANS OF BATTLES, AND NUMEROUS PORTRAITS, ILLUSTRATIONS, AND BATTLE SCENES.

By CHRISTIAN WEBER.

SOLD ONLY BY SUBSCRIPTION.

New York:
J. W. GOODSPEED & CO., 37 PARK ROW,
GOODSPEED & CO., CHICAGO: A. H. HUBBARD, PHILADELPHIA:
H. H. NATT & CO., CINCINNATI, OHIO.
1871.

Entered, according to Act of Congress, in the year 1871,
By L. P. BROCKETT, M.D.
In the Office of the Librarian of Congress at Washington.

THE NEW YORK PRINTING COMPANY,
205, 207, 209, 211 213 East 12th Street.

PREFACE.

THE writer feels that no apology is necessary for the attempt here made to portray the progress of a war which, in its rapid movement, its terrible destructiveness, and its stupendous results, is without a parallel in history.

The ties which bind us to both the great nations which have been engaged in this sanguinary conflict—ties of kindred, friendship, and commercial intercourse—have made every step of its progress more interesting to us as a people than any other war of modern times, except that in which we ourselves were so recently engaged; and these considerations are sufficient to commend to popular interest any work which gives succinctly, lucidly, and accurately, the events of such a contest.

A large experience in historical composition, and especially in the preparation of histories of our own war, has, the writer would fain hope, given him some special qualifications for undertaking this work. It has been his first aim to secure as complete accuracy as possible; and hence he has had recourse to official reports and documents, where they were to be had, and also to the testimony of intelligent and capable eye-witnesses of the various battles. The work is not, however, a mere compilation of war correspondence and official documents. Every battle has been carefully studied, and plans drawn of the position of each army and the course of their movements; and the writer has not felt disposed to rest satisfied without attempting to convey to his readers the same clear and vivid idea of each battle which his careful studies had enabled him to attain.

The preliminary chapters, giving the history of the causes of the war, the military, naval, and financial position of the two countries, the description and comparison of their weapons, and biographical sketches of the prominent actors in the war, will be found, he hopes, to possess intrinsic value, irrespective of the war itself. They are from authentic sources in all cases, and in many instances from such as are not generally accessible.

The maps and plans are compiled from the best German and French sources, and from the official reports of the battles and sieges, and are believed to be remarkably accurate. The portraits are from undoubted originals, and these, as well as the drawings of weapons and battle-scenes, are the work of some of our best artists.

The material for the work has been ample, and while for the official narratives, biographies, &c., we have gone directly to the French and German sources, we have found some of the best descriptions, both of the topography and the actions themselves, in the correspondence of Major Forbes and Mr. Holdsworth with the London *Daily News*, the war-letters of the New York *Tribune*, *Herald*, *World*, and *Times*, the Cincinnati *Gazette* and *Commercial*, and the *Courrier des Etats-Unis*, and the admirable "Diary of the War" of the *Army and Navy Journal*. We have been indebted also for many items to the various statistical and biographical works, in which both England and the Continent so greatly excel us.

If the work shall accomplish its purpose of gratifying the natural anxiety of our people to know more fully, accurately, and minutely, the particulars of the greatest, and, we would fain hope, also the last of modern wars, the ambition of the author will be fully satisfied.

L. P. B.

BROOKLYN, N. Y., April, 1871.

CONTENTS.

CHAPTER I.

The remote and proximate causes of the War.—Encroachments of France upon Germany in the past three hundred years.—Alsace and Lorraine.—Westphalia and the Rhine Provinces.—Belgium.—Restoration of the last three to their rightful owners.—Avenging Waterloo.—The Rhine and Adriatic boundary.—Movements of Napoleon III to accomplish this.—His jealousy of Prussia.—His preparations for War.—The introduction of the Chassepôt rifle and the *Mitrailleuse*.—The want of genuine preparation for the War on the part of France.—Other reasons for the War.—France restive.—The *plebiscite*.—Napoleon's health.—Religious motives.—France in a secondary position.—The occasion of War.—The Hohenzollern candidacy.—Sketch of Prince Leopold.—Protest of the French Emperor.—His interview with General Prim.—Declination of Prince Leopold.—New pretexts.—The alleged insult to Count Benedetti.—The missives sent to German States supposed to be disaffected.—The French declaration of War...pp. 13-19

CHAPTER II.

Biographical sketches.—WILHELM I, King of Prussia.—His birth, education, absolutist principles.—His Accession to the Throne.—His personal appearance, manners and character. NAPOLEON III.—His parentage, birth, education.—Joins the Carbonari.—Involved in Italian Conspiracies.—Attempts authorship.—Becomes the legal heir of Napoleon I.—The Strasbourg affair in 1836.—His banishment to America.—Is coldly received there.—His return to Switzerland.—Death of his mother.—His escape to England.—Publication of his *Idées Napoléoniennes* and *Rêveries Politiques*.—The Boulogne fiasco.—His arrest, trial, and sentence to imprisonment at Ham.—His studies and writings at Ham.—Escape to England in 1846.—His life in England.—The Revolution of 1848.—Election of Louis Napoleon to the National Assembly.—His return to France.—His election as President.—His policy.—His aspirations for permanent and supreme power.—Efforts to change the Constitution.—Uneasiness of the French people.—The *coup d'état* of Dec. 2, 1851.—The first *plebiscite*.—Further steps toward despotism.—Proclaims himself Emperor.—"The Empire is Peace."—His Marriage.—Alliance with England.—The Crimean War.—His policy as Emperor.—Birth of the Prince Imperial.—Overestimation of Napoleon III.—The Italian War.—His mismanagement.—The compact with Cavour.—The threatening attitude of Prussia.—Treaty of Villafranca.—Napoleon's disappointment.—Acquisition of Savoy and Nice.—His failing health.—Troubles.—The attempt to intervene in behalf of the Southern Confederacy.—The War with Mexico.—He makes a dupe of Maximilian.—Sad end of this War.—The Cochin China and Chinese Wars.—The promise of reforms.—The Austro-Prussian War.—Prussian superiority demonstrated.—His offers to and demands upon each of the belligerents.—Their rejection.—His Life of Cæsar.—His determination to bring on a War.—His character in brief........................pp. 20-38.

CHAPTER III.

Biographical sketches continued.—Count von Bismarck-Schonhausen.—His birth and education.—Entrance upon public life.—A Conservative.—His pamphlet, "Prussia and the Italian Question."—Minister at St. Petersburg and Paris.—Premier, and Cabinet Minister.—His bold measures.—The opposition evoked.—The Danish War.—The War with Austria.—The wisdom of his measures demonstrated.—His extraordinary abilities and foresight.—His personal appearance.—His scholarship.—His impaired health.

General von Moltke.—His birth and education.—Military studies at Copenhagen.—Straitened circumstances.—His eminent attainments.—His rapid promotion.—His mission to Turkey and Asia Minor.—Authorship.—His advancement to the position of Chief of Staff.—His herculean labors.—His remarkable topographical and geological knowledge.—His extraordinary prescience and knowledge of the character of his antagonists.—His personal exploration of military routes.—His interview with General de Wimpffen.—Personal appearance and manners.

The French Premiers and War Ministers.—Ollivier and Rouher.—General Leboeuf.—Birth and education.—Promotion.—Commandant of Polytechnic School.—Chief of Artillery.—General of Division, 1857.—Distinguished in the Italian War.—Minister of War in 1867.—His corrupt management relative to the Chassepôt rifle.—His recklessness and dishonesty.

Count de Palikao.—His birth, education and military career.—His experiences in Algeria, France and China.—His stern and cruel disposition.

Other French generals.—The old soldiers.—The three Marshals.—Marshal MacMahon.—His birth and education.—Early career in Africa.—His courage and daring.—Ability as a tactician.—Capture of the Malakoff.—His skilful strategy at Magenta.—Duke of Magenta.—Representative of France at King Wilhelm's coronation.—Subsequent command in France and Algeria.

Marshal Canrobert.—His birth and education.—His African career.—Adhesion to Louis Napoleon.—Service in the Crimean War.—In the Italian War.—Senator of France.

Marshal Bazaine.—His education.—Military experience in Algeria, Spain, and the Crimea.—His part in the Mexican Expedition.—His cruelty, greed, and mismanagement there.—His corruption and rapacity.

The French corps-commanders, Frossard, De Failly, l'Admirault, &c.—General de Wimpffen.—Gen. Trochu..pp. 39–56

CHAPTER IV.

Biographical sketches continued.—Prince Friedrich Karl.—Birth and education.—His entrance into the Army.—His fondness for military studies.—Frederick the Great his exemplar.—A staff-officer under von Wrangel in 1848, in the first Schleswig-Holstein War, and the Baden Campaign in 1849.—Commander of the Prussian Contingent in the Danish War of 1864.—His gallantry in the assault on Düppel.—His command of the first Army in the Austrian War of 1866.—Sadowa.—His pamphlet on improvements in military organizations.—The changes which followed.—His interview with von Moltke.—Prince Friedrich Wilhelm.—Birth, education.—A pupil of von Moltke.—A corps-commander in 1864.—Commander of the Second Prussian Army in 1866, and the hero of Sadowa.—His ability in handling large bodies of troops.

General von Steinmetz.—Birth, education.—Wounded at Dannegkow in 1813.—Entered Paris with the Allies in 1815.—"The Lion of Skalitz."—A stern, imperious old man.—The German corps and army commanders...pp. 57–63.

CHAPTER V.

Financial condition of France and Germany.—Difficulty in arriving at the facts relative to the French finances.—The latest statistics of French revenue and expenditure.—The constant deficits.—Seven loans from 1854 to 1870.—Cost of the Wars during the reign of Napoleon III.—

CONTENTS. 7

Imports and Exports.—The national debt.—Its enormous amount.—Valuation of property in France.
Financial condition of the North German Confederation.—Revenues of 1869-70.—Ordinary and Extraordinary Expenditure.—Revenue of Prussia.—Her Expenditure with about the same population.—Her Expenditure only two sevenths of that of France.—No deficits.—Items of Expenditure.—The national debt of Prussia, small.
Social condition of the two countries.—Intelligence and Morals in Germany.—Condition of France in these respects.—Military and naval strength of the two countries.—Over-statement of French military strength.—Under-estimate of Prussian military power.—Causes.—The French reports of their Army.—Its vast numbers and presumed efficient condition.—The reserves, National Guard and *Garde Mobile*.—Almost two millions of soldiers—on paper.—The actual numbers.—One half the Army only existing on paper.—The German Armies.—Their actual numbers in each arm of the service.—Even these estimates largely exceeded.
The Navies of the two Nations.—Great number of vessels in the French Navy—55 Iron-clad Steamers.—Analysis of the character of these.—Their efficiency more apparent than real.—Their meagre success.
Prussian Navy.—Vessels few in number, but of remarkable efficiency.
The Cannon of the German Army.—Krupp's rifled breech-loaders.—Their great range and accuracy.
The French bronze Napoleons—muzzle-loaders.—The *Mitrailleuse*, its character and destructiveness.—The Needle-gun.—Full description of its mechanism.—The different methods of obturation or closing of the cylinder upon the barrel.—The Chassepôt rifle.—Its construction.—Comparison of the advantages and disadvantages of the two..................pp. 64-91.

CHAPTER VI.

The circumstances attending the declaration of War, in detail.—Gen. Prim's visit to Napoleon III.—His correspondence with Prince Leopold.—His acceptance of the candidacy.—The King of Prussia's disapproval.—The Prince's persistence.—The French demand on Prussia, July 6.—Count Benedetti's instructions.—Mr. Ripley's account of the interviews of Benedetti with the King.—The demand of the French Government.—The offensive way in which they were presented.—Napoleon's preparations for immediate War.—The declaration of War.—The activity which followed, all over Christendom.—Return of King Wilhelm from Ems to Berlin.—His address to the Prussian Legislature.—War-loan voted.—Address of Napoleon III.—Its melodramatic character.—His address to the Army at Metz, July 28th.—The circular of von Bismarck to the Prussian representatives at the courts of Foreign Powers.—Efforts of the French Government to counteract the damaging effect of this exposure.—Attempts of other European Powers to effect a settlement.—Their futility.—Letter of Pope Pius IX to Napoleon III and King Wilhelm.—King Wilhelm's reply.—Forward movements of the French advance-guard.—Skirmishing.—Circulation of addresses by the Emperor among the South Germans, and the people of Schleswig-Holstein and Hanover.—Failure of these addresses to win any adherents to his cause.................................pp. 92-106.

CHAPTER VII.

The War begun.—King Wilhelm takes command of the German forces, August 2d.—His address to the troops, at Mayence.—Strength and position of the French forces on the 2d of August.—The German forces and their positions.—The affair at Saarbruck.—The Emperor's letter to the Empress.—The Tranquil Infant's baptism of fire.—Movements of the two armies.—The French fortify the Spicheren Hills back of Saarbruck.—MacMahon advances to Weissenburg.—Battle of Weissenburg, Aug. 4.—The Crown-Prince's report of the action.—Ad-

dress of Prince Friedrich Karl.—Gen. von Steinmetz's address to the First German Army.—
The battle of Spicheren heights or Forbach, Aug. 6.—Report of von Steinmetz.—Account of
the New York *Tribune* correspondent.—Casualties of the battle.—The advance of the
Crown-Prince toward Woerth.—The Battle of Woerth.—Attempts of the French commander
to rally his troops.—His retreat to Saverne.—Marshal MacMahon's report to the Emperor.—
King Wilhelm's despatch to the Queen.—"Our Fritz."—Napoleon III's despatches.—"He
goes to the Centre."—Gen. Leboeuf's report.—Attempts to keep the news from the French
people.—The proclamation of the Empress.—The statement of the Minister.—Changes in
the French government and military commands...pp. 107-129.

CHAPTER VIII.

Indications of a coming revolution.—Addresses and orders of Prince Friedrich Karl, the King, and von Steinmetz.—Their humane tenor.—Strasbourg summoned to surrender.—Proclamation of Gen. Uhrich in reply.—Proclamation of King Wilhelm to the French people.—Particulars of MacMahon's defeat at Woerth.—His order to his soldiers.—The reënforcements he received from De Failly, Canrobert, and De Caen.—His march towards Paris.—Pursuit by the Crown-Prince of Prussia.—Bazaine falls back upon Metz, and decides to retreat upon Verdun and Paris, leaving a large garrison at Metz.—The rapid advance and severe pressure of the German armies upon his rear.—Crossing of part of the Second Army at Pont à Mousson.—Napoleon III quits Metz, leaving an address to the inhabitants.—The battle of Courcelles, east of the Moselle.—Conflicting accounts.—The German report.—Correspondents' reports.—King Wilhelm's despatches.—French official report.—The Emperor's despatch to Eugenie.—Bazaine's necessity for retreat.—Critical position.—The two routes to Verdun.—His determination to seize and control one or both.—The battle of Vionville, or Mars-la-Tour, on the 16th of August.—Terrible fighting.—The Mars-la-Tour road completely blocked by the Second German Army.—Bazaine falls back to the line of Gravelotte.—The battle indecisive.—Heavy losses.—The German report.—Bazaine's reports.—Statement published in Paris.—Possibility of Bazaine's retreat by the Conflans road.—Napoleon III leaves Verdun with the little prince for Rheims.—The battle of Gravelotte.—The official account in the *Army and Navy Journal.*—King Wilhelm's despatches from Rezonville.—The *New York Tribune* correspondent's account.—Frightful slaughter.—The battle continues into the night. —Account of another correspondent.—The execution done by the Mitrailleuse at close quarters.—French and German artillery practice......................................pp. 130-167.

CHAPTER IX.

Gen. Trochu appointed Governor of Paris by the Emperor.—His proclamation to the people of Paris.—Organization of a committee of defence.—Gen. Trochu's address to the people and appeal to the soldiers.—Gen. MacMahon's movement on Chalons.—He turns northwestward to Rheims.—The attempt to raise the siege of Metz.—The route taken.—The movement a blunder.—Reasons why.—Difficulty of the country for rapid marching.—MacMahon's advance reaches Rethel and Mézières.—The pursuit by the German armies.—The lines on which they moved.—The action of August 30.—The advantage gained by the Germans.—Crossing the Meuse.—The 1st of September.—The intention to rest the German troops that day.—Change of plan.—Orders issued.—The plan of attack.—Position of the German armies.—The French troops forced back to Sedan.—They enter the town with the French.—The white flag raised.—King Wilhelm's account of the battles and surrender.—The terms of capitulation.—Telegrams from the King.—Gen. von Moltke's order for carrying out the capitulation.—Count von Bismarck's letter describing his part.—MacMahon wounded early in the fight.—De Wimpffen's address to his soldiers.—Controversy concerning the Emperor and de Wimpffen.—Description of the battle and surrender by a French officer.—Narrative of the *Tribune's* correspondent with the German army..pp. 167-223

CHAPTER X.

The sortie of Marshal Bazaine on the 31st of August and Sept. 1st.—He attempts to force a passage for his troops to the northeast of Metz.—Why this direction was taken.—Severe fighting.—He is beaten back at all points and retires behind the fortifications of Metz.—General Stieble (chief of staff to Prince Friedrich Karl) telegraphs the repulse of the sortie.—General Manteuffel's despatch.—The minor fortresses still holding out.—Condition of affairs at Paris.—The people deceived.—Their sudden awakening.—Great excitement.—Cries of *La Déchéance*.—Count de Palikao's official statement.—The vote of *déchéance* demanded.—The Revolutionists force the gates of the Tuileries.—The Empress escapes.—The three propositions before the *Corps Législatif*.—Adjournment of the Chamber.—The reassembling of the Chamber amid the turmoil of the mob.—Its dissolution.—The assembling of the Republicans.—The downfall of the Empire declared.—The Republic proclaimed and the members of the government announced.—Emmanuel Arago Mayor of Paris.—Rochefort released from St. Pélagie and made a member.—Address of the new republican government to the people.—The circular of M. Jules Favre to neutral powers.—Its defiant spirit.—Its folly.—M. Favre's negotiations for peace.—His interview with Bismarck.—The preliminary question of the power of the Provisional Government to bind the people of France.—Favre's proposals, and Bismarck's rejoinders.—Rejection of Bismarck's proposals by the French leaders.—Removal of the Government to Toul.—Their proclamation respecting the peace negotiations.—Bismarck's circular on the same subject.—His reasons for the claim made.—Advance of the German armies toward Paris.—Its investment complete on the 20th of September.—Surrender of Toul, Sept. 23d and of Strasbourg, Sept. 27th.—The condition of the French army and people.—Unwisdom of the leaders.—The suicidal policy of suffering an army of 430,000 men and a population of two millions to be besieged.—Losses of the French.—Their whole available force.—The want of leaders.—Condition of Paris.—Exaggeration of the most trifling success and manufacture of wholesale falsehoods in regard to defeat of the Prussians.—The reaction in the feeling of sympathy at first manifested for the French Republic in consequence of these falsehoods.—The two-headed French government.—Efforts to raise the army of the Loire.—The irregular troops of the Republic.—Sorties from Paris and Metz.—The sortie from Paris of the 19th of Sept.—Ducrot defeated and routed.—Subsequent sorties unsuccessful.—The German troops overrun large districts of France.—The new levies unable to resist them.—The report of the German commission in regard to operations in the region of the Loire.—The Partisans of Gers.—Capture of Orleans.—Its value as the centre of a rich district from which supplies could be drawn.—Its strategical importance.—Other towns captured.—Predominance of Red Republicanism in Marseilles and Lyons.—Fear of the German troops in the smaller towns of France.—The desolated tract between the Rhine and Paris.—Surrender of Metz.—Magnitude of the surrender.—Statistics of officers surrendered.—The indignation of the Provisional Government at this surrender.—Their proclamation.—Bazaine denounced as a traitor.—The real condition of France understated in this proclamation.—Hopelessness of its situation.—The energy and executive ability of Gambetta of no avail except to aggravate the severity of the conditions on which peace could eventually be made.—The approach of famine and revolution.—Intense pride and conceit of the French people and their leaders.—Apostrophe to France ....pp. 224-254.

CHAPTER XI.

The siege of Paris.—The capture of the Heights of Sceaux (Battle of Chatillon) by the Germans. - Culpable negligence of Trochu in not fortifying this point.—His folly in attempting to recapture them with a single corps of half-organized troops.—Trochu's reconnoissance and sortie of Sept. 30.—Its failure.—Position of the several corps of German troops around Paris. —Breadth of the cordon; its facilities for rapid concentration on any point.—Its lines never broken.--French sorties.—The sortie of Oct. 28 against Le Bourget.—Its failure.—Temporary Revolution.—Raising armies in the Provinces to compel the raising of the siege.—Gambetta at Tours.—His ability as an organizer.—The establishment of camps.—The expulsion of the

Army of the Seine from Orleans and its vicinity, Oct. 10, by General von der Tann.—Movements of the Germans to drive the French Army of the Loire out of the Loire Valley.—The determination of Gambetta to crush von der Tann and relieve Paris.—Recapture of Orleans by the French after a vigorous resistance by von der Tann, Nov. 9-10.—Exaggerated announcements of the victory.—General d'Aurelles de Paladines' report.—Gambetta's glorification of the General.—The other French commanders, Bourbaki, Ducrot, de Chanzy, and Faidherbe.—General von der Tann falls back, but General d'Aurelles de Paladines does not advance, but fortifies his camp around Orleans.—Gambetta dissatisfied.—Movements of the German commanders, General von Voights Rhetz and the Duke of Mecklenburg.—They pass by the Army of the Loire without an engagement, and move westward.—General d'Aurelles is ready to move the last of November.—His lines too much extended.—The fight at Beaune de Rolande.—Only part of the French force brought into action.—The arrival of Prince Friedrich Karl causes the defeat of the French.—Their heavy losses.—General d'Aurelles attacks the German centre, Dec. 1.—Desultory fighting for five days.—The defense of Orleans. —The attack by the Germans in full force.—General d'Aurelles driven back.—The Army of the Loire cut in two, and two corps pushed across the Loire.—Orleans evacuated and given up by the French.—Retreat of the three Army Corps under General de Chanzy to Blois, and subsequently toward Le Mans.—Heavy losses of the French.—Constant fighting for eight or ten days.—"A blessing in disguise."—The sortie of Generals Ducrot and Trochu from Paris, Nov. 30–Dec. 4.—The district lying on the bends of the Marne selected.—Why.—Large force engaged in the sortie.—Details of the movement.—General Trochu's reports.—Major Forbes' account.—Topography of the battle-ground.—Movements and counter-movements of the two armies.—General Ducrot's order of the day.................................pp. 255-280.

CHAPTER XII.

The situation.—All not yet lost, though imperiled.—Unimproved opportunities.—Orleans.—Ducrot's sortie.—Gambetta's blunders.—Sending Bourbaki to the east of France.—Gambetta's dispatch to General Trochu.—The real state of affairs.—Capitulation of important posts.— Tours surrendered.—The condition and position of de Chanzy's and Faidherbe's armies.—The occupation of Amiens.—Another sortie (Dec. 21 and 22) of the French garrison against the Saxon Corps.—Heavy losses of the French.—The sortie a failure.—Details of the engagement.—Bombardment of Fort Avron, Dec. 27.—Capitulation of Mezières.—Silencing of French forts.—Defeat of General Faidherbe's army, Jan. 2-4, 1871.—Rocroy captured.—The final pursuit and defeat of de Chanzy, Jan. 5-12.—Prince Friedrich Karl undertakes the pursuit in person, and sends the Grand Duke of Mecklenburg-Schwerin to execute a flank movement.—The battle of Jan. 10, near Le Mans.—Description by an eye-witness.—The battle of Jan. 11.—The Grand Duke's flanking movement.—Description.—The night attack.—The French surprise and panic.—General von Voights Rhetz occupies Le Mans.—The losses on both sides.—General de Chanzy's order of the day.—He retires with the remnant of his army to the vicinity of Laval, and attempts no further offensive movements.—Sketch of de Chanzy..pp. 281-299.

CHAPTER XIII.

General Bourbaki's Army of the East.—The position of affairs in Eastern France.—Siege of Belfort.—Its gallant resistance.—Reasons why Gambetta made this eastern movement.—The policy of doubtful wisdom.—The size and condition of the Army of General Bourbaki.—His reputation.—The objects he had in view.—His attacks on General von Werder's force.—Severe fighting, Jan. 13-18.—Bourbaki repulsed and defeated.—He commences a retreat.—His report.—Reënforcement of von Werder.—Approach of Manteuffel.—Bourbaki crowded on to the Swiss frontier.—He attempts suicide.—General Clinchart succeeds him.—Heavy losses.—The French are pushed over the border, and surrender 80,000 men to the Swiss.—General Faidherbe's last attempt to advance on the route to Paris.—He is outnumbered, outflanked, and

CONTENTS. 11

defeated by General von Goeben, and driven into and out of St. Quent'n.—His retreat to Cambrai.—His report.—Heavy losses.—Retreat to Lisle.—Surrender of Longwy.—Perilous condition of Garibaldi in the vicinity of Dijon.—Ineffectual sortie of Jan. 13.—The final sortie of General Trochu.—Details.—Bombardment of Paris.—Removal of General Trochu.—The Outlook.—Summary of the situation.—Condition of the great armies.—De Chanzy, Bourbaki, Garibaldi, Faidherbe.—The schools of instruction for soldiers.—The state of affairs in Paris.—Famine.—Fever.—Morals.—Riots.—Famine and ruin in the provinces.—No hope.—Favre seeks an interview with Count von Bismarck to obtain an armistice in which to negotiate for the conclusion of the war.—The state of affairs different from that in September and November.—The armistice concluded.—Its conditions.—The territory surrendered.—The substantial capitulation of Paris.—Number of French prisoners of war.—Loss of French population.—Meeting of the National Assembly at Bordeaux.—Gambetta's restrictive decree.—It is annulled by his associates, and he removed from office.—The election.—Complexion of the Assembly.—No party has a clear majority.—Choice of M. Grevy as President of the Assembly, and of M. Adolphe Thiers as Provisional President of the Republic.—His Cabinet.—The negotiation of the preliminary treaty.—Its provisions.—A heavy burden for France.—It is ratified by the National Assembly March 1, and by the Emperor Wilhelm I. March 5.—The Germans enter Paris March 1, and leave it March 3.—The Parisian mob quiet, —General d'Aurelles de Paladines in command.—The Emperor's despatch.—Return of the Germans, except the Army of Occupation, to Germany.—Condition in which the war left France.—The Red Republicans.—The future of France.—The Government to be.—What will it be?—The national debt of France.—Its crushing weight.—President Thiers' address to the nation on taking office...pp. 300–324.

CHAPTER XIV.

Review of the whole campaign.—The manner and bearing of the French Emperor and the Prussian King contrasted.—The affair at Saarbruck.—A great boast over a small matter.—The "Tranquil Infant."—Terror of the Emperor at the defeats of Forbach, Weissenbourg, and Woerth.—His despatches.—Bazaine's retreat upon Metz.—His attempt to fall back toward Paris.—Too late.—The sanguinary battles of Courcelles, Vionville, and Gravelotte.—The great blunder of MacMahon.—The pursuit.—MacMahon caught astride the Meuse.—Terrible slaughter of the battle of Aug. 30.—The fighting of August 31st and Sept. 1st.—MacMahon's army forced into Sedan, and then compelled to surrender.—Gen. de Wimpffen in command.—Napoleon's surrender.—The French revolution.—The "Government of National Defense."—Its unwisdom.—Their early peace negotiations.—Their refusal to cede any territory or surrender any of their strongholds.—The elections for a Constituent Assembly indefinitely postponed.--Investment of Paris.—The two-headed French Government.—Surrender of Strasburg.—Capture of Orleans.—Gambetta's exertions to raise new armies.—Regular and irregular troops.—Credit due him notwithstanding all his failings.—Steady progress of German conquest.—Capitulation of Metz, Oct. 27th; of Dijon, Oct. 30th; of New Breisach, Nov. 6th, and of Verdun, Nov. 9th; Thionville surrendered Nov. 25th.—Sorties repulsed.—Temporary success of the French at Coulmiers, Patay, and Orleans.—Failure of the great sortie from Paris, Nov. 29 to Dec. 2.—Recapture of Orleans by the Germans, and division of the Army of the Loire by Prince Friedrich Karl, Dec. 4.—The two Armies of the Loire and of the East.—Removal of d'Aurelles de Paladines from command.—The rising tide of disaster.—Surrender of Rouen, Beaugency, Dieppe, Pfalzburg, Montmedy, Vendome, Nuits, Tours, Sangre, Blois, Bapaume, Fort Avron, and other forts in the vicinity of Paris, during the month of December.—Attempt of General Faidherbe to advance toward Paris.—His repulse, defeat, and route by General von Goeben; General de Chanzy pursued and utterly defeated in the neighborhood of Le Mans.—Garibaldi but just escapes defeat.—Bourbaki's disaster, retreat, and final surrender.—The negotiation of the armistice, the election, and meeting of the National Assembly.—Thiers elected Provisional President.—The preliminary treaty negotiated and ratified.—The closing scenes of the war.—The remarkable character of the war—its slaughter, its surrenders, its weapons.—Its destruction of life and property.—The effect on the two nations—politically, socially, and religiously.—The peril of failing to heed these lessons ....pp. 325–340.

APPENDIX I.

Philanthropy of the War.—Organization of an International Sanitary Commission in 1866.—Its banner and badge.—Formation of Ambulance Corps early in the present War.—Activity of the Empress in France.—The zeal of Queen Augusta, the Crown-Princess Victoria, Princess Alice, the Grand Duchess Louise of Baden, and the Crown-Princess Caroline of Saxony.—The Grand Duchess of Mecklenburg-Schwerin.—Assistance rendered by Miss Clara Barton, Miss Safford, Mrs. Evans, &c.—The organization of Ambulance Corps in both armies.—The aid and service rendered by American gentlemen in Paris, and of others in the German armies.—Their strength overtasked in these labors.—Liberal gifts for the relief of the sick and wounded in France and Germany.—Munificence of Count Henri de Chambord.—Large contributions from Great Britain and the United States.—The wounded French in Germany. —Their general kind treatment.—German wounded prisoners in France.—The organizations for distribution of Bibles, tracts, periodicals, and moral and religious reading....pp. 341–343.

APPENDIX II.

Biographical sketch of LOUIS ADOLPHE THIERS, Provisional President French Republic.
pp. 344–350.

THE YEAR OF BATTLES.

CHAPTER I.

THE war of 1870, between France and Germany, is often denounced as "wanton," "causeless," and "unprovoked;" and in one aspect of the case this is true; for the immediate causes of the war were trivial, and could only have led to a conflict where one or both parties were eager for a pretext for fighting. Had these been the only grounds on which the contest was based, it could not have occurred; for, if the rulers had been such fools as to knock their heads together on the question of a possible Spanish succession, their people would have protested against it.

The true origin of the war, though perhaps unjustifiable on the part of the French Emperor, lies farther back, and appeals to higher motives and jealousies than a petty question of succession to a foreign throne. There have been, for two hundred and twenty years past, almost constant encroachments by France upon the provinces of the old German empire. Some of these, like the old provinces of Alsace and Lorraine (the old Elsass and Lothringen of the Germans), gained by treaty, by seizure, by the intrigues of French Bishop-princes, or by the real or supposed exigencies of mercantile policy, France has been allowed to keep; and though 1,007,477 out of the 1,097,000 inhabitants of Alsace, and 351,681 out of the 1,291,000 inhabitants of Lorraine, were Germans, yet the severest measures of oppression have been resorted to by the French Government to compel the people to abandon all use of the German language, customs, and manners. The natural boundary between France and Germany is the Vosges range of mountains, not the Rhine; and though Napoleon I, among his other conquests of territory belonging to other nations, seized and held, for six or eight years, the German provinces lying west of the Rhine (Dusseldorf, Cologne, Aachen or Aix-la-Chapelle, Coblentz, Hesse, Treves, Birkenfeld, and the Palatinate), and carved out from them the kingdom of Westphalia, over which he placed his brother Jerome, yet the injustice of their being torn from their natural affinities was so great, that, by the treaty of 1815, they were restored to Germany. In the 3,108,000 inhabitants of these provinces, there are not more than 10,000 people to whom French is their mother-tongue.

Napoleon I had also absorbed Belgium, with its 2,667,000 inhabitants of Flemish origin, in his conquests, and, uniting it with Holland, had placed his brother Louis over it. These kingdoms were taken from France by the treaty of 1815, and have since, under different designations, maintained a separate existence.

Under the Bourbons of the Restoration, and under Louis Philippe, France made no effort to recover these territories— Belgium, Holland, and the Rhenish provinces—which were so alien from her in race and language, and which she had possessed but so short a time. Contenting herself with increasing wealth and prosperity, and the possession of Alsace and Lorraine, which she had held from one to two centuries, her policy was rather that of a cordial understanding with the nations adjacent than one of territorial aggression.

But after the Revolution of 1848 and the accession of Louis Napoleon to the Presidency, and especially after the *coup d'état* and the establishment of the Empire, the hearts of the French people were fired by the usurper with the hope of regaining all the territory they had ever possessed under the first Napoleon.

No sooner was the new Emperor firmly seated on his throne, than, while carefully promulgating his declaration that "the Empire was peace," he began to plot for the accomplishment of his long-cherished purposes of avenging Waterloo, and extending the bounds of France to the Rhine on the east, and to the Adriatic on the southeast. Crafty and reticent, yet wholly unscrupulous, he made every move on the political chess-board with a view to these ends. He duped England into an alliance which should enure to his benefit; made war with Russia, ostensibly on behalf of Turkey, but really to cripple her resources and prevent her interference with his schemes; joined Italy in a war with Austria, in the hope of obtaining a large slice of Italy for his reward; and when Prussia, cognizant of his plans, declared that the Rhine must be defended on the Adige, withdrew and accepted, somewhat ungraciously, Savoy and Nice as the compensation for his services. To amuse his people and keep them in training for the great war he purposed to begin as soon as he felt strong enough for it, he made war upon the Cochin-Chinese, and sent his armies to Mexico to establish a throne there for Maximilian, and to be on hand to interfere, if he could drag any other European power into the plot, in behalf of the Southern Confederacy. The blunder he made was a serious one, and he felt it keenly. Meantime, his old foes, the Prussians and Austrians, were fighting each other, and he offered his aid to each in turn, demanding, as his price, the Rhine provinces and Belgium. Austria could not, and Prussia, strong in her military organization and her skilled troops, would not, entertain his proposals. When, after seven weeks of hard fighting, he found Prussia triumphant, Austria humbled, and the North-German Confederation an accomplished fact, with a certainty that a united Germany would follow in time, he was greatly enraged, and his demands for a share of the territory which he had done nothing to earn, being treated with contempt, he began to comprehend that Prussia was becoming too strong for him.

Thenceforward he commenced preparations for a desperate struggle with his enemy, the time and place of commencement to be determined by circumstances. But even in this preparation he blundered sadly, blinded by the demoralizing effects of the corruption which he had encouraged in the nation. The wonderful success of Prussia was not, as he supposed, due to her needle-guns or her improved artillery, excellent as they were, so much as to her admirable military organization, which made every able-bodied man in the realm an experienced soldier, and which required of every officer that thorough topographical knowledge and military skill which enabled them to handle their troops efficiently.

For the needle-gun the French Emperor substituted the chassepôt rifle, in some respects a superior weapon; his bronze cannon were not greatly inferior to Krupp's steel artillery; and he had in the *mitrailleuse* a weapon very efficient at short range; but he lacked what was far more important—skilful and efficient officers, men of thorough honesty, integrity, and military ability; and a large part of his army were untrained and undisciplined.

Official peculation and falsehood had permeated every portion of his army and sapped its very life-blood. That he had converted to his own use a part of the appropriations for the army, was but a small part of the trouble; almost every officer, from the highest to the lowest, had followed his example. Where he supposed he had a hundred soldiers fully armed and equipped, there were found but fifty, and these imperfectly supplied with arms and ammunition. His officers knew nothing of the topography of France or Germany; their military education had been acquired either in Africa, Cochin-China, or Mexico, and they had no experience in fighting an intelligent and educated foe. These things the Emperor neglected to take into account; and, infatuated with his hatred of Prussia, he sought diligently for an occasion to declare war, meantime endeavoring to imbue the French people with the sentiment that the Rhine was the only true boundary of France on the northeast.

There were not wanting other motives to lead to this war. France was restive under his system of repression and espionage. The great cities, Paris, Marseilles, Lyons, Bordeaux, were bitterly hostile to him. The *Corps Législatif*, or popular branch of the Legislature, was at each election increasing the number of opposition members, and on every side were the hoarse growlings of a coming storm. The artfully-phrased ballot, submitted to the popular vote or *plebiscite* in May, 1870, was, by adroit management and no little direct exertion of authority, carried in his favor by a majority of nearly six millions; but the opposition was nevertheless strong and intelligent, and a considerable fraction of his army voted with it. His own health was evidently failing, and the only prospect for his dynasty lay in a war which should rouse the old enthusiasm of the French, and drown their dislike of him in their love of military glory.

Nor were religious motives lacking. Eugenie, whose religious zeal increased as her beauty faded, had for her confessor an artful Jesuit, high in rank in that powerful order. The condition of the Pope was becoming desperate. Italy was in revolt against his temporal power and his new dogma of Infallibility; Austria was no longer his faithful defender; Spain was in revolution, and there remained only the eldest son of the Church, the Emperor of the French, on whom the Pope could call for aid. Prussia, the leading Protestant nation, was gaining strength every day. Its pride must be humbled, and this could only be accomplished by a great war; and, even if the Emperor should fall in the fray, she, the devout daughter of the Church, and the young Prince Imperial, could, under Catholic influence, have a better and stronger hold upon the nation than in any other way. Such were the arguments addressed to the Empress, and through her to the Emperor, by this skilful Jesuit.

Apart from his passion for the perpetuation of his dynasty, which seemed to make war his only alternative, the Emperor may reasonably be supposed to have had some feeling for the position of France as one of the great powers of Europe. Prussia had humbled Austria, and now ranked, or would soon rank, first among the European powers, where she had, till lately, been fourth. Her position menaced France. Should she relinquish her prestige to a State so lately her inferior? If she would not, she must subdue this proud, haughty nation before it became too strong to be subdued.

And so, after years of waiting, during which all Europe had been kept in constant alarm by the defiant attitude of the French ruler, now threatening one and now another, Napoleon III believed he had found or made his opportunity for a war with Prussia.

Spain, which, in the autumn of 1868, had overthrown its Bourbon dynasty and had been drifting along since that time under a Regency and a Provisional Government, had sought widely, but, from one cause or another, ineffectually, for a suitable candidate for her vacant throne. To all who were named there seemed to be some objection, either on the part of adjacent nations and rulers, or of the Spanish people themselves. General Prim, the real though not the nominal ruler of Spain, was a personal friend of Louis Napoleon, and had a long conference with him respecting the succession to the throne in the Spring of 1870. Soon after his return to Madrid it was given out, at first semi-officially, and afterward by the Spanish Government itself, that Prince Leopold Hohenzollern, of Sigmaringen, would be the candidate for the vacant Spanish throne, and on a canvass of the Constituent Assembly, it was ascertained that there was

PRINCE LEOPOLD OF HOHENZOLLERN.

a probability of his election. The Prince Leopold was a cadet of a younger branch, and somewhat remotely connected with the reigning family of Prussia; his mother was a Beauharnais, a niece, we believe, of Queen Hortense, the mother of Louis Napoleon; so that he was a distant relative of both the King of Prussia and the Emperor of France. He was, however, a younger son of the last ruling prince of Sigmaringen, and had entered the Prussian army, where he had risen to the rank of Colonel.

Immediately on the announcement of his candidature, the French Emperor protested most vigorously, and announced his fixed determination to make any effort to put a Hohenzollern upon the Spanish throne a cause of war against Prussia, which power, he assumed, had prompted the movement from hostility to him. Prussia promptly disavowed all previous knowledge of Prince Leopold's candidature, and the King expressed his disapproval of it, though, from the relations which existed between the German princes, he was not in a position to prohibit it absolutely. This difficulty was, however, soon obviated by the prompt declinature of the candidacy by Prince Leopold himself, and by his father for him. It really looked, for the time, as if there would be no war after all; and there were not a few statesmen of surrounding nations who believed that the whole movement was a trap into which Louis Napoleon and General Prim had sought to inveigle Prussia, that the Emperor might have a justifiable pretext for declaring war against her, and that Prussia, understanding the trick, was determined to foil it.

But the inflammatory circulars, addresses, and proclamations distributed by the French Emperor among his people, had roused such bitter hatred against Prussia throughout France, that war was inevitable. He had roused, but could not lay, the storm, even if he desired it. The apparent aversion of Prussia to a war made him more anxious to compel her to accept its arbitrament, and making demands which Prussia could not accept—such as, that Prussia should give substantial guarantees that no Prussian prince should ever become a candidate for the Spanish throne, professing that otherwise the balance of power was likely to be disturbed. The French Minister at Berlin was directed to press the demands offensively upon the King of Prussia, and performed the work so zealously as to cause his dismissal from the Prussian Court. This was used as an additional grievance by the Emperor, who immediately declared war, basing his justification on these grounds: the insult to his minister; the refusal of the King of Prussia to prohibit, absolutely, Prince Leopold's candidature, and his unwillingness to offer material guarantees that he would not permit any Prussian prince to be a candidate for the Spanish throne in the future; and, finally, the danger to the peace and balance of power in Europe from the action of the Prussian King. Every nation in Europe knew that Napoleon III did not really make war on these grounds, but because he wanted the Rhenish provinces and Belgium, and wanted to humble Prussia and her great statesman, Bismarck; and, while some of the European powers were not averse to seeing Prussian arrogance, as they phrased it, a little lowered, they were all aware that no justifiable pretext for war had been made out.

Napoleon III had sent his emissaries and missives throughout Bavaria, Wurtemburg, Baden, and Hanover, in the hope of alienating them from the Prussian cause; but he met with no encouragement from that quarter, and found, when it was too late, that he had all Germany, instead of Prussia, to fight.

Such was the origin and such the immediate causes of the war which, in six weeks, has caused a slaughter of nearly a quarter of a million of men, and produced extraordinary changes in the condition of Europe. Let us next trace the personal history of the two monarchs, their counsellors, and their leading commanders.

WILHELM, EMPEROR OF GERMANY.

CHAPTER II.

AMONG the conspicuous personages in this great contest, the first place belongs to the King of Prussia by right of seniority. He is not a man of as remarkable intellectual abilities as Bismarck, nor of as profound military knowledge as Von Moltke; but, though naturally, and as a result of his early education and prejudices, an absolutist, he has, through the influence of his ministers, become so far liberalized as to grant constitutional privileges to his people; and his manliness, integrity, and straightforwardness have so endeared him to his people, that he may justly be regarded as the most popular monarch in Europe.

WILHELM FRIEDRICH LUDWIG, better known as WILLIAM I, King of Prussia, was born March 22, 1797, and is, therefore, seventy-three years old. He entered the military service very young. As a child, he witnessed the humiliation of his father by the first Napoleon, and he engaged in the avenging campaigns of 1813 and 1814. In 1840 he was appointed governor of Pomerania. The revolution of 1848 drove him from Prussia, for he was at that time a bitter hater of democracy. After nine months in England, he returned, and was elected a member of the National Assembly, but took no part. In the same year he commanded the troops that put down the Baden insurrection. During the Crimean war he was anxious to have Prussia take sides with Russia. October 23, 1857, owing to the ill health and insanity of his brother, Frederick William IV, the government was placed in his hands; October 9, 1858, he was declared regent; January 2, 1861, he became king. For the first four or five years of his reign his tendencies to absolutism brought him into repeated collisions with the popular branch of the Prussian legislature, and rendered him unpopular as a king; but the wise counsels of Count Bismarck, and the material change in his policy, have of late greatly endeared him to his people. He is described as stalwart, deep-chested, with a square, rugged face, and bristling gray mustache, cold, implacable eyes, and a heavy jaw; yet, in his intercourse with his people, and especially with children, the grim face relaxes, and it is easy to see that the stern old man has a kindly and tender heart. His military education was very thorough, and he handles large bodies of troops with great ability. During the war of 1866, as well as the present war, his despatches from the field of battle have always been modest, frank, and truthful, underrating rather than exaggerating his successes, and always giving full credit to others for victories. His messages to Queen Augusta have been so fraught with feeling, and so free from any thing like elation or bombast, as to be models of what war-despatches should be.

His opponent, the originator of the war, though a younger man, has a longer and more eventful record, though not a more creditable one.

With his usual imperiousness, Napoleon I compelled, in 1802, his brother, Louis Bonaparte, to marry Hortense Beauharnais, the daughter of Josephine. The match was repugnant to the wishes of both the parties, Louis being already openly the suitor of Emilie Beauharnais, Josephine's niece, and Hortense secretly, if not openly, betrothed to General Duroc. As might have been expected, the marriage proved an unhappy one, and resulted in a separation in 1810. Hortense became the mother, in this period, of three sons, the youngest bearing the name of CHARLES LOUIS NAPOLEON, being born April 20, 1808. King Louis hesitated long before acknowledging the legitimacy of this third son, and only consented finally at the urgent solicitations and threats of his brother. There was a Dutch admiral at that time on terms of intimacy with Queen Hortense, to whom rumor assigned the paternity of the boy, who certainly resembled him more strongly than he did any of the Bonapartes. After the age of two years, his residence was with his mother, at Paris, until 1815, and he was, as a child, a favorite of Napoleon I.

After the Restoration, the ex-Queen Hortense spent her summers at Augsburg, or at the castle of Arenenberg, near Lake Constance, and her winters in Italy; and her two sons (the eldest child had died in 1807), who accompanied her, received but an imperfect and desultory education. They studied German and the classics, though with such interruptions that they never became remarkable proficients in any thing. Both joined the revolutionary society of the Carbonari, in Italy, and were implicated in several of the Italian conspiracies. After the revolution of July, 1830, and the accession of Louis Philippe to the throne, the younger asked permission for himself and family to return to France; and this being refused, he requested to be allowed to serve as a private soldier in the French army. The French Government answered these requests by a renewal of the decree for his banishment. He concealed his chagrin at this action at the time, but thenceforth did not cease to plot for the overthrow of the Orleans dynasty. In the beginning of 1831, he and his brother left Switzerland, and settled in Tuscany, from whence, a month later, both took part in the unsuccessful insurrection at Rome. The fatigues and exposures of that period led to the death of his elder brother at Forli, March 17, 1831; and Louis Napoleon escaped through Italy and France to England, where he remained a short time, and then retired to the castle of Arenenburg, where his mother still resided. Soon after his arrival there, the Duke of Reichstadt, the only legitimate son of Napoleon I, died, and Louis Napoleon became the legal heir of the family, and the claimant of the imperial throne of France. His efforts were secretly directed, from this time, to the overthrow of Louis Philippe, and he had succeeded in winning the favor of some of the distinguished men of the time to his projects. Outwardly, during this time, he appeared to be very quiet. He wrote, between 1832 and 1835, three works, which attained a small and limited circulation; but he was never sufficiently well educated to be master of a good French style, and his grammatical and rhetorical blunders greatly marred the effect of these and all other of his literary performances. The books prepared at this time—"Political Reveries," "Political and Military Considerations in Regard to Switzerland," and a "Manual of Artillery"—were the crude productions of a young man of imperfect education, unaccustomed to profound thought, and with very little knowledge of human nature. The "Manual of Artillery," a mere technical book, is incomparably the best of the three, and received from some of the military journals a favorable notice.

But he was restless, and sick of this quiet life. Some of his correspondents in France had encouraged him in the belief that France was ripe for a revolution, and he resolved to attempt it. There was always a melodramatic tendency in his mind, and this led him to model his intended attack on the return of Napoleon I from Elba. His associates in the plot were Colonel Vaudrey, of the 4th Artillery, then stationed at Strasbourg, and M. Victor Fialin, afterward better known as the Duc de Persigny.

On the 30th of October, 1836, Louis Napoleon suddenly made his appearance in Strasbourg, was presented to a part of the garrison by Colonel Vaudrey, who at the same time announced to the soldiers that a revolution had taken place in Paris, and was accepted by the 4th Artillery and a portion of

NAPOLEON III., LATE EMPEROR OF FRANCE.

some other regiments. The prompt action of Gen. Voirol and Colonel Tallandier arrested the movement. The troops hesitated; in a few minutes more, the epaulettes and decorations of the would-be Emperor were torn from him. He was arrested without delay, and forwarded to Paris. Louis Philippe felt too secure in his place to be vindictive; the attempt, in fact, illustrated its own impotence; and the culprit was dealt with very leniently. Within three weeks he was shipped to New York, without any conditions being attached to his release, and $3,000, the gift of Louis Philippe, in his pocket. He was first taken to Rio Janeiro, where the vessel delayed but a few days, and then sailed for the United States. He was landed at Norfolk, in March, 1837, and thence made his way to New York, where he remained until some time in May. His residence in America was not marked by any events at all to his credit. His relatives, Joseph Bonaparte, at Bordentown, and the Patterson-Bonapartes at Baltimore, turned the cold shoulder to him. His hare-brained adventure at Strasbourg had stamped him as an adventurer; his personal habits were reckless, and his associations not at all respectable; and he had not the passport to good society.

The news of the serious illness of his mother recalled him to Switzerland. He reached Arenenberg shortly before her death, which occurred on the 3d of October. In the following year his account of the Strasbourg affair was published by Lieutenant Laity, who had also been concerned in it. Louis Philippe took offence at the statements it contained, and demanded his extradition from the Swiss Government, which, in spite of Louis Napoleon's citizenship, would probably have been compelled to accede, had he not relieved it from the embarrassment by migrating to England. Here, in 1839, he published his *Idées Napoléoniennes*, which were widely circulated. They reiterated the assertion of his *Rêveries Politiques*, that France could only be developed by a Napoleonic ruler, and assailed both the policy of the Orleans family and its right to the throne.

Although, in 1840, the Orleanist rule was still firmly established in France, Louis Napoleon, yielding less to the impatience of his small band of followers in London, than blindly and recklessly trusting his fortunes to chance, organized a new attempt. Accompanied by Count Montholon (one of the companions of Napoleon at St. Helena) and about fifty others, he crossed the Channel in a small steamer, and landed at Boulogne. One of the "properties" of the expedition was a tame eagle, which—according to the gossip of the day—had been trained to alight on the Prince's head by the lure of a piece of raw beefsteak attached to his hat. The landing was made, the bluffs ascended, and the garrison summoned to acknowledge their legitimate commander; but the eagle forgot his lesson, and the soldiers had not yet learned theirs. The first alighted upon a post, instead of the selected head, and the second charged upon their self-styled sovereign and his adherents. Plunging into the sea in his endeavor to regain the steamer, Louis Napoleon was dragged out, dripping and collapsed, and forwarded a second time to Paris. This attempt was even more disastrous than the first; for at Strasbourg a part of the garrison (deceived by Colonel Vaudrey) had actually declared for him; whereas at Boulogne not a single soldier appears to have done him reverence.

Louis Philippe, it must be admitted, acted with great moderation. The life of the conspirator, who had abused his first forbearance, was in his power; but he brought him to trial before the House of Peers, where he was defended by Berryer, then the first advocate in France, and acquiesced in the sentence of perpetual imprisonment. Nay, more; it was reported, and generally believed, that the escape in 1846 was accomplished with the knowledge and tacit connivance of the French Government. Louis Napoleon's imprisonment in Ham—a small place near St. Quentin, about half-way between Paris and the Belgian frontier—was voluntarily shared by Dr. Conneau, a physician who had faith in his destiny. During the six years at Ham, however, the prisoner was not idle. He occupied himself chiefly with political studies, and wrote three works—" Historic Fragments" (published in 1841), a comparison between the fall of the Stuart dynasty in England and certain features of French history; an "Analysis of the Sugar Question" (1842), in which he took ground against specially favoring production in the French colonies; and, finally, an essay on the "Extinction of Pauperism," which was the most important of all, inasmuch as it indirectly favored the communistic theories which were then rapidly taking root among the laboring classes of France. He proposed that the Government should advance funds to establish settlement and cultivation in all the waste districts of the country, and that the profits of the undertaking should be appropriated to the support and elevation of the manufacturing classes. He asserted, moreover, his own intention "to act always in the interest of the masses, the sources of all right and of all wealth, although destitute of the one and without any guaranty for attaining the other."

Toward the end of 1845, the ex-King Louis, then ill at Florence, made an appeal to the French Government for the release of the only son who bore his name. After a long consideration, the appeal was refused; but the refusal was followed, in May, 1846, by the escape of Louis Napoleon from Ham. With Dr. Conneau's assistance, disguised as a workman, he walked out of the fortress carrying a board upon his shoulder, easily made his way to the Belgian frontier, and thence to England.

His long confinement, and the evidence of literary ability in his published works, had by this time partly removed the impression of folly and pretension which the attempts at Strasbourg and Boulogne had cast upon his name; and during his second residence in England he appears to have associated with another and better class of society. He was welcomed to Lady Blessington's receptions at Gore House, was a frequent visitor of Sir John (then Dr.) Bowring's, and made a strong impression on Walter Savage Landor at Bath, by declaring to him, confidentially, that he would yet reign in France. Generally, however, he was reticent, impassive, and abstracted; his destiny was credited by very few, and his abilities doubted by most. Disappointment, ridicule, exile, imprisonment, and privation, had taught him prudence.

Then came, startling all Europe, the revolution of February, 1848. Louis Napoleon's shrewdness and self-control at such a crisis contrast remarkably with his former recklessness. The Bonapartist faction in France was not large at that time, but it was very active. Lamartine, originally a Legitimist, knew the power of a name among the people, and the Executive Committee (in May), probably at his suggestion, laid before the National Assembly a proposal to renew the decree of 1832, and banish the Bonaparte family from France. This was rejected by the Assembly, and Louis Napoleon, who had been brought before the people as a candidate by his followers, and had been elected Deputy from four departments, was free to visit Paris. Nevertheless, he still delayed, from an apparent disinclination to create trouble. After having announced to the President of the National Assembly, on the 14th of June, that he was ready to perform any duty with which the people might charge him, he forwarded a letter, the following day, resigning his place as Deputy in the interest of peace and harmony. This step greatly increased his popularity, and he was immediately rechosen Deputy by four other departments.

Thereupon he left England, reached Paris on the 24th of September, and, on the 26th, took his seat in the National Assembly. He made a short address, taking strong ground in favor of the preservation of order and the development of democratic institutions. His manner as a speaker was stiff and unimpressive, his accent was slightly foreign, and General Cavaignac, then temporary dictator, and candidate for the Presidency, seems to have greatly under-estimated both his ability and the chances of his popularity.

The Bonapartists had used every means in their power to unite the numerous discordant elements in the nation upon him; and, thanks to their adroit management and the lack of any popular name for a rallying-cry among the other parties, they were successful. The election was held on the 10th of December, 1848, and the result gave evidence of an almost complete union of all other parties against that of the Republic of Order represented by Cavaignac. The latter received 1,460,000 votes; Louis Napoleon, 5,500,000; and Lamartine a comparatively trifling number. The two monarchical parties designed making use of Louis Napoleon as an instrument to weaken the Republicans, trusting that his own incompetency would complete the work, and hasten a counter-revolution. When, therefore, on the 20th of December, he was installed as President of the French Republic, it was under auspices seemingly very fortunate, because the hostile influences were temporarily held in abeyance. Cavaignac, a noble Spartan nature, had restored France to order, although the blood he had shed in saving the country lost the country to him. The new President, with no record of offence except against the banished dynasty, took quiet possession of the realm which another had made ready for his hands.

His policy, which was speedily developed, was to improve the social and business condition of France, and at the same time to pursue a gradually increasing system of repression, till he had crushed out the last vestige of liberty. The French people of the middle and lower classes love to be ruled with a strong hand, so that their social prosperity is assured and their love of glory gratified; and he succeeded more easily, perhaps, than even he had anticipated. A system of internal improvements was planned and put in execution; industry of all kinds revived, and the change from the depression produced by the uncertainties of the previous year was felt as a happy relief by the whole population. All this time the liberty secured by the Constitution was steadily contracted; the Government became firmer and more repressive in its character; the restless movements of factions were dealt with more severely as the mass of the people became more contented under their new prosperity. Although the point to which this policy tended was now tolerably clear, it was still difficult to point to any act as specially indicative of it. While violating the spirit of the Constitution, while advocating or opposing universal suffrage, according to the exigencies of his policy, his speeches were so worded as to make it appear that *he* was the sole defender of the Constitution, concerned only to shield it from the aggressions of the National Assembly.

In January, 1851, a completely Bonapartist Ministry was appointed; but the Assembly, having voted its lack of confidence, another Ministry was substituted. An attempt was then made to change the Constitution in such a manner that the President's term of office might be extended, since an immediate reëlection was prohibited; but, after a very fierce and stormy discussion, the proposition failed to receive the requisite majority of three fourths. The Assembly was soon afterwards adjourned until November, which gave the Prince-President time to mature his plans. His term would expire the following Spring; the Prince de Joinville was already named as a candidate; the elements of opposition, although without combination, were increasing in strength, and the temper of the French people was anxious and uneasy. In this juncture, he called about him men who were equally cunning, daring, and unprincipled—General St. Arnaud (who was made Minister of War in October, 1851), De Morny, Persigny, and Fleury. All of these appear to have been made acquainted with his plans, and two of them—St. Arnaud and De Morny—were his chief instruments in carrying them into execution.

On the 13th of November, 1851, the National Assembly, by a large majority, defeated the proposition for universal suffrage, and the Prince-President and his co-conspirators speedily determined upon a desperate measure. Before daylight on the morning of the 2d of December, 1851, seventy-eight prominent men were seized, many of them being dragged from their beds, the National Assembly forcibly dissolved (220 of the Deputies having been arrested and imprisoned the same day), Paris declared in a state of siege, and the people called upon to elect a President for ten years, with power to select his own Ministry, and a Government consisting of two Chambers, with limited powers. All legal opposition and protest was crushed under foot. Paris arose against the outrage, and, until the night of December 4, its streets ran with blood. Entire quarters of the city were given up to murder and plunder. Men, women, and children, natives and foreigners, were shot and bayoneted indiscriminately. The greatest pains have been taken to suppress the dreadful details, but the number of persons butchered cannot have been less than 5,000, and may have been twice as many. Within the next month, according to the Bonapartist, Granier de Cassagnac, 26,500 persons were transported to the penal colonies of Cayenne and Africa, where the greater number of them died.

The blow was so sudden and terrible that the spirit of the nation was utterly paralyzed; even indignation was lost in the deeper sense of horror and fear. The mask was removed, and the Empire in a nearly absolute form already existed. The people knew this when they were called upon to vote upon the questions proposed by Louis Napoleon. Public opinion was equally suppressed throughout the provinces; the most alarming socialistic dangers were invented and threatened; every prominent man was ordered to declare himself instantly for one side or the other; the business classes were kept excited by rumors of plots and outbreaks; the press everywhere was effectually muzzled; and when the election was held, a few days later, the result was: 7,500,000 yeas, 650,000 nays.

In January, 1852, he ordered the confiscation of all the property belonging to the Orleans family; in February, the last vestige of liberty was taken from the press; in May, the Napoleonic eagles were distributed to the army; and in December the Prince-President, Louis Napoleon Bonaparte, became Napoleon III, Emperor, "By the Grace of God and the will of the French people"! Having assured himself that resistance was paralyzed for a time, his next objects were, first, to allay the distrust of the other European powers by showing that the Empire was Peace; and secondly, to bring about a war, in order to satisfy his army.

After various unsuccessful attempts to ally himself by marriage with some of the reigning houses of Europe, he abandoned the quest, and in January, 1853, married Eugenie Marie de Guzman, Countess de Téba, a Spanish lady, though descended, on her mother's side, from a Scottish family.

In the summer of 1853 he succeeded in forming an alliance with England, which, a few months later, was riveted by the Crimean war. In this war, through the ability of his generals and the inefficiency of some of the English officers, he managed to secure the lion's share of the glory for France, and, under a great show of disinterestedness, to cause the material successes to enure to his own advantage, while the heaviest burdens came upon his ally.

The Empire was not Peace, but it seemed to be Order. The country was covered with a network of railways, harbors were created, a fleet built and manned, Paris was pierced in all directions with broad and splendid streets, the Empress inaugurated a new era of luxury, labor was plentiful, money was plentiful, morals were pleasantly relaxed, and the French people were free to enjoy the good things of this life, so long as they abstained from meddling with politics. The *material* justification of the Empire became popular throughout Europe, and even with many Americans. An Imperial Prince was born in March, 1856—an only one, and again a resemblance to Napoleon! Even persons not superstitious began to incline toward the theory of " destiny." With his positive power and his increasing prestige, it was now possible to relax somewhat of his former caution, and for a few years the world, convicted of having undervalued him, persisted in atoning for its offence by interpreting his stolidity as depth, his reticence as wisdom, his straining after theatrical effect as the force and daring of genius. From 1853 to 1861 he was the most over-estimated man in the world. Every turn and winding of his apparently subtile policy, every new disclosure of his seemingly impenetrable plans, was accepted as an evidence of greatness by a majority of the civilized races.

It would, perhaps, be unfair to say that sympathy for the Italian cause had no part in bringing on the war of 1859. He was scarcely insensible to so many early associations; he knew the tremendous under current of resistance and aspiration in Lombardy, the Romagna, and the Duchies, and felt that there were the seeds of great popularity, if not power, in his policy. But there were two other equally powerful considerations: he would abolish the relentless determination of the Carbonàri, and he would increase the territory of France by the annexation of Savoy. (There is little doubt that the latter clause was agreed upon when Cavour visited Napoleon III at Plombières, before the war.) His course being decided, there remained only the finding of a pretext, which Austria blunderingly furnished, in April, 1859. Although Napoleon's Ministry were reported to be unfavorable to the war, it was hailed with great enthusiasm by the masses of the people.

After entering Piedmont, the Emperor delayed three weeks, plotting and planning, before commencing hostilities. He had an interview with Kossuth, and agreed with the latter upon a plan for coöperating with the Magyar and Sclavonic population of Austria. Tuscany had already risen, the Romagna was stirring, and there were movements in Naples and Sicily. The Emperor's design was to secure the former for Prince Napoleon and the latter for the Murats; a united Italy was the farthest thing possible from his plans. But he was forced to simulate a generosity he did not feel, and to give battle with no other gain than Savoy and Nice assured in advance. After a small engagement at Montebello, the battle of Magenta, on the 4th of June, gave Milan and Lombardy to the French and Italian armies. The Emperor's reception in Milan was warm and cordial, but a storm of uncontrollable joy surged around the path of Victor Emanuel. Tuscany had by this time claimed the latter's protectorate, and the drift of popular sentiment throughout Italy was no longer to be mistaken. The Emperor found himself embarked on a new current, and his first business was to withdraw successfully.

Taking this view of the matter, the battle of Solferino was a piece of great good luck. The Sclavonic conspiracy had so far succeeded that the Croat regiments in the Austrian army refused to serve; the Emperor Francis Joseph trusted in Gyulai, the most incompetent of generals; and Venice, in the Austrian rear, was thoroughly prepared, and only awaited the signal to rise. On the other hand, Napoleon III appeared to the world as commander of the united French and Italian armies. His mistakes were skilfully concealed by his Marshals, and even the blunder which so nearly made him an Austrian prisoner was so retrieved as to make it seem an act of personal daring. The victory was more complete than that of Magenta; it satisfied French vanity, gave Napoleon III the very position he desired, and enabled him to convert his real disappointment into apparent forbearance.

By this time other forces were fast developing into form, and he took good note of them while seeming impassive and imperturbable. The Pope, in spite of the French garrison at Rome, threatened excommunication. The spirit of Germany was thoroughly aroused, and even in Prussia the phrase was current, "The Rhine must be defended on the Adige." This was geographically false, but politically true; for the plans of Napoleon III, from the moment his rule was assured, embraced the extension of France to the Alps (which was now accomplished), then to the Rhine, from Basle to the sea, including Belgium. This was the price he meant to pay France for the permanency of his dynasty. Moreover, had he not already said, in the *Idées Napoléoniennes*, "After a victory, offer peace"? The peace of Villafranca, which cut Italy to the heart, betrayed Hungary and Croatia, bewildered Europe, but gave relief to the anxious nations, and increased prestige to the Emperor, was the inevitable result of his policy.

His disappointment, however, was bitter. Basing his own imperial power upon the Plebiscite, he was powerless to interfere, when all Italy, except the little Roman territory held by French troops, pronounced for a united nationality under Victor Emanuel. Savoy and Nice were acquired, it is true; the names of Magenta and Solferino were added to those of the Alma and the Malakoff; the influence of France was more potent than ever in the councils of Europe: but more than this was necessary. The doubt in the permanence of his dynasty was general, even among his own adherents. The French appetite for glory, he knew, was only satisfied for a little while by such minor results as he had obtained in the Crimea and Lombardy; it craved undiluted success, overwhelming victory. Meanwhile, the benumbing horror of the *coup d'état* of December, 1851, was beginning to fade from men's minds; the undying Republican instinct of the mind of France began to show signs of its life; and even the intelligent un-Republican classes, who had acquiesced in the Empire, recognized the social and moral degeneration which had followed its establishment. His great successes were beginning to be followed by indications of a change of fortune. His own health, from a complication of disorders, was precarious; his boy had been frail and sickly from his earliest infancy; the Empress, with the already perceptible waning of her beauty, was coming more and more under the influence of her confessor and the Jesuits every year; and her Spanish bigotry was loosing her hold—never very strong—upon the hearts of the nation. The Republican element was becoming strong in the cities, and it was evident that something must be done, or there was slight hope for the continuance of his dynasty. A great European war was not to be undertaken without a better pretext than he could find just then; but he sought a quarrel with Mexico, meaning to use it as a pretext for interfering in our war, and used his best endeavors to drag England into a bold intervention with him on behalf of the Southern Confederacy. How miserably he failed in both projects, is within the recollection of all; and the execution of the gallant but unfortunate Maximilian, whom he made his tool and dupe in his Mexican enterprise, and the plaintive laments and lifelong insanity of the hapless Carlotta, must even now fill his soul with horror for his treachery.

He also made some small experiments in the way of war in Cochin-China and China, but his success was not commensurate with his expenditure, and there was not glory enough to satisfy the greed of the French nation. He promised constitutional and political reforms, the freedom of the press, the liberty of interpellation, the partial control of the finances by the *Corps Législatif*, or House of Representatives; but his reforms were so much less than his promises, that they only excited discontent and induced no gratitude.

In the midst of these vain strivings after a success which constantly eluded his grasp, a severer blow fell upon him than any he had yet experienced. Prussia, which he had ever regarded as a second-rate power, declared war against Austria in 1866, and his tender of assistance to Austria for a consideration (the Rhine provinces and Belgium) being rejected, he offered his assistance to Prussia on similar terms (Baden and Wurtemberg being substituted in this case for the Rhenish provinces), only to have it rejected with contempt. In seven weeks Prussia had thoroughly defeated Austria, fighting a great battle (that of Sadowa), which entirely overshadowed his own battles of Magenta and Solferino; and this seven weeks' war had led to changes in the map of Europe the most important which had occurred since 1815; changes, too, in regard to which he had not been consulted. He was rash and foolish enough to demand from the victorious party a share of their territory; but his demand was promptly and justly refused.

It had been his boast that he had made his uncle, Napoleon I, his model, and he had written a "Life of Caesar," for the purpose of demonstrating the divine right of great commanders to absolute authority over the people, and their right and duty to transmit this power to their nephews, or other heirs; but here was a state of things to which there was no parallel in his uncle's career, and he was wholly at fault. The prestige of the Bonaparte name was fast passing away both at home and abroad, and it was a serious question how it could be recovered. From the day of the rejection of his proposed treaty with Prussia, in 1867, it had been evident to him that he must fight Prussia, and seize and hold the Rhenish provinces and Belgium, or lose his throne. The measures he had taken for the reorganization of his army, and for arming them with improved weapons, we have already detailed. What the result was, we shall see presently. It is, nevertheless, a sad commentary on our boasted progress in the nineteenth century, that an unprincipled adventurer, with no higher intellectual ability than Louis Napoleon possessed, and guilty of so many and so great crimes, could have ruled one of the foremost nations of the world for twenty-one years, and have been recognized by the other monarchs of Europe as their peer.

CHAPTER III.

THE ruling spirit of Prussia, since 1862, has been Count Karl Otto von Bismarck-Schönhausen, one of the most able and remarkable statesmen of the present century. His great ability has been shown quite as much in his skill in leading, controlling, and influencing King William I to adopt measures which were directly in opposition to his views and prejudices, as in any of his direct ministerial acts. The King was, partly by nature and partly as a result of his education, a firm believer in the divine right of kings, an intense absolutist, opinionated, wilful, and stubborn, and it required the utmost tact and magnetic power to lead him in any other direction than that in which he had determined to go. But this stern, positive, wilful old man has been moulded by Count Von Bismarck into almost another being, and has now the personal love of those who, in 1864 and 1865, were bitterly hostile to his measures. The man who could accomplish such results, and, while keeping peace between king and people, lead both forward in unity, harmony, and progress, to a higher and better condition as ruler and ruled, is deserving of honor and fame as a great statesman.

Karl Otto von Bismarck was born at Schönhausen, in the province of Saxony, April 1, 1814. He was of an ancient and noble family, who had long been in the service of the Prussian and Saxon rulers. He was educated for the legal profession, at Göttingen, Berlin, and Greifswald, and entered the army for a time after obtaining his degree of Doctor of Philosophy, serving first in the light infantry, and afterward as an officer of the

Landwehr, or Reserves. He did not enter on public political life till his thirty-second year, being elected to the Diet of Saxony in 1846, and to the general or United Diet in 1847. In the latter he soon became the leader of the Junkers, or conservative party, and distinguished himself for eloquence and logical ability. He opposed the adoption of the constitution offered to Prussia, fought most vehemently against the prevalent democracy of the period, and, it is said, declared, in one of his most brilliant speeches, that the great cities of Europe ought to be razed to the ground, because they were the centres of democracy and constitutionalism. He has grown, since that time, to like a constitutional government better than he did, but he is, to-day, far from being a democrat.

His course in the Diet attracted the attention of the King, Frederick William IV, and, in 1851, he assigned him to the difficult and important post of Privy Councillor to the Prussian embassy at Frankfort. In this position he laid down the principle that Prussia could not fulfil her mission in Germany until Austria should be driven out of the Confederation. In 1852 he was sent on a special mission to Vienna, and there, as at Frankfort, showed himself the constant and vigilant adversary of Count Rechberg, the Austrian premier. A pamphlet, written with great ability, appeared in 1858, entitled "Prussia and the Italian Question," and was very generally—and probably correctly—attributed to him. It had no small influence in shaping the subsequent course of Prussia in the war between Austria and France and Italy, in the ensuing year. In 1859, Von Bismarck was Minister to St. Petersburg, and in 1860 he visited Paris. In May, 1862, he was transferred by the present King of Prussia to the French embassy, but remained at Paris only till September, when he was summoned to Berlin as premier of the new Cabinet, with the double duty of Governor of the King's household and Minister of Foreign Affairs.

v. BISMARK
v. MOLTKE
FRIEDRICH WILHELM
FRIEDRICH-CARL
ALBERT v. SACHSEN

He had already attained high distinction as a diplomatist and parliamentarian, but his new position was one of much greater difficulty, and requiring a higher order of talent, than any he had previously filled. He inherited from the Ministry which had preceded him a chronic quarrel with the House of Deputies (answering to our House of Representatives) of the Prussian Legislature. The King and his Cabinet had deemed it indispensable to reorganize the army, and substitute for the militia a system of military training which should make every able-bodied man in the realm an educated soldier, owing and giving to the nation three years of military service, and subsequently forming a member of the Landwehr, or reserve force, liable to be called upon for service in actual war. Connected with this were changes promoting greater efficiency among the officers of the army, and training the whole nation in the use of arms. The necessity of this reorganization grew out of the position of Prussia in relation to Germany. Either she, a nearly pure German power, or Austria, whose population was largely made up of non-German nationalities, must lead Germany. If Prussia was to take this place, she must be prepared to fight for it; if she yielded it to Austria, she became only a second-rate power, without any considerable influence in Europe. If, as was probable, Austria would not relinquish her position without fighting, Prussia must be prepared to contend with a power superior to her in numbers and her equal in resources. It was the duty of the Prussian Government to be prepared for such a conflict, yet to give any hint of its probability would be to court defeat. The King, therefore, under Bismarck's advice, though himself opposed to a war with Austria for any cause, went forward and reorganized the army, expending large sums and doing his work very thoroughly, and then demanded from the Diet the necessary appropriations for it. These the House of Deputies persistently refused, and, when the House of Nobles voted them, impeached their action as illegal. The Ministry insisted on the appropriations, and were vehemently denounced by the Deputies. At length the King, finding the Deputies intractable, closed their session by a message through Bismarck. The next House elected under this excitement proved equally intractable; they could not or would not understand the necessity for this reorganization of the army, and urgently demanded that no money should be withdrawn from the Treasury for the purpose. Bismarck was firm and decided against all this opposition, and, when the press became abusive, he warned and finally suppressed the most noisy of the papers. Meanwhile the war with Denmark drew off a part of the opposition; and when, in 1866 the crisis came, and Prussia, having formed an alliance with Italy, declared war with Austria, defeated her in seven weeks, and reorganized the German Confederation, with herself at its head, and all the German States, except Austria, either confederated or bound to her by treaties offensive and defensive, the wisdom of Bismarck's course became obvious, and those who had denounced him most bitterly were now loudest in his praise. Gifted with a remarkable insight into the motives of men, and especially of monarchs and political leaders, Count Von Bismarck has measured his strength as a diplomatist with the ablest men in Europe, and has invariably maintained his position. He was aware, after the battle of Sadowa, that war with France would come as soon as Louis Napoleon could find a tolerable pretext for it; and, while carefully avoiding any act of provocation, he had been quietly using all his energies in making ready for it. Thus it happened that, when the declaration of war came, Prussia was all ready to take the field, and France was not.

In person, Bismarck is a portly but intellectual-looking man, with a keen, brilliant eye, great self-command, yet with a quick, nervous manner, partly perhaps the result of ill health. He is a fine scholar, thoroughly familiar with most of the languages of Europe, and speaking them fluently, and even idiomatically. His herculean labors for the past five years have permanently impaired his health, and compelled him to take long vacations for its partial restoration ; but he possesses great executive ability and remarkable powers of endurance.

While Germany is indebted to Count Von Bismarck for the political and diplomatic measures which accompanied and followed her recent remarkable reorganization, the strategical plans of the successful war of 1866, as well as those of the Franco-German war of 1870, are due to the extraordinary scientific and military ability of General Von Moltke, a man every way as remarkable in his special department as Von Bismarck is in his.

KARL HELLMUTH BERNHARD, Baron VON MOLTKE, was born in Parchim, Mecklenburg, October 26, 1800. He was from an old and distinguished Mecklenburg family, which had contributed several statesmen to both Denmark and Germany. Soon after his birth, his father, a military officer, left Mecklenburg, and acquired an estate in Holstein, where young Von Moltke spent the first twelve years of his life ; and this has led some of his biographers incorrectly to speak of him as a native of Holstein. He and his brother were sent to the Military Academy in Copenhagen, and the iron discipline, thorough training, and military frugality of that institution, exerted a favorable effect upon a mind constituted as his was, and laid the foundation of an admirable character. In 1822 he entered the Prussian army as cornet. His parents having at this period lost their entire fortune, he was left without any means whatever, and suffered very many hardships in maintaining himself in his position, the pay of the subordinate officers in the Prussian army being at this time very small ; yet he managed to save enough to acquire a very thorough knowledge of the modern languages of Europe, which subsequently proved of great advantage to him. His favorite studies, however, then and since, were the physical sciences. Not Alexander Von Humboldt himself studied with more care and zeal the minute topography and the geological structure of the adjacent countries, than did this young and accomplished officer. Though without powerful friends to facilitate his promotion, his eminent abilities soon procured him a favorable position in the general staff; and his advance, solely from his merit, was remarkably rapid for a Prussian staff-officer. In 1835 he was sent by the Prussian Government to Turkey and Asia Minor, to make inquiry concerning the war between the Sultan and Mehemet Ali. He remained in the East for four years, and his report shows that he had made himself a complete master of the whole Oriental question.

After his return, he published anonymously several works of great merit, descriptive of the country and the Egyptian war. He was advanced, in a short time, through the different ranks to that of lieutenant-general, and, finally, to be chief of the general staff of the Prussian army. In this capacity he drew up, even to its minutest details, the plan of the reorganization of the Prussian army and Landwehr, or Reserve, and to the perfection of this plan is unquestionably due much of the success which has since attended the Prussian warfare. At the commencement of the Austro-Prussian war of 1866, his wonderful topographical knowledge was made manifest. His plans for the movement of the Prussian armies indicated a most intimate and thorough acquaintance with every hill, mountain, defile, ravine, and stream in their course. Even their places of encampment were designated, and the progress they would be expected to make and the obstacles they would have to encounter, were all designated. His strategic prescience was equally remarkable. He foresaw the fatal delays of Benedek and the unavailing impetuosity of Clam-Gallas, and had so arranged the time of marching of the different armies as to render their junction at the right time morally certain. The unexpected obstacles which delayed the Crown-Prince, and prevented his reaching the battle-field of Sadowa till afternoon, had well-nigh produced a disaster; but even here Von Moltke's careful allowance of time brought all right in the end. Both Prince Friedrich Karl and the Crown-Prince had been his pupils in military science, and especially in strategics; and the latter especially was a great favorite with him. That he had for years foreseen the Franco-Prussian war of 1870, is certain; and more than one of the French peasants and bourgeois have recognized in the grave, silent general-in-chief, so absorbed in his maps, a venerable Professor of Geology, who, some three years ago, hammer in hand, and with a younger companion (the present Crown-Prince) who had a great predilection for botany, rambled over the ramparts and suburbs of Strasbourg, Weissenburg, Toul, and Metz, examining most carefully the fortifications, chipping off here and there a bit of stone as a geological specimen, and, with his companion, exploring every stream, ravine, and hill, in search of botanical specimens for their herbariums. So careful was their survey, that, with the aid of their excellent maps, they were far more familiar with the minute topography of the entire theatre of the war, and the weak points of all the fortifications, than all the French staff together.

When General Wimpffen hesitated in regard to surrendering at Sedan, General Von Moltke demonstrated to him, in the fewest possible words, that such was the position of the German troops, and so complete their command of every avenue of escape or of resistance, that his surrender had been a foregone conclusion since the previous day.

General Von Moltke is a man of dignified and imposing personal appearance, but of great modesty and simplicity of manners. He is reserved and taciturn, but always, whether in conversation, in giving commands to his officers, or in the heat of battle, maintains the same composure and equanimity. The army have given him the surname of "The Silent;" but when he does speak, his words are well worth hearing. He is said to be, to this day, more fond of physical than military science; but his reputation in the future will rest mainly on the fact that he has been, in a much higher sense than the distinguished Carnot, "an organizer of victories."

Of the French premiers, war ministers, and chiefs of staff in the last days of the Empire, there were none who compared with Bismarck and Von Moltke for ability or diplomatic skill. The diplomacy was of less consequence, since the Emperor himself managed the intercourse of France with foreign powers, and inspired the correspondence, which his Ministers put in form.

The position of Chief of Staff, which was often, in France, associated with the office of War Minister, was one of great importance and responsibility; but Napoleon III's theory of government required that this officer also should be his tool and do his bidding. It resulted from this theory that, whether the premier were Ollivier or Rouher, and the chief of staff Leboeuf or De Palikao, they were alike the creatures of their master, bound to do his will and discarded at his pleasure.

Of Ollivier and Rouher it is hardly necessary to say much. The latter was a man of considerable ability, but intensely absolutist in his views, and the supple tool and mouthpiece of Napoleon III. Ollivier had been a Republican, and for some years a leader of the Opposition, but, since 1863, his fidelity to that party had been suspected. He continued from that time to cultivate more and more friendly relations toward the Emperor, whom he had formerly attacked with great bitterness, and, after receiving from him several lucrative temporary appointments, he was, in the winter of 1870, called to take Rouher's place as Prime Minister. His administration was every way weak and unfortunate. Irritable, and possessing little dignity of manner or character, he was goaded most unmercifully by his former associates, the Republicans; and, uneasy in his position, which he could not but feel was a false one, he lost his temper under their sharp questioning, and alternately wrangled and threatened, till he presented a most pitiable spectacle. Questioned concerning government delinquencies which he knew, but had neither the tact to conceal or defend, he became, at times, furious in his threats, which he had not the courage to put in execution. At the declaration of war, there was a momentary hush of the discord; the feeling of patriotism for the time dominated over the hostility of the Opposition to the Emperor, and a man of shrewdness and tact would have availed himself of this opportunity to regain the prestige he had lost; but Ollivier had not the ability to accomplish this, and very soon he was again wrangling with Favre, Gambetta, and the other Republican leaders.

At his first reverses the Emperor did not hesitate to throw overboard this man, who had sacrificed his reputation and character for his favor, and for a brief period the Count of Palikao took his place as premier.

Of the Count we shall have occasion to speak hereafter.

General EDMOND LEBOEUF, Minister of War and Chief of Staff of the French army at the beginning of the war, had a good, though by no means the highest, reputation as a military leader among the French generals. He was born November 5, 1809, and received his military education at the Polytechnic School in Paris and the School of Artillery at Metz. At twenty-eight years of age he was a captain, and, nine years later, major of a regiment of artillery. In 1848 he was made assistant commandant of the Polytechnic School, where he remained till 1850. In 1852 he was promoted to a colonelcy, and during the whole of the Crimean war served as chief of artillery. In 1854 he was made brigadier-general, and in 1857, general of division. In the Italian war of 1859 he was again chief of the large artillery force there engaged, and distinguished himself for bravery and skill, receiving the rank of Grand Officer of the Legion of Honor from the Emperor in August, 1859. He was subsequently appointed aide-de-camp to the Emperor, and made head of the Artillery Bureau. On the death of Marshal Niel, in 1869, he was made Minister of War, and introduced some essential reforms in the organization of the army. The taint of corruption, however, had attached to him. On the appointment of a commission to decide upon a new breech-loading rifle for the French army, there were many patterns offered, but he excluded all except the chassepôt, in the manufacture of which he had a large interest; and this gun, though inferior to several of the others, was supplied in immense quantities to the French army. With his downfall, the reputation of the rifle fell also; and in the midst of the war, the French Provisional Government, and, indeed, the successor of Leboeuf, began to order American patterns of rifles, which stood the test of actual warfare much better, but which Leboeuf had rejected because he could make no profit on them. It is averred, also, that large quantities of the chassepôt rifles, of imperfect and defective construction, were passed by the inspectors and placed in the hands of the soldiers, by the orders of this corrupt War-Minister. Subsequently to his removal from office, he is said to have acknowledged that he knew that neither the nation nor the army were prepared for war, but that he did not dare to tell the Emperor so, lest he should excite his displeasure.

Charles Guillaume Marie Appolinaire Antoine, Cousin-Montauban, Comte de Palikao, the successor of Leboeuf as Minister of War, and subsequently for a brief period also premier, is an old man of higher military reputation, more executive ability, and probably of greater honesty and integrity, than his predecessor; but, educated in the Algerian wars, and naturally of a stern and cruel nature, he was not the man to be the leader

OLLIVIER · FAVRE

MAC MAHON · BAZAINE

CANROBERT · PALIKAO · TROCHU

either in war or diplomacy of a great and generous people. He was born June 24, 1796; educated at the Polytechnic school. At twenty-eight years of age he was a cavalry officer, and had won distinction in Algeria. At forty years of age he was major; and, nine years later, colonel of Spahis (the irregular but terrible dragoons of the African army). In 1851 he had been promoted to be brigadier-general, but was actually in command of a division. His promotion to the rank of major-general came in 1855, and with it the military governorship of Constantine. Not long after, he was recalled to France and placed in command of one of the grand military divisions—a post to which his forty years of active service entitled him. In 1860 he was appointed commander-in-chief of the joint expedition against China of the French and English forces. His movements here were marked by great celerity and success. The forts of Taku, at the mouth of Peiho, were captured, after a severe engagement, on the 20th of August; the successful battle of Palikao fought September 21st; the summer palace of the Chinese Emperor destroyed, and the victorious troops entered Peking, October 12th; the treaty of peace negotiated, and General Montauban left China in December of the same year. Abundant honors were heaped upon him for this service. The Grand Cross of the Legion of Honor (its highest decoration) was conferred upon him in December, 1860. He was appointed Senator in 1861, and created Count of Palikao in 1862, with a liberal dotation, which, however, was strongly resisted by the Corps Législatif. He was made commander of the Fourth Army Corps in 1865, and a member of the Cabinet in 1870. His lifelong experience in fighting Kabyles, Berbers, and Chinese, had not qualified him specially for civilized warfare, and it was alleged by the Prussians that to his counsel was largely due the employment in this war of the savage Turcos and Spahis, whose excesses and brutality have here, as elsewhere, brought down upon them the reprobation of the civilized world.

Of the French military commanders distinguished in former wars, several, as General Changarnier—a Republican in politics, but one of the ablest of the French generals in his day—Marshals Randon, Vaillant, and Baraguey d'Hilliers, and the Count De Palikao, were too old for active service; others, as General Trochu, were not specially in favor with the Emperor, and were only grudgingly allowed inferior commands. Those designated to the three armies were Marshals MacMahon, Canrobert, and Bazaine. A brief sketch of the previous career of these men may be of interest, as throwing light upon their action during the war.

Marshal MARIE EDME PATRICK MAURICE DE MACMAHON, Duke of Magenta, born at Sully, July 13, 1808, is a descendant of an old Irish Catholic family attached to the Stuarts. He entered the military school of St. Cyr in 1825, won his first laurels in Algeria, where he fought in numerous battles and minor engagements. An incident in the African campaign shows his intrepid character. At the close of the successful battle of Terchia, General Achard wished to send an order to Colonel Rulhieres, at Blidah, between three and four miles off, to change the order of his march. This commission he entrusted to MacMahon, and offered him a squadron of mounted chasseurs as an escort. He declined their protection, and rode off alone. His journey lay entirely through the enemy's country, which was rugged and irregular. About six hundred yards from Blidah was a ravine, broad, deep, and precipitous. MacMahon had ridden close to the ravine, when suddenly he beheld a host of Arabs in full pursuit of him from every side. One look told him his chances. There was no alternative but to jump the treacherous abyss or be butchered by his pursuers. He set his horse's head at the leap, put spur and whip to it, and cleared the ravine at a bound. The pursuing Arabs, dismayed, ventured no further, and only sent after the daring soldier a shower of bullets as horse and rider rolled over on the other side, with the poor steed's leg broken. At the attack on Constantine he received further promotion. His superiority as a tactician became soon apparent, and was fully appreciated and rewarded by rapid advancement. His long career as a military commander in the colony, and his never-ceasing activity in behalf of the firm establishment of French authority in Northern Africa, were interrupted, for some time at least, by his recall to France in 1855. It was not, however, the intention of the Government to let him remain inactive; he was, on the contrary, immediately assigned to the command of a division of infantry forming part of the army under Marshal Bosquet. Here he laid the foundation of his military glory. On the 8th of September, the perilous honor devolved on him of carrying the Malakoff, which formed the key of the defences of Sebastopol. The impetuous ardor of his troops proved irresistible. They entered the works and maintained for hours a desperate conflict with the Russians. Pellissier, the commander-in-chief, believed the fort was mined. He sent MacMahon orders to retire. "I will hold my ground," was the reply, "dead or alive." Success crowned his bravery, and the tricolor soon floated above the fortress. In 1857 he returned to Algeria, forced the revolting Kabyles into submission, and was soon after appointed commander-in-chief of all the French forces there on land and sea. The outbreak of the Italian war, in 1859, caused his return to France, when he was assigned to the command of the Second Corps of the Army of the Alps. Here his brilliant movement on the Austrians, turning a threatened defeat into a victory at Magenta, and concealing the blunders of his imperial master, were rewarded by the conferring on him the titles of Duke of Magenta and Marshal of France, on the field of battle. In November, 1861, he was sent to Berlin to represent France at the coronation of William

I, the present King of Prussia; and in the splendor of his appointments, and the magnificence of his retinue, outshone all the other representatives of foreign courts. In October, 1862, he succeeded Marshal Canrobert in the command of the Third Army Corps; and, two years later, was made governor-general of Algeria, where he introduced many administrative reforms. He was recalled from Algeria shortly before the opening of the Franco-German war, and took an active part in organizing the army for service. Marshal MacMahon bears the reputation of a gallant, manly, and honest officer; and though his long experience in Algeria had partially disqualified him for civilized warfare, and made him reckless of those details on which, in a contest with an able and intelligent foe, all success depends, yet he deserves the reputation of being the best of the French army commanders.

Marshal FRANÇOIS CERTAIN CANROBERT, born in the Department of Gers, June 27, 1809, was admitted to the military school of St. Cyr in 1825, which he left in 1828, to enter the 47th Regiment of the Line as second lieutenant, and soon after joined the military expedition to Mascara, fought bravely in several engagements against the hostile tribes in Northern Africa, and assisted at the storming of Constantine in 1837. He was sent back to France in 1839, for the purpose of forming a battalion for the foreign legion out of the dispersed bands of Carlists. He succeeded in this, and returned to Africa in 1841, where he was entrusted with the command of a battalion of light infantry and of the 64th Regiment of the Line, suppressed the rebellion of Bon Maza, and, during eight months of desperate fighting, forced most of the revolting tribes of Kabyles into submission. He was engaged in various parts of Northern Africa for nearly eight years, led some of the most daring and adventurous expeditions into the interior, and everywhere distinguished himself by his coolness, bravery, and quick adaptation to the warfare to which he had to resort. Returning to France he proved, by his services to Louis Napoleon, that he meant to be a firm supporter of the new *régime*, and has ever since been one of the stanchest friends and adherents of the second empire. He was made general of division in 1853, took part in the expedition to the Crimea, and when Marshal St. Arnaud felt his end approaching, he transmitted the command of the entire French army to Canrobert. This was in accordance with an order given in a private letter by the Emperor Napoleon himself. Having won new laurels at the sanguinary battles of Inkermann, Balaklava, and Eupatoria, he conferred with Lord Raglan, commander of the British forces, and urged him to participate in an immediate assault on Sebastopol. The two commanders being unable to agree, and Lord Raglan sternly refusing to coöperate in the intended movement, Canrobert resigned in favor of General Pelissier, and left the Crimea two months after. During the Italian campaign, in 1859, he commanded the Third Army Corps, fought at Magenta, and afterwards contributed most essentially to the decisive victory of the French army at the battle of Solferino, sustaining Marshal Niel at a critical moment against the furious assault of a powerful Austrian column. By virtue of his rank as Marshal (to which he was promoted in 1856), Canrobert is a Senator of France, and, in that capacity, opposed strongly the maintenance of the temporal power of the Pope in March, 1861. He commanded the camp at Chalons from June to October, 1862, and was then promoted to the command of the Fourth Army Corps at Lyons, which he yielded, two years later, to Marshal MacMahon. During a few years past he has been residing in Paris, attending the sessions of the Senate, and watching over the interests of the army. He is a man of considerable ability, but not free from the taint of the corruption and demoralization which has pervaded all classes in connection with the imperial court.

The third of these army-commanders, and incomparably the worst, was Marshal FRANÇOIS ACHILLE BAZAINE, born February 13, 1811, a descendant of a family well known in French military history, who studied at the Polytechnic School in Paris, and entered the army in Africa when twenty years old. After six years of uninterrupted warfare against the Kabyles and other hostile tribes, he was assigned to the foreign legion, and sent into Spain, in 1837, to suppress the Carlist movement in that country. He returned to Algeria in 1839, joined the expedition against Milianah and Morocco, and was for several years governor of the Arabian subdivision of Tlemcen. During the Crimean war, where he was in command of a brigade of infantry, he is said to have distinguished himself by his bravery and by his talent for organization. When the Russians had evacuated Sebastopol, Bazaine was made Governor of the place. He took no part in the campaign against Austria in 1859, but was entrusted with the command of the first division of infantry of the expedition to Mexico, in 1862. The Emperor Napoleon, taking advantage of the civil war then raging in the United States, conceived the idea of establishing an empire at our Southern frontier, hoping thus to prepare the way for the final supremacy of the Latin race on this continent. The attempt proved a failure. French pride was humiliated, and the army compelled to reëmbark, towards the close of 1866.

General Bazaine succeeded Marshal Forey in the command of the expedition in October, 1863, and continued to be its chief till his hasty departure in 1866. His whole course was marked by a cruelty and barbarity which would have been disgraceful in a savage chief. Regarding the Mexicans as barbarians, he showed himself far more cruel than they. He organized, from the vilest desperadoes he could hire, what he called "counter-guerilla bands," to fight the irregular Mexican troops; and the atrocities committed by these wretches, and never reproved by him, exceed belief. His unscrupulous rapacity, and his constant intrigues against the heroic Maximilian, would of themselves be sufficient to stain a character none too fair without these blots. In 1864, Bazaine was made Marshal of France, having, the year before, received the Grand Cross of the Legion of Honor. Corrupt, rapacious, and false even to his friends, Bazaine's appointment to a high command in the army in the war of 1870 was the most discreditable to the Emperor of any act of his in connection with the war; and it is no more than fair to believe that it was only because Napoleon III was too fully in the power of this bold, bad man, to help himself, that he assigned him to this position.

Of the corps-commanders, General Frossard, the late chief of the Emperor's household, and governor of the Prince Imperial; General De Failly, first distinguished in the Italian war, and subsequently (in 1867) sent to Rome to put down the Garibaldian movement; Count Ladmirault, late commander of the Second Army Corps; General Douay, an active officer of the Mexican expedition, and General Bourbaki, an officer of Greek family, distinguished both in the Crimean and Italian wars, were the most prominent.

Later in the war, General DE WIMPFFEN, a brave and gallant officer, came from Algeria, where he had served for several years, to join MacMahon's army, to take command in consequence of MacMahon's being severely wounded, and to surrender the army, all within thirty-six hours.

General TROCHU, who was at first ignored as being out of favor with the Emperor, but eventually, in the time of his distress, assigned to the command of Paris and its fortifications, bears the reputation of being an honest, brave, and capable officer, on whose character, public or private, there is no stain. He was born in the department of the Morbihan, March 12, 1815; was educated at St. Cyr, and at the staff school. A lieutenant in 1840 and a captain in 1843, he was attached to Marshal Bugeaud's staff in Algeria, and, like all the rest of the French officers, took his ten years' or more of training there. In 1853 he was aide-de-camp to Marshal St. Arnaud in the Crimea, with the rank of colonel; and, in 1854, had risen to the rank of brigadier-general. In 1859, as major-general, he went through the Italian campaign, winning distinction for bravery and military skill. He was made grand officer of the Legion of Honor in 1861. As we shall see further on in this history, he has displayed, since the commencement of his command in Paris, great skill and remarkable executive ability under the most trying circumstances in which a commander could be placed, and has won the confidence of all as a patriot, who sought his country's good in preference to his own, or that of any aspirant to power. Such men are so rare, that it is but right that their names should be honored when they are found.

GENERAL TROCHU, GOVERNOR OF PARIS.

CHAPTER IV.

WITH brief sketches of a few of the principal German commanders, we hasten to the consideration of another branch of our subject.

The ablest of the Prussian commanding generals—the venerable chief of staff always excepted—though by no means the oldest, is Prince FRIEDRICH KARL ALEXANDER, son of Prince Karl, and nephew of the King of Prussia. He was born March 20, 1828. Like all Prussian princes, Friedrich Karl had to enter the Prussian army when scarcely ten years old, it being considered necessary that every descendant of the house of Hohenzollern, no matter what his individual inclination may be, should become fully acquainted with the military service of his country, and that, whatever career he may ultimately follow, he may be called upon at any moment to draw his sword for the defence of Fatherland in times of danger. With Friedrich Karl, however, there was no need of compulsion. The warlike spirit of his ancestors animated him even in his earliest youth, and induced him to devote himself with enthusiasm to his military studies. The result of this innate love of every thing connected with the army soon became apparent in the rapid progress he made in the military school of instruction. The study of the life and glorious deeds of Frederick the Great filled his leisure hours, and it is said that he was on several occasions severely reprimanded for passing entire nights over the history of the "Seven Years' War," and the study of the plans of battle adopted by that illustrious captain. At the outbreak of the first war of Schleswig-Holstein, in 1848, he was assigned to the staff of the commander-in-chief of the Prussian forces, General Von Wrangel, when, at the battle of Schleswig, his impetuosity and his entire disregard of all danger, while imperilling his life at every instant, did not fail to encourage the troops, and materially aided in securing the victory to the Prussian eagle. During the campaign in Baden in 1849, he likewise distinguished himself on various occasions. Fifteen years of peace now followed, during which the Prince resumed his theoretical studies of the science of war, made himself familiar with all branches of the army, and showed conclusively his superior talent for the organization as well as for the skilful disposition of large armies. The disregard of treaties by Denmark resulting in a declaration of war against that power by Austria and Prussia, the second campaign in Schleswig-Holstein was soon entered upon, and, although General Von Wrangel was at first appointed commander-in-chief of the combined armies, the command of the Prussian division was intrusted to Prince Friedrich Karl, December 15, 1863. He at once recognized the fortified place of Düppel to be one of the greatest Danish strongholds, and a formidable barrier to the advance of the German armies into Danish territory. He therefore decided upon a regular siege and investment of the position. The severity of the winter in these northern latitudes interfered considerably with his operations, and it was not until April, 1864, that he thought safe to order first the bombardment and then the storming of the fortifications. Twice the assault was repulsed with serious slaughter, until, at last, the intrepid commander grasped the flag of the regiment of Royal Guards, and, personally leading his troops to a third attack, drove the enemy out of his stronghold and gained a decided victory, the Danes losing over 5,000 men and 118 pieces of artillery. Being defeated in several other important engagements, the Danes saw the impossibility of further resistance, and a treaty of peace was signed on October 30, 1864. At the outbreak of hostilities between Prussia and Austria in 1866, Prince Friedrich Karl was called to the command of the first division of the Prussian army, immediately marched his troops to the frontier, which he crossed on June 23, and, in ordering the attack upon the forces of the enemy, addressed his men with the words: "May your hearts beat toward God, and your fists upon the enemy." A succession of splendid victories at Liebenau, Turnau, Podol, Münchengrätz, and Gitschin, having forced the enemy into the interior of Bohemia, Prince Friedrich Karl, who knew the Austrians to have occupied a formidable position on the heights beyond the Bistritz, requested the Crown-Prince Friedrich Wilhelm to come to his assistance with the second division of the army, but attacked the enemy on the morning of July 3, without awaiting his arrival. The Prussians fought desperately, but the position of the enemy was so well chosen and their artillery so favorably placed, that the Prince could not gain a decided advantage over them, and it was not until the arrival of the second division, under the Crown-Prince, that the enemy lost ground, retreated under the deadly fire of the Prussians, and was finally completely routed, running in all directions and in the wildest confusion. This ended the celebrated battle of Sadowa. The enemy was pursued from the 5th to the 12th. Brünn was taken, and the Prussian troops found themselves near the capital of Austria, ready, at a moment's notice, to march upon Vienna. The interference of France resulting in the treaty of Prague, this ever-memorable campaign was at an end, Austria humiliated, and her former military prestige lost forever. As might be anticipated from a man who had taken such a conspicuous part in the brilliant achievements of the Prussian army, our hero, although proud of his troops, and willingly admitting their superiority over any European army which could then be marshalled against them, had nevertheless become aware of some serious drawbacks and errors hitherto overlooked in the organization of the Prussian army, and at once concluded to advocate such reforms as his experience had convinced him to be absolutely necessary. Meeting with opposition in high quarters, he is said to have resolved to submit his opinions to the approval of the highest military authorities; and it is generally believed that he is the author of an anonymous pamphlet published in Frankfort, which has attracted the greatest attention from the Government, and has been the cause of the recent important reforms in the Prussian army.

It appears that the views expressed in this publication gained the approbation of the Chief of Staff, Von Moltke; and the consequence was that, after a free conference with the Prince, changes were made which have, during the recent campaign, demonstrated that the Prussian army is in every respect by far the best in Europe. Of the part taken by the Prince in the war of 1870, we shall have occasion to speak hereafter.

Scarcely inferior to Prince Friedrich Karl in general military ability, and, judging from his admirable generalship in the recent campaign, fully his equal in handling his troops, is the Crown-Prince FRIEDRICH WILHELM, eldest son of the King of Prussia, and heir-apparent to the German throne. The Crown-Prince was born October 18, 1831, and received the thorough scientific and military education which all the Prussian princes are required to obtain. He was a diligent student, and particularly fond of physical science. Later, he was a pupil of Von Moltke, and learned from him the principles of strategy and tactics which he has since so skilfully reduced to practice. He took part as a corps-commander in the Danish war of 1864, came to the rescue at Sadowa in 1866, and turned what had nearly been a drawn battle, if not a defeat, into an overwhelming victory. In the campaign of 1870, as we shall see, he has

GENERAL STEINMETZ.

had the command of the army which has done the hardest fighting; and, in the full prime of manhood and the maturity of his powers, he has displayed a tact, judgment, and skill in handling his troops, and in his rapid movements and persistent pursuit of his enemy, which rank him among the great generals of our time.

The other general who has been most distinguished in the campaign of 1870 is the veteran KARL FRIEDRICH VON STEINMETZ, "The Lion of Skalitz." He is one of the veterans of the Napoleonic wars (1812-15), and, though a little too much inclined to adhere to the old traditions of the Prussian army, is nevertheless a very able and skilful officer. Von Steinmetz was born December 27, 1796, was sent to the military school at Culm at the age of ten years, and soon showed a decided predilection for the army. He was a little over sixteen years old when he was ordered to Berlin and assigned to the corps of General York. Two years later he received his commission as lieutenant, was wounded at the battle of Dannigkow, fought with distinction at Königswartha, where a ball took away one of his fingers, while another wounded him severely in the thigh. But such was the ardor of his warlike temper, that, although unable to walk, he insisted upon taking part in the battle at Bautzen, in May, 1813, on horseback. He fought in France in nearly all the engagements of 1814, and entered Paris with the armies of the Allies. During the long term of peace which now followed, he studied military science to great advantage, and, after advancing rapidly to the rank of captain, he was soon after assigned to the staff. During the dispute between Austria and Prussia, in 1850, on account of the Electorate of Hesse, Von Steinmetz was ordered to Cassel, and afterward appointed commandant of the place. Although it was his earnest desire to participate in the second campaign in Schleswig-Holstein in 1864, he was ordered elsewhere, and had to remain inactive against his will. During the campaign against Austria, Von Steinmetz commanded the Fifth Army Corps, and vanquished and dispersed three different Austrian army-corps within the almost incredible short space of four days. Here it was that the Prussian cavalry, who had been hitherto considered as inferior to the Austrian, or rather Hungarian, horsemen, proved that they were not only their equal, but in many respects their superiors. His triumphant victory at Skalitz, against forces of more than twice the numerical strength of the corps he commanded, procured for him the name, "The Lion of Skalitz." Throughout the entire campaign Von Steinmetz did not meet with a single reverse, although he was often compelled to fight with the odds decidedly against him. He has been accused, like many other great generals, of being too reckless of the lives of his troops when intent upon gaining a victory, and this fault is said to have led to his being relieved of the command after the battle of Gravelotte; but while there may be truth in the charge, these men of relentless wills, after all, sacrifice fewer lives by delay, sickness, and despondency, than men of less decided purpose and energy. At the beginning of the war General Von Steinmetz was assigned to the command of the First German Army, consisting of the First, Seventh, and Eighth Army Corps; the Second Army being under the command of Prince Friedrich Karl, and including the Second, Third, Ninth, and Tenth Army Corps; and the Third Army under the Crown-Prince of Prussia, composed of the Fifth, Sixth, and Eleventh, and the two Bavarian Army Corps. There was also a Fourth Army, composed of the Fourth and Twelfth Army Corps and the Saxon and Prussian Guards, under the command of Friedrich August Albert, Crown-Prince of Saxony, a well-educated and skilful officer, born in 1828, and who commanded the Saxon contingent of Austria in the war of 1866. A Fifth Army, composed of the Wurtemberg and Baden contingents, under the command of General Werden, has also participated in the war, being engaged in the siege of Strasbourg; while the Landwehr, or Reserves, formed the Sixth and Seventh Armies, the former under the command of Friedrich Franz, Grand Duke of Mecklenburg-Schwerin, a brave and accomplished officer, and the latter under General Von Canstein, at Berlin, and General Loewenfeld, in Silesia. The corps-commanders were all men of experience and ability; and the whole army, composed as it was of different nationalities of the German race, manifested the most remarkable harmony and obedience.

CHAPTER V.

THE financial condition of the two countries which are the principals in this war is an important item in its relations to their ability to endure a great war. It is, however, a matter of no small difficulty to arrive at the exact facts in relation to the financial condition of France, since the statements of her Ministers of Finance under the empire were irreconcilable with themselves and with each other. In the first place, they gave the "project of the budget," or estimate of the receipts and expenses of the next year; then, a year or two later, the "rectified budget," or corrected estimate for the same year; and, a year or two later still, the "definitive budget," or ascertained amount of the expenses of perhaps three years before; and these estimates would vary from forty-five to fifty millions of dollars from each other. And, what was worse even, these definitive statements did not represent the actual expenditure; and, in the course of sixteen years, loans were contracted in all to the amount of five hundred and fifty million dollars, to supplement the current revenue. There is too much reason to believe that fraud and peculation were rife in every department of the Government. As nearly as can be ascertained, however, the following statement represents pretty accurately the financial condition of France in the beginning of 1870.

The total revenue received in France, in 1869, was $425,-744,360, being $54,800,612 in excess of that of the United

States. This sum was raised by customs duties and an elaborate system of inland revenue, which directly affects all interests in the empire.

The principal items of this revenue were:

Direct taxes	$65,903,732
Registration, duties, and stamps	86,789,200
Customs and salt duties	20,724,600
Departmental and Communal taxes	45,649,166
Wine and spirit duties	46,943,200
Tobacco monopoly	49,531,600

These figures serve to show the sources relied upon for revenue in France, and which will have to bear, in the future, a large portion of the present war expenditure.

The estimated expenditure for the same period was $440,668,130, formed of items such as the following:

Interest on the funded and floating debt	$74,449,153
Ministry of the Interior	40,049,587
Ministry of War	74,172,155
Ministry of Finance	23,889,565
Ministry of Marine and Colonies	32,267,684
Collection of revenue	46,855,022

The military expenditure of France during a year of profound peace was, it appears, in round numbers, $74,000,000; such being the burden entailed by the French standing army of 404,000 men, irrespective of their forced withdrawal from productive industry. The marine, in addition, exacted, including colonial expenditure, the sum of $32,267,684. In the presence of this large revenue it cannot be said that France has been, as the United States were at the commencement of hostilities, free for years from heavy taxation, and consequently all the better prepared to meet the burdens of war. On the contrary, her expenditure was augmented in the following extraordinary proportions, and has since these years rather increased than diminished.

1852... $371,000,000
1853... 441,600,000
1854... 416,800,000
1855... 434,000,000
1856... 422,400,000
1857... 457,400,000

The ordinary revenue in the twelve years from the establishment of the empire till the end of 1863, increased from $297,400,000 to $452,800,000; while the expenditures augmented in the same twelve years from $302,600,000 to $457,400,000. With the exception of 1855, when the revenue was raised high above the average by special means, there was not a year without a large deficit. To cover the ever-recurring financial deficits, the Government, between the years 1854 and 1870, procured a series of loans, seven in number, in sums, as to nominal capital, varying between $50,000,000 and $150,000,000. These loans were raised on a new principle—that of borrowing not from a few large banking-houses acting as agents, but directly from the people, or the mass of small capitalists, both in France and other countries. This course was highly successful. The fifth loan, for instance, which was offered in 1859 and issued at 66 francs, 30 centimes—bearing 3 per cent. interest, was received with the offer, on the part of half a million persons, of 4,487,000,000 francs, or sixteen times the amount required.

The following shows the cost of the three principal wars of the empire, and the drain upon the population which they caused:

	Cost.	Loss of men.
Crimean war..................	$1,700,000,000	80,000
Austrian war..................	300,000,000	60,000
Chinese and Mexican wars.....	200,000,000	65,000
Total................	$2,200,000,000	205,000

In connection with the increased expenditure referred to, it should be borne in mind that the material wealth of France has rapidly increased, mainly owing to the intervals of peace which she enjoyed. Her home industries have suffered from the operation of the commercial treaty with England, but, despite that, their expansion has been great and general, if we except shipbuilding. The imports and exports in 1860 and 1868 contrast as follows:

	Imports.	Exports.	Total.
1860	$379,466,965	$455,425,223	$834,892,188
1868	679,714,400	581,358,000	1,261,072,400

One legacy which Napoleon III will leave France is an enormous increase in her national debt. It was, in 1853, $1,103,238,940. In 1868 it was $2,766,344,622, or two and a half times greater. This is exclusive of a floating debt amounting to about $173,200,000, consisting of Treasury bills, funds from savings banks, the Army Dotation Fund, and other liabilities.

This debt, as stated in the revenue returns, entails an annual interest of $74,449,153, which is, however, much below the total expenditure, on account of interest, pensions, and annuities, which, in 1869, amounted to $128,225,000, or very nearly the interest on our debt the same year. Despite the increase in the national debt, French credit has improved. On June 29, 1870, before the fears of war awakened the tremulous capitalists, Rentes bearing 4½ per cent. interest sold for 104, and 3 per cents. for 72.65.

The computed value of the real property in France is $16,000,000,000: the rural properties are valued at $10,000,000,000, and the town properties and buildings at $6,000,000,000.

Turning now to the financial condition of Germany and Prussia, we find a different state of affairs. The finances of both the North German Confederation and the Prussian kingdom were in a good condition, and the debt comparatively small.

The revenue and expenditure of the North German Confederation for federal purposes is not large. The federal budget for the year 1870, passed by the Diet, April 24, 1869, was based upon an estimate of expenditure, in round numbers, of $56,000,000, to be covered to the extent of $39,000,000 by Prussia, and the remainder by the other States of the Union. The total expenditure for 1869 was calculated at 72,734,601 thalers, or about $54,550,950, of which the ordinary and extraordinary disbursements were distributed as follows:

	Thalers.		
For the Federal Chancellery, &c....	193,913	=	$145,435
For Consulates....................	275,650	=	206,788
For the Federal Army.............	66,340,275	=	49,755,206
For the Federal Navy.............	1,868,979	=	1,401,734

EXTRAORDINARY EXPENDITURE.

	Thalers.		
For the Federal Chancellery........	150,000	=	$112,500
For the General Post Administration	27,999	=	21,000
For Telegraphs	322,780	=	242,085
For the Federal Navy.............	3,550,000	=	2,662,500

The estimates for this year are, of course, now far below what will be required.

The revenue of Prussia, according to the budget accounts in 1869, was $125,652,370, and the expenditure the same. The revenue and expenditure of Prussia has, since 1865, been almost stationary, and no deficits have marked her annual financial returns—a feature unusual in most European budgets. This revenue, in 1869, was raised to the extent of $31,500,000, from direct and indirect taxes, to the amount of $14,180,443, which includes the share of the Zollverein customs.

The State railroads, mines, forges, and other Government monopolies, yielded the greater part of the balance. In the estimate for 1869, the branches of expenditure were as follows:

EXPENDITURE FOR THE YEAR 1869.

Current Expenditure.

	Thalers.
Ministry of Finance............	17,617,117
Ministry of Commerce and Public Works......................	41,603,775
Ministry of State.............. ♦	73,256
Total current expenditure....	59,294,148

Administrative Expenditure.

Ministry of Finance.............	32,026,658
Ministry of Commerce and Public Works......................	9,018,874
Ministry of Justice..............	15,943,780
Ministry of the Interior..........	8,242,488
Ministry of Agriculture..........	2,283,648
Ministry of Public Instruction and Ecclesiastical Affairs.....	6,222,004
Ministry of State..............	394,659
Ministry of Foreign Affairs......	914,630
Charges for the Hohenzollern territory......................	220,628
Total administrative expenditure.	75,267,369

Charges on Consolidated Fund.

Addition to the "Krondotation" of the King................	1,500,000
Interest on Public Debt, including railway debt.............	16,973,637
Sinking fund of debt...........	8,178,433
Annuities........	429,753
Chamber of Lords...	40,910
Chamber of Deputies....	243,000
Miscellaneous..................	122,807
Total charges on Consolidated Fund	27,488,540
Total ordinary expenditure......	162,050,057 = $127,537,543
Extraordinary expenditure.......	5,486,437 = 4,114,828
	167,536,494 = $125,652,371

The public debt of Prussia is very light, and has been almost entirely incurred since 1850. While six and a half years of the large French annual revenue is represented by the amount of the French debt, that of Prussia amounts to only one and a half years of her moderate annual receipts. The total debt of the kingdom, both old and new provinces, amounts to $188,497,520, exclusive of the small liabilities incurred by the annexed provinces for the establishment of State railroads.

The revenue and expenditure of the other German States is unimportant. The same economy is apparent in their financial affairs as in the Prussian, the standing armies being the only serious burden.

It follows, from the solvency and well-managed finances of Prussia, that her credit is untarnished. During fifty-five years the German people have (excepting the recent Austrian war) been undisturbed by war, and have been enabled to develop the immense resources of their fertile territory and accumulate large material wealth.

The social condition of the two countries offers an equally striking contrast. In Germany, and especially in Prussia, education is well-nigh universal. The population of the North German Confederation, in 1867, was 29,653,038, and that of South Germany 8,869,328; making a total of 38,522,366. Of this population, only an infinitesimal proportion are unable to read and write, while the greater part have a good public-school education.

The great advantages of this thorough education have made themselves visible in the improved social condition and greater intelligence of the masses, and have made them vastly better soldiers in a cause where their patriotic feelings were enlisted. It has resulted, too, in a larger measure of thrift and business enterprise throughout the whole of Germany. Nearly every town has its thriving manufactory; and though the price of labor is low, it is advancing, and with it the wealth of the community.

The social condition of France is not so good. The wealth, intelligence, and business activity of the country, and, to a large extent, its poverty and crime also, have been concentrated in Paris and two or three other large cities. Education is very much neglected. Thirty per cent. of the conscripts (who represent very fully the male adult population of France) cannot read or write. The school-age of children is only from seven to thirteen, and nearly a million, or about one fifth of the entire number of children between these ages, do not attend school. Morals are, as is well known, at a very low ebb. One eighth of the births (taking city and country together) are known to be illegitimate, and a still larger proportion are concealed by infanticide, which is so prevalent as to make the percentage of increase of population in France smaller than that of any other European State. As a nation, the French are brave, full of dash, and, when properly trained, good soldiers; but under existing circumstances they have been badly led and but indifferently trained, and the lack of high intelligence has made them less effective as soldiers than the Germans. The country communes are, for the most part, very poor, and there is much less intelligence and enterprise than in Germany. The peasantry in Germany do not live any too well, but they have more and better food than the same class in France.

The statements which were at first put forth in regard to the military and naval strength of the two countries proved subsequently to be erroneous, the errors being, however, in opposite directions—the army of France being greatly overrated, and that of Prussia and the North German Confederation singularly understated. In regard to France, the overestimate was the result of two causes: one, the national tendency to exaggeration, and to regard the official statements of the army on paper as having their full equivalent in the actual dépôts and barracks; and the other, that neither the public, the Emperor, nor any one of his officials, knew the full extent of the system of frauds which had pervaded every department of the service.

The underestimate of the Prussian Government of its forces was also attributable to two causes: the natural cautiousness of the Prussians leading them to make allowances beyond the actual deficiencies; and the indisposition on the part of the Government to lay before the people the vast amount of their military strength, lest, as in previous years, it should be regarded as in excess of their need, and a useless expenditure.

The French army, it was reported, when war was first declared, including the active army, the reserve, the National Guard, and the numerous less important branches, would make up the imposing array of 1,350,000 men. The active army, according to the official statistics, comprised: staff, 1,082; gendarmes, 24,548; infantry, 250,900; cavalry, 61,583; artillery, 37,959; engineers, 7,845; military train, 8,954; commissariat, 11,208. It was said to be commanded by 8 marshals, 86 generals of division, and 160 generals of brigade. To this active army of 404,794 men was to be added the reserve of 400,000; 318 battalions of infantry of the National Guard, numbering 508,800 men in all, and 123 batteries of artillery, and 5 companies of pontoniers, numbering together 29,923 men.

Beyond this vast force, it was said, were the Garde Mobile, answering to the English disembodied militia, as the National Guard did to the Volunteers. The Garde Mobile consisted, it was said, of about 600,000 men, who had a skeleton organization of officers, but had not been called out for any actual service; but it was believed by the French people that they would be a very formidable addition to their military force, and probably be fully capable of meeting on equal terms the German soldiers of the line. Here, then, were military organizations which could,

THE ASTRONOMICAL CLOCK IN THE CATHEDRAL
OF STRASBURG.

on an emergency, throw nearly two million soldiers into the field. This was not, to be sure, an extravagant estimate, as the population of France was about thirty-eight millions. But the sanguine French people forgot, or rather did not know, that such had been the facilities for procuring substitutes by a money payment, that not less than one fifth of the conscripts of any year released themselves from service by the payment of a commutation, which, instead of being employed by the Government in hiring substitutes, was perverted to private purposes; another fifth was declared exempt for various causes more or less just; and a third fifth, though nominally on the rolls, and pay and rations drawn for them, had their existence only there. Thus it happened that, of a conscription nominally of 125,000 men, not over 50,000 or 55,000 were actually in the service. Thus, though, as stated above, the army on the peace-footing amounts to 404,000 men, and the first reserves to as many more, yet from both there were at no time more than 350,000 men to take the field, and it is doubtful if even this number ever actually reported for duty.

On the 2d of August the strength and position of the French army were reported as follows:

First Corps, MacMahon's, 45,000 men, at Strasbourg; the Second Corps, Frossard's, 30,000 men, at St. Auld; the Third Corps, Bazaine's, 30,000 men, at Metz; Fourth Corps, L'Admirault's, 30,000 men, at Thionville; Fifth Corps, De Failly's, 30,000 men, at Bitche and Saorguemines; Sixth Corps, Canrobert's, 30,000 men, at Chalons; Seventh Corps, Douay's, 30,000 men, at Besançon and Belfort; the Eighth Corps, Bourbaki's, 30,000 men, at Metz. (This was the Imperial Guard.) Cavalry, 34,000. Total, 309,000. With artillery and the reserve cavalry, nearly 350,000 men. It is not probable that these army-corps were all full, or indeed, very nearly so. Far sooner than should have been necessary, both the National Guard and the Garde Mobile were called out; and yet, outside of the garrison of Paris and the other great cities, it would seem to have been impossible to keep up an army of much more than 300,000 men. Early in the war there were bands of *Franc-tireurs*, a kind of guerillas, not uniformed, and recognizing no special allegiance to any particular corps, organized in all parts of France; and these, like guerillas generally, while fighting in their irregular way the common enemy, took occasion also to do some plundering on their own account among their countrymen. Including these irregular troops, the armies in the field, and the garrisons of Paris and other cities, there may have been possibly a million of men in all in the field; but deducting the dead, wounded, and prisoners, and the deserters, it is doubtful if there were, on the 15th of October, 650,000 French troops under arms.

The following statement of the military strength of Germany at the beginning of the war is condensed from an elaborate article in the *Frankfurter Zeitung* (*Frankfort Gazette*), the highest German authority on the subject, and is undoubtedly drawn from official sources. It is evident, from several circumstances, that the computation was made in April, 1870, and, therefore, when there was no immediate prospect of war. It is remarkable that, before the 1st of October, the King of Prussia should have been able to bring into the field a force considerably exceeding this computation, notwithstanding the inevitable shrinkage of troops when called into the field.

The North German Confederation comprises 23 States, including Hesse, the northern part of which alone belongs to the Confederation. Prussia has military conventions with the kingdom of Saxony, with several Thuringian States, with Hesse, Mecklenberg-Schwerin and Strelitz, with Oldenburg, &c., whereby the armies of all these States are closely bound up with the Prussian forces.

The forces of the North German Confederation are as follows:

LINE.—*Infantry:* 4 Prussian regiments of Foot Guards, 4 Prussian regiments of Grenadier Guards, 1 Prussian regiment of Fusilier Guards, 15 regiments of Grenadiers of the line, 77 regiments of Infantry, 13 regiments of Fusiliers, 4 Hessian regiments of 2 battalions each, 1 Prussian battalion of Chasseurs of the Guard, 1 battalion Sharpshooters, 16 battalions of Chasseurs; total infantry, 118 regiments and 18 battalions—368 battalions in all.

Cavalry: 10 regiments Cuirassiers (including two regiments of Guards), 11 regiments Dragoons (including 2 regiments of Guards), 18 regiments Hussars (including 1 regiment of Guards), 21 regiments Lancers (Uhlanen), (including 3 regiments of Guards), 6 regiments Light Cavalry (including 2 regiments of Guards). Total cavalry, 76 regiments.

Artillery: 1 regiment of Field Artillery (Guards), 12 regiments of Field Artillery, 1 Hessian division of Field Artillery, 1 regiment of Siege Artillery (Festungs Artillerie) (Guards), 8 regiments of Siege Artillery, 4 divisions of Siege Artillery, 1 division Rocket Train; in all, 13 regiments and 1 division Field Artillery, and 9 regiments and 1 division of Siege Artillery.

Engineers: 1 battalion of Pioneers of the Guard, 12 battalions of Pioneers, 1 Hessian company of Pioneers.

Train: 13 battalions and 1 division of Baggage, Ammunition, &c., Train.

LANDWEHR.—97 regiments of infantry, two battalions each—194 battalions; 12 reserve battalions—12 battalions; 4 regiments of the Guard, three battalions each—12 battalions. Total, 218 battalions.

If we summarize the foregoing, we have the following result:

FIELD-ARMY.—Infantry, 394,310 men; Cavalry, 53,528 men; Artillery, 1,212 pieces.

Reserve.—Infantry, 145,944 men; Cavalry, 18,991 men; Artillery, 234 pieces.

Garrison Troops.—Infantry, 143,924 men; Cavalry, 10,208 men; Artillery, 234 pieces.

In the above computation are not reckoned the armies of the allied South German States, which now follow:

Bavaria.—16 regiments of Infantry of 3 battalions each; 10 battalions Chasseurs; 10 regiments of Cavalry; 2 brigades of Artillery; which give 69,064 men in Field troops, 25,757 men Reserve, and 22,614 Garrison troops; making, in all, 117,435 men and 240 guns.

Wurtemberg.—8 regiments of Infantry of 2 battalions each; 2 battalions of Chasseurs; 4 regiments of Cavalry; 2 regiments of Artillery; which give, in Field troops, 22,076 men; Reserve, 6,540; Garrison troops, 5,064; making, in all, 34,680 men and 66 guns.

Baden.—6 regiments of Infantry of 3 battalions each; 3 regiments of Cavalry; 3 Field divisions of Artillery; giving 16,656 Field troops; 3,995 Reserve, and 9,640 Garrison troops; making, in all, 30,291 men and 64 guns.

Thus the auxiliary troops which the three South German States would bring to the aid of the North German Confederation amount to the respectable figure of 169,802 men, and 370 guns.

The aggregates are: Field Army, 555,634 men and 1,584 guns; Reserves (*Landwehr*), 201,207 men and 234 field-pieces; Garrison troops, 192,450 men and 234 pieces of artillery. Grand total, 949,291 men and 2,052 guns. That the German army in the field since the beginning of the war has considerably exceeded 1,200,000 men, does not admit of a doubt.

But if the Germans had a decided preponderance in military strength, the French were, in turn, greatly their superiors in naval power. In this direction, indeed, France claimed to be second to no nation in the world, and only equalled by Great Britain, which for so long a period had boasted of "ruling the waves." The French people, it is true, do not naturally take to maritime pursuits; their commercial marine has been at all times smaller and less efficiently manned than that of many smaller nations, and their very large and well-appointed navy was not so well manned as that of Great Britain, its vessels being supplied with crews by conscription, and these not always from the coasts; so that, though the French navy has had no important naval battles to test its prowess, it is hardly to be supposed that it would be found much superior in fighting ability to its old reputation.

The French naval force consisted, in January, 1870, of 74,664 officers and men. There were 2 admirals, C. Regnauld de Genouilly and F. T. Trehouart; 6 active vice-admirals, and 30 active counter-admirals. The fleet, on the 1st of January, 1870, was composed as follows:

	Number.	Guns.
Screw steamers, iron-clad	55	1,032
Screw steamers, non-iron-clad	233	2,618
Wheel steamers	51	116
Sailing-vessels	100	914
Total	439	4,680

Besides these there were 8 screw steamers, iron-clad, with 68 guns, and 23 non-iron-clad, with 144 guns, building.

If this large number of vessels were all in commission, or capable of being rendered readily effective, it would indeed have been the most powerful of navies; but this was very far from being the case. A little analysis of the vessels composing the navy will readily demonstrate this. Of the 63 iron-clads afloat and building in 1869, 2 only were ships of the line—the Magenta and Solferino; 18 were iron-clad frigates, varying from 800 to 950 horse-power, carrying from 12 to 32 guns, and having crews of from 570 to 600 men, and the greater part were costly experiments of untried models; 9 were iron-clad gunboats, of several different models, carrying usually 12 guns and 310 men, and probably, for real service, the most efficient vessels of the navy; 7, described as iron-clad coast-guards, were of very varied capacity and horse-power, for the most part carrying only 1 or 2 guns. Among these was the Rochambeau, originally named the Dunderberg, built in New York for our Government, but, not exactly meeting its views, sold, in 1867, to the French Emperor; another was a cupola-ship with a powerful ram, named the Taureau. The remaining 27 were floating batteries, of use for the protection of their own rivers and coasts, but not adapted to offensive warfare. Of these, 12 were so constructed that they could be taken to pieces and transported overland to navigable rivers for warfare along their banks: 6 or 8 of these were sent to Strasbourg, to be put together there and sent down the Rhine, but fell into the hands of the Germans on the capture of that city. Of the non-armored screw steamers very few were in commission, 27 of the 29 ships of the line of this class being laid up in ordinary, with very little probability of their ever being commissioned again; 112 were despatch boats or transports, as were 44 of the paddle steamers. The 100 sailing-vessels were mostly employed as guards of the fisheries. Still, after making these deductions, there remained a formidable naval force, from which great things were expected. The blockade of the German coast was assigned to 16 of the iron-clads, mostly of the frigate class, and to 11 of the best of the despatch boats not armored. Other vessels of the navy hovered around neutral ports, like Liverpool and New York, in the hope of catching some of the German steamers. Owing to their great draught, however, the iron-clads were not capable of approaching near enough to the German ports to do any mischief, and their only exploits up to the 15th of October had been the capture of 15 or 20 unarmed merchantmen.

THE FRENCH MITRAILLEUR.

The Prussian navy was small, but its vessels were well constructed, and some of them were more than a match for any single vessel of the French navy. The following was their number, January 1, 1870:

	Number.	Guns.
Iron-clads	6	70
Frigates and corvettes	9	202
Gunboats	23	54
Yachts	1	2
Paddle-corvettes	3	15
Sailing-vessels	59	315
Total	101	658

The aggregate horse-power of the steam portion of the fleet was 7,020, and the crews, officers, and marines numbered 3,878 men. The great success of the Prussian armies soon rendered naval action of very little importance, and, shortly after the revolution occurred, the blockade of the German ports—never very effective—was practically abandoned. Let us next consider, as one of the problems materially affecting the success of the war, the armament of these forces, whether on the land or the sea. It has often been said, though incorrectly, that Prussia owed her victories over Austria, in 1866, to her superior artillery and her needle-guns. These victories were due, in the first place, to the genius of von Moltke and the thorough organization and training of the Prussian forces; but it is not to be denied that the artillery and needle-guns in the hands of thoroughly trained soldiers contributed largely to the result.

The cannon in use in the German army are mostly of steel, breech-loaders, of different sizes and calibres as required, but mostly of one general pattern, devised by Herr Krupp, a Prussian founder, at whose extensive works most of them were made. The steel of which they are made is of the low but malleable grade produced by the Bessemer and other kindred processes. Most of these cannon are rifled, and their range, accuracy, and toughness is extraordinary. A French authority, writing of the battles around Sedan, states that, on the morning of the surrender, the Emperor was, with his staff, suddenly subjected to a terribly severe cannonade, the shot and shell being thrown with most uncomfortable accuracy, and, on inquiry, found that they came from a Prussian battery 4,900 metres (a little more than three miles) distant. One of the best of the French batteries was put in position to reply to it, but its shot and shells fell into the Moselle, not over 1,500 metres, or less than one mile, from the battery.

The French cannon are mostly of bronze, muzzle-loaders, and of the pattern claimed by the Emperor as his own, and named " Napoleons." They are greatly inferior to the Prussian guns in range, accuracy, and ease of handling, and not superior to them in tenacity. The French, in the war of 1870, have, however, introduced one weapon which, with some modifications, seems likely to play an important part in wars hereafter. It is the *mitrailleuse*, or, as it is sometimes called, the *mitrailleur*, a weapon analogous to, though hardly as effective as, our Gatling battery. The principle of this new and destructive weapon is somewhat like that of the revolver, or the many-chambered pistol, applied to a species of field-piece. A number of barrels of a calibre sufficient for an inch-ball are grouped around a central steel staff, and, metallic cartridges being supplied, they are, by a simple crank-movement, forced into the several barrels, and discharged with great rapidity, from two to three hundred per minute. The range which presents any considerable accuracy, in the French mitrailleuse, does not much exceed a mile, but within this range the weapon is exceedingly destructive. The Prussians had examined the Gatling battery, acknowledged to be the most effective of all the guns of this class, but had not been favorably impressed by it; but their late experiences have probably changed their opinion. The

BETWEEN FRANCE AND GERMANY.

THE CHASSEPÔT.

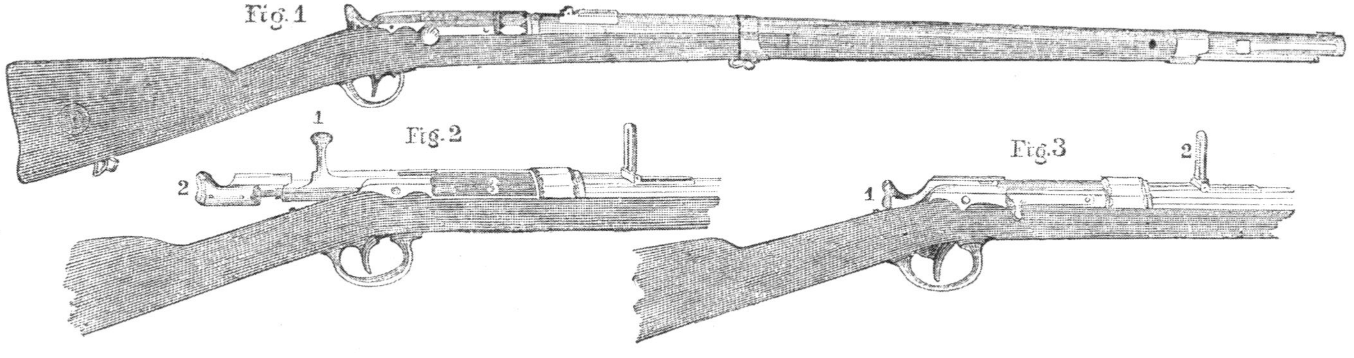

Fig. 1.—Chassepôt Rifle: breech closed. Fig. 2.—Ready for reception of cartridge: 1. Lever for opening and locking breech; 2. Head of the plunger, containing needle for exploding cartridge; 3. Chamber for cartridge. Fig. 3.—Rifle loaded and closed: 1. Plunger drawn out ready for explosion of cartridge; 2. Sight raised for long range.

Fosberry battery, or mitrailleuse, does not seem to be the most perfect form of this destructive weapon, experiments in England proving the decided superiority of the Gatling battery to it in all respects; but there can be no doubt that it will in some form add a formidable weapon to the armament of civilized nations. It will not take the place of cannon, and it will be liable to be destroyed by cannon-shot and shell at long range; yet the experience of the war proves that it has its place, and an important one, in both offensive and defensive warfare. There have been rumors of a steam mitrailleuse worked with the frightful velocity of which that powerful agent is capable, but there are evidently difficulties to be overcome before this combination can be made practicable.

The weapons with which the rank and file of the two armies were provided also deserve our attention. The *Nädelgewehr*, or needle-gun of the Prussians, has now been in use in their armies more than twenty years. It has been slightly modified and improved in such a way as to increase its certainty of discharge, and, perhaps, slightly its accuracy, but the principle of the gun is the same as in 1848.

The Prussian needle-gun is the invention of HERR DREYSE, a gun-manufacturer, who spent thirty years in trying to construct a perfect breech-loading rifle that would be of practical use in war.

There is no necessary connection between a breech-loading gun and the method of firing by the penetration of a needle into a detonating cap or fulminating powder within the cartridge; but the desire to dispense with the separate application of the percussion cap, as his predecessors had done with the more clumsy mechanism of the flint and match-locks, led Herr Dreyse to seek the best and simplest method of combining these two qualities—loading at the breech, and firing by a needle. The greatest, as it was the earliest, objection to breech-loading fire-

BETWEEN FRANCE AND GERMANY.

THE PRUSSIAN NEEDLE-GUN.

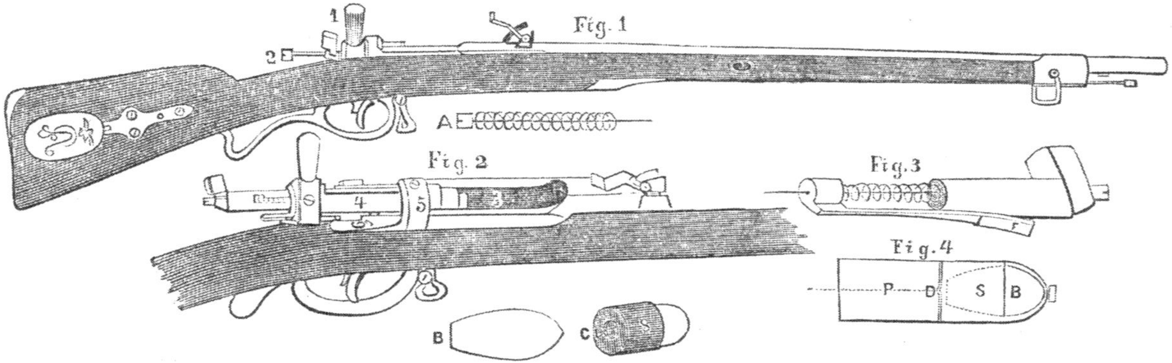

Fig. 1.—1. Lever that locks in cylinder; 2. Needle drawn back ready for projecting into cartridge. Fig. 2.—3. Chamber for cartridge; 4. Cylinder holding needle-case; 5. Cylinder that passes under band; 6. Trigger that pushes on spring, F, in Fig. 3. Fig. 3.—Case containing needle: F, spring lifted by trigger, 6, in Fig. 2. Fig. 4.—Section of cartridge: P, powder; D, detonating powder in hole of sabot; S, sabot holding the ball; dotted line shows passage of needle on to detonating powder at D, through the gunpowder, marked P. A, needle in spiral spring; B, ball; C, sabot containing ball; D, detonating powder at end of sabot.

arms has been their tendency to foul by the escape of a portion of the gases of the powder and the residuum of water and in-combustible, or, at least, unconsumed matters left after repeated firing. There are two methods of overcoming this difficulty, which is in danger of preventing the perfect closure of the breech upon the barrel. The first is by a method of closing which shall effectually prevent the escape of gas at the breech; the second, by the adoption of a cartridge which shall cleanse the barrel and joint at each discharge. There are difficulties in both. Obturation, or the complete closing of the breech upon the barrel, is effected in three distinct ways:

1. By inserting a cylinder into the barrel, or by inside or internal obturation.

2. By shoving the open end of the barrel into the movable closing-piece so that the latter encompasses the end of the barrel, called outside or external obturation.

3. By closing the end of the barrel with a flat, massive piece of metal, which method is denominated flat obturation, and can only be resorted to where metallic cartridges are used, like those invented for the Lefancheux gun, the Spencer or Henry rifle, &c., &c.

Of these three methods of obturation, the first is objectionable and imperfect, inasmuch as the cylinder to be inserted into the barrel of the gun comes into immediate contact with the gas-development, and with the dirty residue of the powder, in consequence of which the free forward and backward movement of the closing mechanism is soon materially checked, and the rapid loading of the gun seriously interfered with. The third method depends wholly upon the use of metallic cartridges, which are too expensive for a large army. The firing of these breech-loaders is also much less rapid than that of the Prussian needle-gun and the Chassepôt, as it is necessary, after each discharge of the gun, to remove the metallic cap or the cartridge, often firmly inclosed in the rear end of the barrel, except where, as is the case with some American rifles, there is an automatic arrangement for throwing out each shell by the firing of its successor.

The Prussian needle-gun is, we believe, up to this day, the only one in the manufacture of which the external obturation has been resorted to, in preference to the other methods. And just to the application of this system one of the most essential advantages of the needle-gun can be attributed, as the metallic plates coming into contact in the process of obturation are not directly exposed to the danger of becoming overheated, and the closing mechanism is kept free from all obstruction by the residue of powder, from which the Chassepôt, with its internal obturation, suffers so severely. This inconvenience, which is called, in French, "*crachement*," has been partly overcome by the application of India-rubber knobs, which, however, become in their turn dangerous to the working of the needle.

The needle-gun consists, as regards its breech apparatus and needle-lock, of three concentric hollow cylinders, with a solid cylindrical bolt, to which the needle is affixed, inside the innermost. The rear end of the barrel is firmly screwed into the head of the chamber which is fixed to the stock of the piece, and is open at the rear end. The upper half of the cylinder is cut away at the front end for rather more than the length of the cartridge, to secure its ready admission. From the rear of this opening to the back of the chamber a groove is cut sufficiently wide to allow the square pillar of the breech-handle to pass along it. In the middle of this groove is a right-angled shunt stopping the breech-handle when drawn backwards, unless it is turned downwards, when it may be completely drawn out at the rear end. This breech-handle is connected with and forms part of the breech-piece, a solid steel cylinder moving within the chamber, and having its front end bevelled with an inward slope to fit the external bevel of the rear end of the barrel, thus closing it perfectly, and forming the external obturation of which we have already spoken. Firmly screwed within the breech-piece is a solid block of metal, with a conical projection extending to the base of the cartridge, called a *tige*, or pillar. Through this block is the channel in which the needle works. Inside the breech-piece cylinder is another, with its springs constituting the lock of the gun. It slides within the breech-piece, and is retained from falling out by a spring, which catches in a notch at the rear end of the breech-piece. Along the bottom of this cylinder is a groove to admit the passage of the trigger, and at the back of the chamber is a short upright handle, by means of which the weapon is cocked. Lastly, within the lock is a solid steel bolt having the needle firmly fastened in its front end, and its motions regulated by a strong spiral spring. When the cartridge (which is of paper) is thrust into the chamber, and moved forward by the act of half-cocking to its place, the point of the needle and the end of the *tige* touch the base of the cartridge, but the spiral spring is relaxed, and without power; when the gun is at full-cock, the spring is compressed, the bolt to which it is attached drawn back and held in place by the trigger, which catches upon a shoulder of the bolt in front of the spring. In the act of firing, the trigger releases this shoulder of the bolt, the spring asserts its power, and the bolt shoots forward, driving the needle unerringly to the fulminate in the centre of the cartridge. Here is no opportunity of fouling, for the cartridge wipes out the barrel, and the closely-fitting bevel allows no escape of gas. The construction of the gun is so simple, that, without screw-driver or any other implement, it can readily be taken to pieces and cleaned or repaired. Its weight —eleven or twelve pounds—is an objection to it, but it has good qualities sufficient to balance this.

The Chassepôt rifle is a needle-gun, but varying in many

and important particulars from the *Zünd nadelgewehr*, or Prussian needle-gun. It was invented by M. Chassepôt, the French Inspector-General of arms, in 1863 (but improved in 1866), to supply the demand of the French Government for a gun which should be different from, yet equal to, the Prussian weapon. A much smaller amount of time has been expended over it than over its rival, and it has several serious defects. Its method of closing the breech is by internal obturation, or the thrusting the chamber into the barrel; and hence, for the reasons already stated, is more liable to foul, and to have its free movement in loading checked and obstructed. This difficulty has proved so great in the war of 1870, that the French have abandoned the gun, and are supplying their troops as fast as possible with the Remington rifle, an American weapon. Its spiral spring is shorter and weaker than the Prussian, and hence more liable to fail; and the rubber knob on the end of the cylinder, intended to close the joint completely against fouling, is apt to press on the needle and form a crust, which interferes with its free motion. The French fire rapidly, and after a number of rounds, in all the recent battles, they invariably manifested their impatience at the foulness and obstruction of their rifles by blowing into them, shaking them, and trying to clear them—which only made them worse.

M. Ignatius Neumann, of Liege, Belgium, a gun-manufacturer of great intelligence and experience, an acknowledged atuhority on all subjects relating to fire-arms, after long experimenting with the two guns, thus gives his verdict in regard to them:

THE NEEDLE-GUN.	THE CHASSEPÔT.
"1. It is impossible to open the gun as long as the spiral spring is strained, while, on the other hand, the spring cannot	"1. The mechanism of the gun is such as to necessitate the straining of the spiral spring previous to the opening of the

be strained unless the gun is completely closed. Thus all danger from want of precaution in opening and in closing the gun is averted, and it is just as fully secured against an unforeseen or accidental explosion when loaded as when unloaded. This may be considered the best and most perfect "rest."

"2. The Prussian needle-gun is the only breech-loader which has the external obturation, by which it is protected against all '*crachement*,' as well as against all other obstructions to the free movement of its closing mechanism.

"3. The gun can be taken apart by any soldier without the

chamber. Therefore, the loading of the gun takes place, and all the movements of the cylinder have to be executed, with strained spring; and the slightest touch on the trigger is sure to cause the projecting of the needle into the percussion-wafer, thus exploding the gun and endangering the lives of those around. Admitting the Chassepôt to be a weapon the efficiency of which it would be imprudent to question or to sneer at, we cannot be blind to the fact that, in the hands of a nervous and excited French soldier, it may eventually prove almost as dangerous to his own comrades and superiors as to the enemy.

"2. The internal obturation produces '*crachement*,' and interferes with the proper loading of the gun through accumulation of dirt from powder-residue and gas. This takes place as soon as the India-rubber knob at the head of the cylinder loses its elasticity and is not replaced in due time.

"3. The closing mechanism is not as easily taken apart as

necessity of using special tools for that purpose; its cleaning is very easy, and repairs, while seldom necessary, require but little time and skill.

"4. The cartridge is undoubtedly the best hitherto invented, while its manufacture is easy for the initiated; the igniting material lies in the solid case of the fulminate, cannot be pushed forward through the action of the needle, and is sure to cause the explosion of the powder-charge without fail. The position of the fulminate, between the projectile and the powder, insures its instantaneous removal from the barrel of the gun at every shot.

"5. The needle-gun is of simple and solid construction, and just heavy enough to make it useful in a bayonet-charge whenever the contending armies come into close contact."

is the case with the Prussian weapon. The closing cylinder moves up and down in its encasement on a little screw, which is easily broken by any imprudent or too forcible pull, when the gun is rendered unfit for use.

"4. The cartridge is of difficult construction, and is not sufficiently protected against spoiling when on the road for any length of time. The projectile does not always get free from its paper cover in due time, in all which cases the ball drops short of its destination.

"5. The Chassepôt is too light, and its construction is not sufficiently solid for a weapon of thrust. In a close encounter its inferiority will no doubt soon become apparent."

Besides the defects and disadvantages above enumerated, the Chassepôt labors under another serious drawback in the rapid formation of a crust on and near the point of the needle, composed of India-rubber and the residue of the igniting matter and the powder-charge; the needle becomes useless, as it fails to effect the explosion of the powder through the percussion-wafer. If the percussion-wafer was placed in front of the powder-charge, so that the needle would have to pierce through the same before reaching the igniting matter (as is the case with the Prussian needle-gun), the needle would not become inefficient, and would remain clean without any interference on the part of the soldier. But the spiral spring of the Chassepôt is too short and too weak to admit of any such change of construction. The objection recently made to the Prussian needle-gun, that its spiral spring was apt to get weakened and unable to propel the needle with sufficient force to pierce the cartridge, is futile, as nothing occurred either during the campaign in Schleswig-Holstein in 1864, or during the memorable ten days' campaign in Bohemia in 1866, to warrant such a surmise. It is also asserted that the calibre of the Prussian gun is too large, and the projectile consequently too heavy, rendering the carrying of a great number of cartridges extremely onerous to the soldier. We are enabled to refute this statement also, for the construction of the needle-gun is such as to admit of the use of small projectiles in spite of the large calibre. The circumstance that the ball is imbedded in the fulminate, wherewith it forms one compact mass, and obtains its rotation by means of the fulminate entering into the four grooves of the barrel, facilitates the firing of smaller projectiles than those originally used. To sum up, Neumann says:

"The Prussian needle-gun does not shoot better nor fire further than any other breech-loader, but its material advantages over all those invented in France, Belgium, England, and elsewhere, cannot be denied. It is entirely erroneous to suppose that it was not introduced into the armies of other European powers on account of its real or alleged shortcomings or defects. France especially was actuated in its decision in the premises by petty jealousy only. They didn't want it because they did not want it; they were unwilling to admit its superiority because somebody else had possessed it before them whom they couldn't think of ever imitating. Such is human nature."

CHAPTER VI.

WE have deemed it necessary, to a full understanding of the position of the two contending powers, to go thus fully into the history of their antecedents, their financial, social, and military condition, the history of their leaders, and the peculiar weapons of the opposing parties. We now proceed with the narrative of the opening of the war. There had sprung up, partly, perhaps, from the coldness and jealousies of France, a very cordial feeling between the Spanish Government since the revolution of 1868, and Prussia, and there had been a more than usually frequent interchange of civilities. General Prim, who was personally very friendly to the French Emperor, had sounded the Prussian Minister to Spain in regard to the candidacy of one of the Hohenzollern princes for the Spanish throne, indicating his preference for the elder brother of the family of Hohenzollern-Sigmaringen, but the proposition not being very favorably received, it had been allowed to drop, not, however, till the General had alluded to its possibility before the Cortes. In May, or early in June, General Prim had an interview with the French Emperor at Biarritz, and, almost immediately after his return, proposed to the Spanish Cortes the name of Prince Leopold, second son of Prince Carl Anton, the head of the house of Hohenzollern-Sigmaringen, for the vacant throne of Spain, and a large majority of the Cortes accepted his candidacy. A correspondence with the Prince resulted in his expression of his willingness to be the candidate of the Cortes for the position.

Prince Leopold was from an independent branch of the Hohenzollern family, having no claims on the succession to the Prussian throne, and were not in any sense directly responsible to it for their action, unless it was treasonable to the reigning house of Prussia to the Prussian King. The Prince was about thirty-five years of age, highly educated, very wealthy, and a Catholic, and held the nominal rank of colonel in the Prussian army. The King of Prussia was, when the matter was laid before him, prompt to express his disapprobation of it, believing that it would prove another Maximilian affair, and that the Prince would lose his head.

In spite of this disapproval, the Prince gave his consent to be a candidate. On the 4th of July, 1870, General Prim advised Señor Olozaga, Spanish Minister at Paris, of his selection of Prince Leopold, and the sanction of it by the Cortes. On the 5th of July, Baron Werther, Prussian Minister at Paris, left that city for Ems to consult with the King relative to this affair. On the 6th of July, the French Government sent a note to Count Benedetti, the Emperor's Minister at Berlin, instructing him to demand the disavowal of Prince Leopold's candidacy by Prussia, and the withdrawal of his name from the list of candidates for the Spanish crown, on the ground that France would consider his elevation to that position as a check and menace to her, which she would not under any pretext permit.

Count Benedetti, himself a Corsican, and of very fiery temper, acting also evidently under instructions from the Emperor, made haste to present the matter as offensively as possible to the King of Prussia. Mr. George Ripley, of the *Tribune* staff, was in Berlin at this time, and has given a most accurate and graphic account of the series of interviews between the Count and the King, the truth of which is certified to by the King and his personal suite.

The first audience, Mr. Ripley says, took place on July 9,

at the request of Count Benedetti. It was demanded by him that the King should require the Prince of Hohenzollern to withdraw his acceptance of the Spanish crown. The King replied that, as in the whole affair, he had been addressed only as the head of the family, and never as the King of Prussia, and had, accordingly, given no command for the acceptance of the candidature, he could also give no command for withdrawal. On the 11th of July, Count Benedetti requested a second audience, which was granted. In this interview he was urgent with the King to prevail upon Prince Leopold to renounce the crown. The King replied that the Prince was perfectly free to decide for himself, and that, moreover, he did not even know where he was at that moment, as he was about to take a journey among the Alps. On the morning of July 13, the King met Benedetti on the public promenade before the fountain, and gave him an extra sheet of *The Cologne Gazette*, which he had just received, with a private telegram from Sigmaringen, relating the withdrawal of the Prince, remarking, at the same time, that he himself had heard nothing from Sigmaringen, but should expect letters that day. Count Benedetti replied that he had already received the information the evening before from Paris, and, as the King regarded the matter as thus settled, the Count wholly unexpectedly made a new demand, proposing to the King that he should expressly pledge himself never to give his consent in case the question of the candidature should at any subsequent time be revived. The King decidedly refused to comply with any such demand, and, when Benedetti returned to his proposal with increasing importunity, stood by his answer. In spite of this, a few hours after, the Count requested a third audience. Upon being asked what subject was to be considered, he gave for answer that he wished to renew the discussion of the morning. The King declined another audience, as he had no answer but that already given, and, moreover, all negotiations must

M. BENEDETTI.

LOUIS II. OF BAVARIA.

now take place through the Ministry. Benedetti requested permission to take leave of the King upon his departure from Ems, which was so far granted that the King bowed to him as the latter was leaving the railway station the next day for Coblenz. Each of the interviews of Benedetti with the King had the character of a private conversation. The Count did not once pretend to be acting in his official capacity.

In the preceding statement, which is sanctioned by the King himself, no mention is made of the rudeness of Benedetti in forcing himself upon His Majesty while indulging in the recreation of a walk on the crowded promenade of Ems. It is generally regarded, however, as a studied insult on the part of the French Minister, and is commented on with indignation by the German press. Such a violation of diplomatic courtesy could hardly have been accidental. Not even the excitement of a sudden surprise could excuse the incivility; but there was no surprise in the case; the Count had received the news the night before, and had at least twelve hours to meditate his course of action. The affair was witnessed with astonishment by the numerous spectators of the scene, who drew their own augury of its probable consequences. It was interpreted as a sign of hostility toward Prussia, and two days after came the declaration of war.

The actual demands of the French Government upon the King are contained in a subsequent despatch from Baron Werther, the Prussian Minister at Paris. In a conversation with the Duke de Gramont, the latter remarked that he regarded the withdrawal of Prince Leopold as a matter of secondary importance, but he feared that the course of Prussia in regard to it would occasion a permanent misunderstanding between the two countries. It was necessary to guard against this by destroying the germ. The conduct of Prussia toward France had been unfriendly. This was admitted, to his certain knowledge, by all the great powers. To speak frankly, he did not wish for war, but would rather preserve amicable relations with Prussia. He hoped that Prussia had similar dispositions. He was satisfied with the intentions of the Prussian Minister, and they could accordingly freely discuss the conditions of reconciliation. He would suggest the writing of a letter to the Emperor by the King, disavowing all purpose of infringing upon the interests or the dignity of France in his authorizing the acceptance of the Spanish crown by Prince Leopold. The King should confirm the withdrawal of the Prince, and express the hope that all ground of complaint between the two Governments would thus be removed. Nothing should be said in the letter concerning the family relations between Prince Leopold and the Emperor.

The refusal of the King to accept the humiliating conditions proposed by the French Government has called forth the liveliest approval and sympathy in all parts of Germany.

As early as the 8th of July, the Emperor had ordered two *corps d'armée* to be ready for immediate movement, one under the command of Bazaine, the other of Lebœuf. This, it will be noticed, was the day before Benedetti's first interview with the King. On the 12th, French troops passed through Paris on their way to the frontier. On the 14th, the French fleet sailed to blockade the German ports. On the 15th, war was declared by the French *Corps Législatif* against Prussia, at 1.50 p. m., on these grounds: First, the insult offered at Ems to Count Benedetti, the French Minister, and its approval by the Prussian Government; second, the refusal of the King of Prussia to compel the withdrawal of Prince Leopold's name as a candidate for the Spanish throne; and third, the fact that the King persisted in giving the Prince liberty to accept the crown.

On the same day Count Bismarck warned German vessels to hasten to ports of shelter; Holland ordered the mobilization of her army; Austria professed neutrality, unless a third power intervenes; King William returned to Berlin from Ems; the German army was ordered to be put in motion; the President of the United States recommended to Congress a temporary and partial relaxation of the navigation laws.

On leaving Ems at an early hour on the morning of the 15th, King Wilhelm found a great crowd of citizens assembled to witness his departure, and said to them in parting, "God is my witness that I have not desired war; but if I am forced into it, I will maintain the honor of Germany to the last man." The enthusiasm for the war, forced upon them by France, was intense throughout Germany, the patriotism and war-like spirit of the people of South Germany and Schleswig-Holstein, both of which had been a few years before at war with Prussia, apparently rising higher even than that of the citizens of the North German Confederation. Addresses of the most earnest character to the King were adopted everywhere, and the legend, "With God for King and Fatherland," blazed out all over Germany. The Prussian Legislature, called in extraordinary session at Berlin, was a unit for prompt and vigorous war. The King opened the session with a brief address, which was greeted with the wildest enthusiasm. The King said Prussia had no interest in the selection of the Prince of Hohenzollern for the Spanish throne, except that it might bring peace to a friendly people. It had, nevertheless, furnished the Emperor of the French with a pretext for war unknown to diplomacy, and, scorning peace, he had indulged in language to Germany which could only have been prompted by a miscalculation of her strength. Germany was powerful enough to resent such language and repel such violence. He said so in all reverence, knowing that the event was in God's hands. He had fully weighed the responsibility which rested on the man who drives into war and havoc two great and tranquil nations yearning for peace and the enjoyment of the common blessings of Christian civilization and prosperity, and for contests more salutary than those of blood. Those who rule France have shrewdly studied the proper methods of hitting the sensitive pride of that great neighbor-nation, and, to promote selfish interests, have misguided it. "Then," concluded the King, "as our fathers before us have done, let us fight for liberty and our rights against the wrongs inflicted by a foreign conqueror; and as He was with our fathers, so God will be with us in a struggle without which Europe can never enjoy lasting peace."

After the King's speech had been delivered, a loan of 120,000,000 thalers was carried unanimously, amid the wildest expressions of enthusiasm by all parties. The enthusiasm was not so great in France, nor the Legislature so unanimous; there were a considerable number of the Republican members who perceived that the war was proclaimed in the interests of the Napoleonic dynasty, and therefore opposed it; but the French people are excitable, and the cry of glory and conquest rendered most of them deaf to reason for the time, and the war could be said, in general, to be popular with them.

As we have already said, the Emperor delayed his departure, as it was thought at the time very singularly, from Paris, after the declaration of war. It is now known that he was astounded to find how utterly unprepared his army was for moving, and made vain and desperate efforts to undo the evil wrought by years of corruption and fraud. Finding, at length, that his enemy was fully ready for him on the frontier, he issued, on the 23d of July, the following address to the people of France:

"FRENCHMEN: There are in the life of a people solemn moments, when the national honor, violently excited, arouses itself irresistibly, rises above all other interests, and applies itself with the single purpose of directing the destinies of the nation. One of those decisive hours has now arrived for France. Prussia, tc whom we have given evidence, during and since the war of 1856, of the most conciliatory disposition, has held our good-will of no account, and has returned our forbearance by encroachments. She has aroused distrust in all quarters, necessitating exaggerated armaments, and has made of Europe a camp where reign disquiet and fear of the morrow. A final incident has disclosed the instability of the international understanding, and shown the gravity of the situation. In the presence of her new pretensions, Prussia was made to understand our claims. They were evaded and followed with contemptuous treatment. Our country manifested profound displeasure at this action, and quickly a war-cry resounded from one end of France to the other.

"There remains for us nothing but to confide our destinies to the chance of arms. We do not make war upon Germany, whose independence we respect. We pledge ourselves that the people composing the great Germanic nationalities shall dispose freely of their destinies. As for us, we demand the establishment of a state of things guaranteeing our security and assuring the future. We wish to conquer a durable peace, based on the true interests of the people, and to assist in abolishing that precarious condition of things when all nations are forced to employ their resources in arming against each other.

"The glorious flag of France which we once more unfurl in the face of our challengers, is the same which has borne over Europe the civilizing ideas of our great revolution. It represents the same principles; it will inspire the same devotion.

"Frenchmen: I go to place myself at the head of that gallant army, which is animated by love of country and devotion to duty. That army knows its worth, for it has seen victory follow its footsteps in the four quarters of the globe. I take with me my son. Despite his tender years, he knows the duty his name imposes upon him, and he is proud to bear his part in the dangers of those who fight for our country. May God bless our efforts. A great people defending a just cause is invincible.

"NAPOLEON."

In this address there is evident not only a disposition to misrepresent the real causes of the war, but a somewhat flippant appeal to the French passion for glory, and a manifestation of that tendency to theatrical effect which has given a tinge of the ludicrous to so many of his public performances. The allusion to his son, a backward and very mediocre boy of fourteen, was, to say the least, in very bad taste.

The Emperor did not, however, leave at once on the promulgation of this address; at least, he did not reach Metz, with his very luxurious and amply provided train, until the 28th of July, when he at once issued the following address to the soldiers on taking command of the army. When we consider that he knew fully the condition and weakness of his army, and was, at least, tolerably informed concerning the powerful and perfectly organized foe with whom he had to contend, some of its assertions will be thought remarkable:

"SOLDIERS: I come to take my place at your head to defend the honor of the soil of our country. You go to combat against one of the best-armed of European countries; but other countries, as valiant as this, have not been able to resist your valor. It will be the same to-day. The war which now commences will be long and hardly contested, for its theatre will be places hedged with obstacles and thick with fortresses; but nothing is beyond the persevering efforts of the soldiers of Africa, Italy, and Mexico. You will prove once more what the French army is able to accomplish, animated by a sentiment of duty, maintained by discipline, influenced by love of country. Whatever road we may take across our frontiers, we will find upon it glorious traces of our fathers, and we will show ourselves worthy of them.

"All France follows you with ardent prayers, and the eyes of the universe are upon you. Upon our success depends the fate of liberty and civilization. Soldiers, let each one do his duty, and the God of Battles will be with us.

"NAPOLEON.

"At the General Headquarters at Metz, July 28, 1870."

During this period, when both nations were summoning their forces into the field, but before any serious conflicts had occurred, Count von Bismarck, the Prussian Premier, on the 29th of July, addressed to the Representatives of Prussia at the Courts of neutral powers a circular giving an *exposé* of secret propositions made by Napoleon III to Prussia in May 1866, and since repeated with slight variations, and always accompanied with threats, which showed most conclusively what were the motives which prompted him to declare the war just commenced.

Before the Danish war, says Count Bismarck, the French Legation at Berlin urged an alliance between France and Prussia for purposes of mutual aggrandizement. France, anticipating war with Austria as a consequence of the Danish war, made overtures relative to the restoration of the Luxembourg frontier of 1814, the acquisition of Saarburg and Landau, while a broader settlement of the boundary question on the basis of language was not to be excluded. These instances, in May, 1866, took the form of propositions for an alliance offensive and defensive, the manuscript original of which is in the Foreign Office here. These propositions are as follows:

First. Should the Congress of the powers assemble, Italy to have Venetia and Prussia the Duchies.

Second. Should the Congress disagree, alliance offensive and defensive will be made between France and Prussia.

Third. Prussia to open hostilities against Austria within ten days after the dissolution of the Congress.

Fourth. Should no Congress meet, Prussia to attack Austria within thirty days after the signature of the present treaty.

Fifth. Napoleon to begin hostilities against Austria as soon as Prussia begins, despatching 300,000 men during the first month across the Rhine.

Sixth. No separate treaty shall be made by either power with Austria. When a joint treaty is made, the following are to be the conditions: 1. Venetia to go to Italy. 2. Prussia to select German territory at will for annexation, the number of inhabitants not to exceed 8,000,000 of souls; the territory thus acquired to become a part of the kingdom of Prussia, without federal rights. 3. France to have a liberal share of the Rhine provinces.

Seventh. A military and maritime allegiance to be made between France and Prussia, to which Italy may be a party should she so desire.

This programme, the circular states, was rejected in June, 1866, in spite of the threatening urgency of France. The proposals were incessantly renewed with modifications sacrificing Belgium and South Germany, but they were never seriously entertained by Prussia. For the sake of peace, however, it was thought best to leave Napoleon to his delusions. No word implying approval was returned; time was counted on to revolutionize France, and extinguish the scheme; hence the long delay and silence. The attempt against Luxembourg failing, France repeated her former propositions, making the specifications clear in regard to the acquisition of Belgium by France, and South Germany by Prussia. These last propositions were formulated by Count Benedetti himself, and it is improbable that he wrote them without the authority of the Emperor, as they are the same which were made four years ago under threat of war as the alternative of their refusal. Any one acquainted with these antecedents must have known that, had Prussia acquiesced in the seizure of Belgium, France would soon have found another Belgium in Prussian territory.

Some effort was made by the imperial Government to weaken the force of this damaging exposure, and to convince the neutral powers that the propositions had been suggested by Prussia, but the falsity of this was so apparent that it obtained no credence from any body. The neutral powers, which had at first given indications of sympathy with the Emperor, were, after the publication of this document, and the circulation of photographic copies of the manuscript of Benedetti, much less disposed to depart from the strictest neutrality, and thus the contest was narrowed down to the two belligerents.

Efforts, however, were not wanting on the part of other powers to effect a reconciliation, and to avert a war which, it was evident, must be so terrible in its results. Great Britain, Russia, and Austria exerted all their power with both parties, but in vain; the French Emperor would not, and Prussia, as she was situated, could not, make any such concessions as would have secured peace. One of the most noteworthy of these efforts for reconciliation was that of Pope Pius IX, who, in the midst of troubles which shortly after deprived him of his temporal power, which France had for some years maintained for him, addressed letters both to the Emperor and King Wilhelm, of which latter the following is a copy:

"Your Majesty: In the present grave circumstances it may appear an unusual thing to receive a letter from me; but, as the Vicar on earth of God and peace, I cannot do less than offer my mediation.

"It is my desire to witness the cessation of war-like preparations, and to stop the evils—their inevitable consequences. My mediation is that of a sovereign whose small dominion excites no jealousy, and who inspires confidence by the moral and religious influence he personifies.

"May God lend an ear to my wishes, and listen also to those I form for your Majesty, to whom I would be united in the bonds of charity.

"Pius.

"Given at the Vatican, July 22, 1870."

A postscript adds:

"I have written identically to the Emperor."

What reply, if any, the Emperor made to the letter addressed to him, is not known; but the King of Prussia promptly returned the following courteous answer, which, however, effectually forbade all hope of any successful result from the proffered mediation:

"Most August Pontiff: I am not surprised, but profoundly moved at the touching words traced by your hand.

"They cause the voice of God and of peace to be heard. How could my heart refuse to listen to so powerful an appeal? God witnesses that neither I nor my people desired or provoked war.

"Obeying the sacred duties which God imposes on sovereigns and nations, we take up the sword to defend the independence and honor of our country, ready to lay it down the moment those treasures are secure.

"If your Holiness could offer me, from him who so unexpectedly declared war, assurances of sincerely pacific dispositions, and guarantees against a similar attempt upon the peace and tranquillity of Europe, it certainly will not be I who will refuse to receive them from your venerable hands, united as I am with you in bonds of Christian charity and sincere friendship.

(Signed)   " Wilhelm."

The blockading fleet sailed from Cherbourg on the 25th of July, and the Emperor being unable to be present at their departure, sent the Empress with a proclamation to be read to the officers and crews. The Vice-Admiral of the squadron having delivered a somewhat boastful address, full of laudation of the imperial family, the Empress read, it was said, in tones full of emotion, the Emperor's proclamation, as follows:

"Officers and Seamen: Although I am not in your midst, my thoughts will follow you upon those seas where your valor is about to be displayed. The French navy has glorious reminiscences. It will prove itself worthy of the past. When, far from the soil of our country, you are face to face with the enemy, remember that France is with you; that her heart throbs with yours; that she invokes upon your arms the protection of Heaven. While you are combating at sea, your brethren in arms will be struggling with the same ardor for the same cause as yourselves. Do you reciprocally second each other's efforts, the same success will crown them. Go! display with pride our national colors. On beholding the tri-colored flag floating over our ships, the enemy will know that in its folds it bears everywhere the honor and the genius of France.

" Napoleon.

"Palace of St. Cloud, 23d July, 1870."

The headquarters of the French army and its Emperor and commander were at Metz, but the advance was thrown forward to the Rhine as early as July 19, though in small force. On that day a company of French skirmishers crossed the frontier and seized a small custom-house on the frontier near Saarbruck. No resistance was offered. On the 20th a French soldier was shot by a Prussian fusileer. On the 23d a Prussian force from Saar-Louis crossed the border, and made a reconnoissance in the direction of St. Avold and Metz. There was some skirmishing, but no serious engagement. On the 26th there was another slight engagement, and the French were repulsed. The 27th of July was observed as a day of fasting and prayer throughout the North German Confederation. The period between the declaration of war and the 1st of August was industriously occupied by the agents of the Emperor in circulating hundreds of thousands of addresses to the people of South Germany, of Hanover, and of Schleswig-Holstein, urging them to unite with France against their old enemy, Prussia, or at least to paralyze her by their determined neutrality. Never was so vast an amount of advice so perfectly wasted. Without a dissenting voice, the South German States—Hanover, and foremost of all Schleswig-Holstein—had hastened to declare their adherence to Prussia and Germany in this war for God, King, and Fatherland, and there was no evidence that, among those twelve millions of people, the Emperor Napoleon III had a single adherent.

CHAPTER VII.

AS we have already said, the Emperor reached his headquarters at Metz and took command of the army in person on the 28th of July. King Wilhelm left Berlin for the front with his chief of staff, General von Moltke, on the 31st, and, arriving at his temporary headquarters at Mayence on the 2d of August, issued the next day the following brief address to his troops:

"All Germany stands united against a neighboring state, which has surprised us by declaring war without justification. The safety of the fatherland is threatened. Our honors and our hearths are at stake. To-day I assume command of the whole army. I advance cheerfully to a contest like that in which, in former times, our fathers, under similar circumstances, fought gloriously. The whole fatherland and myself trust with confidence in you. The Lord God will be with our righteous cause."

On the 1st of August the French attacked the Germans near Saarbruck in small force, and after some fighting were repulsed.

On the 2d of August the strength and position of the contending armies were reported as follows:

The French army.—First Corps, MacMahon, 45,000 men, at Strasbourg. Second Corps, Frossard, 30,000 men, at St. Avold Third Corps, Bazaine, 30,000 men, at Metz. Fourth Corps, l'Admirault, 30,000 men, at Thionville. Fifth Corps, De Failly, 30,000 men, at Bitche and Saarguemines. Sixth Corps, Can robert, 30,000 men, at Chalons. Seventh Corps, Douay, 30,000 men, at Besançon and Belfort. Eighth Corps (Guards), Bourbaki, 30,000 men, at Metz. Cavalry, 34,000. Total, 309,000. With artillery and reserve cavalry, about 350,000 men.

The left wing had before it at this time the Moselle and the French Nied, the centre the Saar, and the right wing the Lauter in front.

The German armies having been assembled at camps on the Rhine, began to move forward. The entire regular German force consisted of eighteen *corps d'armée*, containing 40,000 men each at their normal strength. The First Army, under Steinmetz, had the First, Seventh, and Eighth Corps; the Second Army, under Prince Friedrich Karl, the Second, Third, Ninth, and Tenth Corps; the Third Army, under the Prussian Crown-Prince, the Fifth, Sixth, and Eleventh Corps, and the two Bavarian Corps. The Fourth Army, under the Crown-Prince of Saxony, containing the Fourth and Twelfth Corps, and the Saxon and Prussian guard, occupied in the regular advance the right of the Crown-Prince; the Fifth Army, under General Werden, had the Wurtemberg and Baden divisions, engaged in the siege of Strasbourg; the reserves were composed of the Sixth Army, under the Grand Duke of Mecklenberg-Schwerin, on the Rhine, and the Seventh Army, under Generals von Canstein at Berlin, and Loewenfeld in Silesia. The defence of the northern coast was committed to these reserves. The advance to the French lines was made by the First Army, against the French left wing; Second Army, Prince Friedrich Karl, against the centre; and the Third Army, Crown-Prince of Prussia, against the French right wing.

The French forces being scattered over a line of eighty-five to ninety miles in length, MacMahon, after a council at Metz, received orders to make a flank march toward De Failly, at Bitche. He sent the corps of General Douay to Weissenburg to cover the movement. General Frossard, with the Second Corps, advanced on Saarbruck, and, after seven hours' fighting, drove out the three battalions of infantry, three squadrons of cavalry, and three guns, which formed the German force there. The Emperor was present with the Prince Imperial.

On his return to Metz, after the battle, the Emperor sent the following despatch to the Empress:

"Louis has received his baptism of fire. He was admirably cool and little impressed. A division of Frossard's command carried the heights overlooking the Saar. The Prussians made a brief resistance. Louis and I were in front, where the bullets fell about us. Louis keeps a ball he picked up. The soldiers wept at his tranquillity. We lost an officer and ten men."

On the 3d of August the French commenced fortifying the Spicheren hills, back of Saarbruck. The next day, August 4th, the Third German Army, under the Crown-Prince of Prussia, crossed the Lauter and advanced upon the corps of General Douay, posted behind the fortifications of Weissenburg, thus entering upon French territory as the French had the day previous invaded Germany. A glance at the map and a reference to the position of the two armies will show that this movement was made by the advance-guard of the German army of the left, under the Crown-Prince of Prussia, against the French right, under Marshal MacMahon. The defences behind which the French general and his troops were posted extended from the town of Lauterburg, northwesterly to Weissenburg. After crossing the Rhine at Maxau, the Baden and Wurtemberg troops marched against Lauterburg; the Fifth and Eleventh Prussian Corps marched west of the Rhine against the centre of the works; and the Bavarian Fourth Division against Weissenburg. The first shot was fired at 8.30 A. M. The Crown-Prince stood on the Schweigen hill, north of the town. Weissenburg was occupied by the Seventy-fourth French regiment, and on the Gaisberg hill, south of the place, were the First Turco regiment, Fifth and Fiftieth line, three light batteries of artillery, and one of mitrailleurs. These troops also occupied Altstadt, on the right of the French position. Altstadt was quickly taken by the Ninth Prussian Division; Weissenburg, after sharp resistance, by the Bavarians and some battalions of the Forty-seventh and Forty-eighth regiments, and the Grenadiers marched against the Schafenburg hill, where the mitrailleurs were stationed. The mitrailleurs did not, in this action, do the terrible execution expected of them; the German columns steadily advanced without firing a shot, and the position was taken. There was no fight at Lauterburg, which was found to be unoccupied by the French, and, after midday, all the German troops were concentrated for the action at Weissenburg. The defeat of the French became a rout, which was continued in disorder to Woerth. Thus in this first combat between the veteran troops of the French and the citizen-soldiers of Prussia, the former were not only completely beaten, but showed an ominous lack of steadiness and *morale*. The German losses were over 700 in killed and wounded. The French losses were much greater in killed and wounded, and one gun and 1,000 prisoners were also taken from them.

The report of this action, made to the King by the Crown-Prince of Prussia, adds the following particulars:

" The French infantry in action at Weissenburg and Gaisberg belonged to the First Corps, the cavalry to the Fifth Corps. Except an attack undertaken to cover the retreat, the French stood on the defensive during the whole engagement. Most of the French troops in the engagement conducted themselves with much spirit, and held their ground manfully. Only after retreat had become inevitable did they appear as if seized by a sudden panic. At this crisis troops of the Corps MacMahon, which had not yet been under fire, threw away their caps, knapsacks, tents, &c., and decamped, leaving even their provisions behind them. The Algerian troops exhibited the same temper as the French. There was no perceptible difference between them and their European comrades.

"The infantry, whose battalions were not above 800 strong, opened fire at 1,500 paces. This makes hitting a mere matter of chance, and has a tendency to demoralize a man in the use of his weapon. Our practice of forming company columns and outflanking the enemy's tirailleurs has fully answered. The French cavalry, even if numerically equal to our own, invariably declined attack. Our artillery fired slower, but much more effectively than the French. The mitrailleuse battery fired three rounds at a distance of 1,800 paces against our artillery, but did no damage. It was soon silenced by our guns."

The next day, in their onward march, the Third German Army (the left wing) found all the villages filled with French wounded, and the impression made by the defeat at Weissenburg far more profound than they had expected. The inhabitants of these villages had believed a defeat of the French impossible. Leaving the left wing of the German forces to pursue their enemy to Woerth, let us turn our attention westward along the German line to Homburg, in Rhenish-Bavaria, almost forty miles distant, where the German centre (the Second Army, under Prince Friedrich Karl) are preparing to cross the Saar. The Prince, who is accounted the ablest of the Prussian generals, issued, on the 5th of August, the following order to his troops:

"SOLDIERS: By command of the King you begin to-day the forward march against the enemy. The sons of Prussia have always distinguished themselves in presence of the enemy. On this occasion, too, you will win laurels, so that the fatherland can look upon you with pride. Show, by a calm demeanor toward friend and foe, that you are worthy children of Prussia."

The point toward which this army, like the others, is marching, is Metz, then the headquarters of the French armies; but all three of the armies on the frontier are destined to see severe fighting before they reach that city.

The First German Army, under the veteran General von Steinmetz, also move forward upon Saarbruck, crossing the Saar on the 5th of August, and as they are about to come into conflict with the enemy, the lion-hearted old commander addresses them in these words:

"SOLDIERS: You will very shortly have the opportunity of standing in presence of the enemy. With God's help you will maintain your old fame, and add new laurels to those on your standards of the year 1866, when I had the honor to lead you; and the fatherland will look with pride upon her sons. Show that you belong to an army worthy of the civilization of centuries, by a calm and friendly demeanor, temperate bearing, respecting the positions of strangers, whether friend or foe. On each one of you rests the responsibility of maintaining the honor and fame of the whole fatherland."

Sooner even than their commander had expected, the First German Army was called to a fierce and bloody battle; one fought at such odds, and under such discouraging circumstances, that it is a wonder that the Germans could ever have won the victory. The losses on both sides were very heavy; heaviest, of course, on the German side, since they were the attacking party, and had to climb the very steep Spicheren hills under a terrible fire; but their victory was complete. The battle is known as the battle of Spicheren heights, or as the battle of Forbach. The official report of the battle by von Steinmetz states the facts without exaggeration, and with more complete fairness than most reports of its class. It is as follows:

"On the forenoon of August 6, the Seventh Corps d'Armée pushed its vanguard to Herchenbach, one and a quarter German miles northwest of Saarbruck, with outposts stretching as far as the river Saar. The preceding night the enemy had evacuated its position on the drilling-ground of Saarbruck.

"Toward noon the cavalry division under General Rheinhaben passed through the town. Two squadrons formed the van. The moment they reached the highest point of the drilling-ground, and became visible to spectators on the south, they were fired at from the hills near Spicheren.

"The drilling-ground ridge overhangs a deep valley stretching toward Forbach and Spicheren, and bordered on the other side by the steep and partly-wooded height named after the latter village. These hills, rising in almost perpendicular ascent several hundred feet above the valley, form a natural fortress, which needed no addition from art to be all but impregnable. Like so many bastions, the mountains project into the valley, facing it on all sides, and affording the strongest imaginable position for defence. French officers who were taken prisoners on this spot confess to having smiled at the idea of the Prussians attacking them in this stronghold. There was not a man in the Second French Corps who was not persuaded in his own mind that to attempt the Spicheren hills must lead to the utter annihilation of the besiegers.

"Between 12 and 1 o'clock the Fourteenth Division arrived at Saarbruck. Immediately proceeding south, it encountered a strong force of the enemy in the valley between Saarbruck and

Spicheren, and opened fire forthwith. Upon this General Frossard, who was in the act of withdrawing a portion of his troops when the Prussians arrived, turned round and reoccupied the Spicheren hills with his entire force. A division of the Third Corps, under General Bazaine, came up in time to support him.

"The Fourteenth Division at first had to deal with far superior numbers. To limit the attack to the enemy's front would have been useless. General von Kamecke, therefore, while engaging the front, also attempted to turn the left flank of the enemy by Stiring; but the five battalions he could spare for this operation were too weak to make an impression upon the much stronger numbers of the French. Two successive attacks on his left were repulsed by General Frossard. Toward 3 o'clock, when all the troops of the division were under fire, the engagement assumed a very sharp and serious aspect.

"Eventually, however, the roar of the cannon attracted several other Prussian detachments. The division under General von Barkenow was the first to be drawn to the spot. Two of its batteries came dashing up at full speed to relieve their struggling comrades. They were promptly followed by the Fortieth Infantry, under Colonel Rex, and three squadrons of the Ninth Hussars. At this moment the vanguard of the Fifth Division was espied on the Winterberg Hill. General Stülpnagel, whose van had been stationed at Sultzbach the same morning, had been ordered by General von Alvensleben to march his entire division in the direction from which the sound of cannon proceeded. Two batteries advanced in a forced march on the high road. The infantry were partly sent by rail from Nuenkirchen to Saarbruck.

"At about 3.30 o'clock the division of Kamecke had been sufficiently reënforced to enable General von Göben, who had arrived in the meantime and assumed the command, to make a vigorous onslaught on the enemy's front. The chief aim of the attack was the wooded portion of the declivity. The Fortieth Infantry, supported on its right by troops of the Fourteenth Division, and on its left by four battalions of the Fifth Division, made the assault. A reserve was formed of some battalions of the Fifth and Sixteenth Divisions as they came up.

"The charge was a success. The wood was occupied, the enemy expelled. Penetrating further, always on the ascent, the troops pushed the French before them as far as the southern outskirts of the wood. Here the French made a stand, and, combining the three arms of the service for a united attack, endeavored to retrieve the day. But our infantry were not to be shaken. At this juncture the artillery of the Fifth Division accomplished a rare and most daring feat. Two batteries literally clambered up the hills of Spicheren by a narrow and precipitous mountain-path. With their help a fresh attack of the enemy was repulsed. A flank attack directed against our left from Aislingen and Spicheren was warded off in time by battalions of the Fifth Division stationed in reserve.

"The fighting, which for hours had been conducted with the utmost obstinacy on both sides, now reached its climax. Once more the enemy, superior still in numbers, rallied his entire forces for a grand and impetuous charge. It was his third attack after we had occupied the wood; but, like the preceding ones, this last effort was shortened by the imperturbable calmness of our infantry and artillery. Like waves dashing and breaking against a rock, the enemy's battalions were scattered by our gallant troops. After this last failure the enemy beat a rapid retreat; fifty-two French battalions, with the artillery of an entire corps, stationed in an almost unassailable position, had thus been defeated by twenty-seven Prussian battalions, supported by but the artillery of one division. It was a brilliant victory indeed. We had every thing against us—numbers, guns, and the nature of the locality—yet we prevailed.

"Darkness fast setting in afforded its valuable aid to the enemy in effecting his retreat. To cover this backward movement the French artillery were stationed on the hills skirting the battle-field on the south, where they kept up a continuous but harmless fire for a considerable time.

"The ground was too difficult for the cavalry to take any part in the action. Nevertheless, the fruits of the victory were very remarkable. The corps under General Frossard being entirely demoralized, dispersed. The road it took in its hasty flight was marked by numerous wagons with provisions and clothing; the woods were filled with hosts of stragglers, wandering about in a purposeless way, and large stores and quantities of goods of every description fell into our hands.

"While the battle was raging at Spicheren Hill, the Thirteenth Division crossed the Saar at Werden, occupied Forbach, seized vast magazines of food and clothing, and thus forced General Frossard, whose retreat was covered by two divisions of General Bazaine, which had come up for this purpose, to withdraw to the southwest, and leave free the road to St. Avold.

"The losses were very serious on both sides. The Fifth Division alone has 230 dead, and about 1,800 wounded. The Twelfth Infantry has 32 officers and 800 men dead or wounded; next to this the Fortieth, Eighth, Forty-eighth, Thirty-ninth, and Seventy-fourth have suffered most. The batteries, too, have encountered terrible loss. The number of killed and wounded on the enemy's side is at least equal to our own. The unwounded prisoners in our hands already exceed 2,000, and are increasing hourly. We have also captured 40 pontoons and the tents of the camp."

A correspondent of the New York *Tribune*, who was on the field four days later, and carefully gleaned the particulars of the battle, sent to that paper a very graphic description of it. Under date of August 11, he says:

"Yesterday I went over the field of Spicheren, where there was a very sharp fight on Saturday—in fact, what would have been called a battle before the present century, there having been more than 20,000 men on each side engaged. Taking the road from Saarbruck to Forbach, one climbs a hill which commands the town, and which was used by the French, in their attack, as a place for their batteries. Once on top of the hill, a level plateau, from 1,000 to 1,200 yards deep, extends as far as the hills which rise to the left of the village of Spicheren. On these hills the French took position on Saturday last, their line extending for about a mile from the hills, across the highroad for Forbach, in front of a manufactory, and down to the railway-cutting. They were enabled completely to sweep the plain in front of them; and, looking at its level, unbroken expanse, one wonders how a single Prussian ever passed it alive.

"The French position on the hills was naturally a very strong one, and that on the plain had been strengthened by an intrenchment thrown up in front of the troops. About 10 o'clock in the morning the Prussians began the attack with eight pieces of artillery in position on the crest of the hill above Saarbruck. But these pieces did small execution, as their fire had little effect on the French sharpshooters on the rocks above them.

"After about an hour of artillery-fire from the Prussians, with slight effect, the heights were ordered to be stormed by two battalions of the Fourteenth Regiment (from Pomerania); these men, some 2,000 strong, flung down their knapsacks and rushed across the intervening plain and up the hill, the artillery and the rest of the division covering the advance by their fire. But the French fire from the brow of the hill was too fearful, and, in spite of the leading companies having actually reached the top, it was impossible to drive out the French; nor was the attack on the plain directed against the village of Spicheren more successful. The French were strongly posted in a manufactory at the entrance to the village, and swept all the plain for nearly a mile with their Chassepôts. After a little time the Seventy-fourth Regiment, Hanoverian (this should be noted as showing how little foundation there is for the idea that the Hanoverians will not fight against the French), went at the heights again. They succeeded in gaining the top, but could only just maintain themselves there, and were thinking of retiring, as night was coming on and the French had brought three mitrailleuses, which did much execution at close quarters, into action. Suddenly drums were heard on the right of the French position, in a wood which they believed would effectually protect their left flank. This was the advance-guard of General Zastrow's corps, and their arrival settled the battle, the French being completely outflanked, and compelled to retire in some disorder to Forbach, losing many prisoners, as some of their men were caught between the two bodies of Prussians.

"But the Prussian victory was not obtained without terrible loss on their side. Of some 20,000 men engaged, there were over 2,000 killed and wounded, or more than one in ten. On Wednesday, when I visited the heights, there were still many French and Prussians unburied, some of them looking as if only asleep. What has been said about the frightful effect of the Chassepôt bullet does not seem to have been exaggerated, for many of the wounds on the Prussian bodies were horrible to look at. I noticed one man whose whole face was one big wound, a ball having struck him just under the eye and made a hole one could have put one's fist into. There was little contortion in the bodies, as was to be expected, most of the wounds being gunshot ones. There was, however, some hand-to-hand fighting in the final struggle for the top of the hill. The muskets and bayonets which covered the ground were broken and bent with blows given and received. Even the French officers taken prisoners admit the great dash and bravery shown by the Prussians in their attack on hills which I can say from experience were difficult to climb without an alpenstock. They own that the mitrailleuses used by the French were very deadly at close quarters, but they affirm that at any distance the balls fly so wide that they are little to be dreaded. Though some of the bodies are still unburied, most of them are interred, and pious hands have raised rough wooden crosses above the graves, with the names of those who sleep below inscribed on them. Frossard's division made so precipitate a retreat from Forbach, that they left many baggage-wagons and the whole of their pontoon-train behind them. Thus it happened that they did not break the railway up at Forbach; not a rail, as far as I can see—and I have been all along the line from St. Avold to Saarbruck—has been disturbed."

The casualties of this battle, as subsequently ascertained, were: General François, killed; the French (Frossard's Second Corps) retreated in great disorder, losing 3,000 to 4,000 prisoners, and probably as many more in killed and wounded; quantities of stores, trains, and camps were captured. The Fifth German Division lost 239 dead, and 1,800 wounded; the Twelfth Regiment, 832 dead and wounded; other regiments and the batteries also lost very heavily.

While this severe fighting was in progress between Saarbruck and Forbach, and the First German Army were gallantly and successfully struggling against superior numbers, a greater and more destructive battle was raging the same day between the Third German Army (the left wing, commanded by the Crown-Prince, Friedrich Wilhelm, of Prussia) and the French right wing, led by Marshal MacMahon, the bravest and ablest of the French generals.

We left the Crown-Prince in close pursuit of the French, whom he had defeated and routed on the 4th of August at Weissenburg, and who fled toward Woerth. This is a village of about 1,300 inhabitants, on the eastern slope of the Vosges, twelve miles S. W. of Weissenburg. On the heights west of Woerth the French found a favorable situation to make a stand against the Crown-Prince, and being largely reënforced, and commanded by MacMahon in person, they were sanguine of victory. Nowhere during the war did the French troops manifest more determined and desperate valor, and nowhere did they approach more nearly to a great success than in this battle. The Crown-Prince's report of it does full justice to the bravery and skill of his antagonist. He says:

"On the 5th of August reliable intelligence was received at the headquarters of the Third Army, that Marshal MacMahon was busily engaged in concentrating his troops on the hills west of Woerth, and that he was being reënforced by constant arrivals by railway. In consequence of these advices it was resolved to lose no time in effecting a change of front, which had been determined upon a few days previously, but not yet executed. The Second Bavarian and the Fifth Prussian Corps were to remain in their respective positions at Lembach and Prenschdorf; the Eleventh Prussian Corps was to wheel to the right and encamp at Hölschloch, with van pushed forward toward the river Sauer; and the First Bavarian Corps was to advance into the neighborhood of Lobsann and Lampertsloch. The Cavalry Division remained at Schönenburg, fronting west. The Corps Werder (Würtemberg and Baden Divisions) marched to Reimerswiller, with patrols facing the Haguenau forest.

"The Fifth Prussian Corps, on the evening of the 5th,

pushed its van from its bivouac at Prenschdorf on to the heigh east of Woerth. On the other side of the Sauer numerous camp-fires of the enemy were visible during the night, the French outposts occupying the heights west of the Sauer, opposite Woerth and Gunstett. At dawn of the 6th skirmishes commenced along the line of the outposts, which caused the Prussian vanguard to send a battalion into Woerth. At 8 o'clock steady firing was heard on the right (Bavarian) flank. This, and the fire the enemy directed against Woerth, caused us to station the entire artillery of the Fifth Prussian Corps on the heights east of this place, and try to relieve the Bavarians. A little later the Fifth Corps was ordered to break off the engagement, it being the intention of our generals to begin the battle against the concentrated forces of the enemy only when the change of front had been effected, and the entire German army was ready to be brought into action. At 7.45 o'clock the Fourth Division (Bothmer) of the Second Bavarian Corps (Hartmann), induced by the heavy fire of the outposts near Woerth, had left their bivouac at Lembach, and, proceeding by Mattstall and Langen-Salzbach, after a sharp engagement penetrated as far as Neschwiller, where they spread, fronting to the south. At 10.30 o'clock this Bavarian Corps, supposing the order to break off the engagement, which had been given to the Fifth Prussians, to extend to themselves, withdrew to Langen-Salzbach. The enemy being thus no longer pressed on his left, turned all his strength with the greatest energy against the Fifth Prussians at Woerth. Reënforcements were continually thrown in by rail. Finding the enemy in earnest on this point, and perceiving the Eleventh Prussians to approach vigorously in the direction of Gunstett, the Fifth Prussians immediately proceeded to the attack, so as to defeat the enemy, if possible, before he had time to concentrate. The Twentieth Brigade was the first to defile through Woerth, and marched toward Elsasshausen and Froschwiller; it was promptly followed by the Nineteenth Brigade. The French stood their ground with the utmost pertinacity, and their fire was crushing. Whatever the gallantry of our Tenth Division, it did not succeed in overcoming the obstinate resistance of the enemy. Eventually, the Ninth Division having been drawn into the fight, the whole Fifth Corps found itself involved in the sanguinary conflict raging along the heights west of Woerth.

"At 1.15 P. M. orders were given to the First Bavarian Corps (Von der Tann) to leave one of its two divisions where it stood, and, sending on the other as quick as possible by Lobsann and Lampertsloch, seize upon the enemy's front in the gap between the Second Bavarian Corps at Langen-Salzbach and the Fifth Prussian Corps at Woerth. The Eleventh Prussians were ordered to advance to Elsasshausen, skirt the forest of Niederwald, and operate against Froschwiller. The Würtemberg Division was to proceed to Gunstett and follow the Eleventh Prussians across the Sauer; the Baden Division was to remain at Sauerburg.

"At 2 o'clock the combat had extended along the entire line. It was a severe struggle. The Fifth Prussians fought at Woerth, the Eleventh Prussians near Elsasshausen. In his strong position on and near the heights of Froschwiller, the enemy offered us a most intense resistance. The First Bavarian Corps reached Görsdorff, but could not lay hold of the enemy fast enough; the Second Bavarian had to exchange the exhausted troops of the Division Bothmer, who had spent their ammunition in the fierce fights of the morning, for the Division Walther. While the Division Bothmer fell back, the Brigade Scleich of the Division Walther marched upon Langen-Salzbach. The Würtemberg Division approached Gunstett.

"At 2 o'clock fresh orders were given. The Würtemberg Division was to turn toward Reichshofen by way of Ebersbach, to threaten the enemy's line of retreat. The First Bavarian was to attack at once and dislodge the enemy from his position at Froscnwiller and in the neighboring vineyards. Between 2 and 3 o'clock the enemy, bringing fresh troops into the field, and advancing with consummate bravery, assumed the offensive against the Fifth and Eleventh Prussian Corps. But all his assaults were beaten off. Thus the fight was briskly going on at Woerth, neither party making much progress, till at length the brilliant attack of the First Bavarian Corps at Görsdorff, and of the First Würtemberg Brigade on the extreme left at Ebersbach, decided the fate of the day.

"Toward the close of the battle the French attempted a grand cavalry charge against the Fifth and Eleventh Corps, especially against the artillery of these troops. Our artillery awaited them in a stationary position, and repulsed them with severe loss. The infantry did so likewise. This last experiment having failed, the enemy, at 4 o'clock, evacuated Froschwiller, and retreated through the mountain-passes in the diréction of Bitche. The cavalry of all our divisions were despatched in pursuit.

"The cavalry division which, on account of the difficult ground, which allowed little scope for its manœuvres, had been left at Schönburg, were ordered, at 3.30 o'clock, to advance to Gunstett. On the morning of the 7th this cavalry corps began the pursuit in the direction of Ingweiler and Bronstweiler. All the troops who had taken part in the engagement bivouacked on the battle-field, the cavalry at Gunstett, the Baden Division at Sauerburg.

"Our losses are great, but cannot, as yet, be exactly estimated. The enemy lost 5,000 unwounded prisoners, thirty guns, six mitrailleuses, and two eagles. The enemy's troops arrayed against us were General MacMahon's army, and the Second and Third Divisions of the Sixth Corps."

The French attempted to make a stand at Niederbronn with their artillery, but the guns were captured by the Bavarian troops, and active pursuit was made on all the roads by the German forces, the French flying in confusion. The military chest of the Fourth French Division was captured. At Saverne, twenty-five miles S. W. of Woerth, Marshal MacMahon rallied his disheartened troops, and from thence, on the 7th of August, despatched his official report to the Emperor. As the army of the Crown-Prince, however, occupied the territory between him and Metz, his communication with the Emperor was broken, and was not resumed for several days; so that, for ten days or more, the right wing of the French army was entirely cut off from the remainder.

The Marshal's report was as follows:

"SAVERNE, August 7.

"SIRE: I have the honor to acquaint your Majesty, that, on the 6th of August, after having been obliged to evacuate Weissenburg on the previous evening, the First Corps, with the object of covering the railway from Strasbourg to Bitsche, and the principal roads connecting the eastern and the western slopes of the Vosges, occupied the following positions: The First Division was placed, its right in advance of Freichsweiller, and its left in the direction of Reichshoffen, resting upon a wood which covers that village. Two companies were detached to Neunviller, and one company to Joegersthal. The Third Division occupied, with the First Brigade, some low hills which run from Freichsweiller and slope toward Guersdorff. The Second Brigade rested its left on Freichsweiller, and its right on the village of Elsasshausen. The Fourth Brigade formed an uneven line to the right of the Third Division, its First Brigade facing toward Gunstedt, and its Second Brigade opposite the village of Marsbroun, which, on account of insufficient strength, it was unable to occupy. The Division Dumesnil, of the Seventh Corps, which had rallied to me early on the morning of the 6th, was placed in rear of the Fourth Division. There were held in reserve the Second Division, in rear of the Second Brigade of the Third Division, and the First Brigade of the Fourth Division. Finally, still further in the rear, was the Brigade of Light Cavalry, under the command of General Septeuil, and Division of Cuirassiers, under General de Bonnemain. Michel's Cavalry Brigade, under the command of General Dechesmes, was stationed in the rear of the right wing of the Fourth Division. At 7 o'clock in the morning the enemy appeared before the heights of Guersdorff, and opened the action with a cannonade, which he immediately supported with a sustained fire from his *tirailleurs* upon the First and Third Divisions. The attack was so vehement that the First Division was obliged to effect a change of front, advancing upon its right wing, in order to prevent the enemy from turning the general position. A little later the enemy largely increased the number of his batteries, and opened fire upon the other position which we occupied on the right bank of the Sauerbach. Although even more heavy and more strongly marked than the first, which was still maintained, this second demonstration was but a feigned attack, which was warmly repulsed. Toward noon the enemy directed his attack toward our right. Clouds of sharpshooters, supported by considerable masses of infantry, and protected by upward of sixty pieces of artillery placed upon the heights of Gunstedt, rushed upon the Second Division and upon the Second Brigade of the Third Division, which occupied the village of Elsasshausen. Despite repeated offensive movements vigorously executed, and notwithstanding the well-directed fire of the artillery and several brilliant cavalry charges, our right was broken after many hours' obstinate resistance. It was 4 o'clock. I ordered a retreat. It was protected by the First and Second, which presented a bold front, and enabled the other troops to retire without being too closely harassed. The retreat was effected upon Saverne by Niederbronn, where the Division of General Guyot de Lespard, belonging to the Fifth Corps, which had just arrived there, took up position, and did not withdraw until nightfall. I submit inclosed with this report to His Majesty the names of officers wounded, killed, or missing, which have been reported to me. This list is incomplete, and I will forward a complete return as soon as I shall be in a position to do so.

"MacMahon."

King Wilhelm telegraphed to the Queen, on the night after this battle, as follows:

"Good news. A great victory has been won by our Fritz. God be praised for His mercy. We captured 4,000 prisoners, thirty guns, two standards, and six *mitrailleurs*. MacMahon, during the fight, was heavily reënforced from the main army. The contest was very severe, and lasted from 11 o'clock in the morning until 9 o'clock at night, when the French retreated, leaving the field to us. Our losses were heavy."

The two defeats (of Frossard and MacMahon), both occurring on the same day, were a very severe blow to Napoleon III, but, with his accustomed stoicism, he telegraphed to the Empress:

"Marshal MacMahon has lost a battle. General Frossard, on the Saar, has been obliged to retire. His retreat was effected in good order. All can be reëstablished."

The next day further disasters to the French cause were reported. Haguenau, a considerable town of Alsace, was captured by the Baden Cavalry, the French taken prisoners, or driven out, and the town occupied by the Germans. The same cavalry overran the greater part of Alsace, taking many prisoners, and beleaguering Pfalzburg, Bitche, and Luneville. At the west, Saargemund was occupied, and Forbach taken after a slight action. On the 7th of August the Emperor telegraphed to the Empress:

"My communication with MacMahon being broken, I had, until yesterday, but little news of him. General Laigle informed me that MacMahon had lost a battle against very considerable forces of the enemy, and that he had withdrawn in good order. The battle began at 1 o'clock, and did not appear very serious until gradually increasing reënforcements came up on the enemy's side, without, however, compelling the Second Corps to fall back. Only between 6 and 7 o'clock, as the enemy became constantly more compact, did the Second Corps, and the regiments from other corps which served as his supports, fall back upon the hills. The night was quiet. I go to the centre of our position."

Major-General Lebœuf, commanding the French forces, reported the same day to the Minister of the Interior:

"After a series of engagements, in which the enemy brought heavy forces into the field, Marshal MacMahon was forced to fall back from his first line. The Corps of General Frossard had a fight yesterday, from 2 o'clock in the afternoon, with an entire army of the enemy. Having held his position until 6 o'clock, he ordered a retreat, which was made in good order."

Up to the evening of the 7th of August all unfavorable news had been carefully kept from the people of Paris. The battle of Weissenburg had been represented as a French victory; but this deception was suspected and resented by the people, and the Empress found herself compelled to acknowledge partially the misfortunes which had befallen the army. Accordingly, the following proclamation was made public in the evening, though dated in the morning.

"FRENCHMEN: The opening of the war has not been favorable to us. We have suffered a check. Let us be firm under this reverse, and let us hasten to repair it. Let there be but one party in the land—that of France; a single flag—that of the national honor. I come among you, faithful to my mission and duty. You will see me the first in danger to defend the flag of France. I adjure all good citizens to maintain order. To agitate would be to conspire with our enemies.

"Done at the Palace of the Tuileries, the 7th day of August, 1870, at 11 o'clock A. M.

  (Signed)   "The Empress Regent,
            "EUGENIE."

This proving unsatisfactory, as giving no details, the Ministers very reluctantly published the despatches of the Emperor and Marshal Lebœuf; and as they were by this time thoroughly alarmed, they appended also the following appeal, signed by the Ministers then in Paris.

"Details of our losses are wanting. Our troops are full of *élan*. The situation is not compromised; but the enemy is on our territory, and a serious effort is necessary. A battle appears imminent. In the presence of this grave news our duty is plain. We appeal to the patriotism and the energy of all. The Chambers have been convoked. We are placing Paris with all possible haste in a state of defence. In order to facilitate the execution of military preparations, we declare the capital in a state of siege. There must be no faint-heartedness, no divisions. Our resources are immense. Let us pursue the struggle without flinching, and the country will be saved.

"Paris, the 7th of August, 1870, at 10 P. M.

"By order of the Empress Regent."

In connection with these demonstrations, other changes were dictated by Napoleon III and made by the Government. Among these were the dismission of Marshal Lebœuf from the command of the army, and the appointment of Marshal Bazaine in his place, and the promotion of General Trochu to be Major-General in the army and commander of Paris. Ollivier was also compelled to resign his premiership, and Palikao made Premier.

CHAPTER VIII.

THERE were, indeed, at this time, indications of the speedy approach of a revolution in Paris, hoarse mutterings of the coming storm which was destined to overthrow the dynasty of the Man of December—the despot who for twenty-one years had crushed pitilessly the liberty which he professed to cherish, and to which he owed his own elevation to power. A few days more of grace were left to him, but most of them were passed in fierce battles and overwhelming defeats.

We resume our narrative in chronological order. While the First Army (General von Steinmetz's) and the Third Army (the Crown-Prince Friedrich Wilhelm's) had both done some desperate fighting with the French, and the latter, in particular, had signalized its valor both at Weissenburg and Woerth, the Second, or Army of the Centre, commanded by Prince Friedrich Karl, and with which the King of Prussia had his headquarters, had not been in any engagement. Indeed, they did not leave their position around Homburg, in Rhenish-Bavaria, until the 6th of August, and the King did not move forward until the 8th or 9th. On the 6th, before marching to the frontier-line on the Saar, Prince Friedrich Karl issued the following order, bearing evidence, like most of the German proclamations, of the desire of the German commanders to conduct the war on civilized and Christian principles:

"SOLDIERS OF THE SECOND ARMY: You enter upon the soil of France. The Emperor Napoleon has, without any reason, declared war upon Germany, and his army are our enemies. The French people has not been asked if it wished to carry on a bloody war with its German neighbors. A reason for enmity is not to be found. Meet the feeling of the peaceable inhabitants of France with a like sentiment; show them that, in our century, two civilized people do not forget their humanity even in warring with each other. Bear always in mind how your fathers would have felt if an enemy—which God forbid!—overran our provinces. Show the French that the German people confronting its enemy is not only great and brave, but also well controlled and noble-minded."

Two days later the King issued from his headquarters at Homburg the following general order to all the armies in the field:

"SOLDIERS: The pursuit of the enemy, forced back after bloody fighting, has already carried a great part of our army over the frontier. Many corps will enter upon the French soil to-day and to-morrow. I expect that the self-discipline with which you have heretofore distinguished yourself will be also especially maintained in the enemy's territory. We carry on no war against the peaceable inhabitants of the land; it is, on the contrary, the duty of every honest soldier to protect private property, and not to allow the good reputation of our army to be marred by even *one* example of lawlessness. I depend upon the excellent feeling which possesses the army, but also upon the vigilance and rigor of all commanders."

On the same day the veteran von Steinmetz, from his headquarters at Saarbruck, addressed his troops, already baptized in blood in the fierce fight for the possession of the heights of Spicheren, in the following determined language:

"Soldiers of the First Army: By command of His Majesty the King, the First Army will to-morrow cross the French boundary. Let us greet this first result of our previous efforts as we enter upon the enemy's territory with a hearty hurrah for our wise, supreme war-leader. Of your good conduct in the struggle which awaits us with an equally brave army, I am assured by your love of the fatherland, your courage, and your just pride, which forbid you to suffer the insults cast upon us by an intemperate opponent, to remain unnoticed. But the peace-loving citizen and countryman, as you will say yourselves, stands under the protection of the humanity which is comprehended in Prussian discipline. I trust that you will never falsify either the one or the other by excesses which can never be countenanced by your superiors. When and where the enemy confronts us, I expect that he will be attacked with the greatest determination. For the cavalry it is already a principle of long standing that it always attacks first. The excuse, that there was nothing to be done, I can never allow, when the thunder of the cannon can be heard. On the contrary, each detachment of troops must march toward that direction, and, arrived upon the battle-field, inform itself upon the condition of the fight, in order to attack at once, in the best way. The same sound must also serve as a guide to each superior commander in a pitched battle. One thing more. What can be done on one day must never be distributed over two days. Only with the greatest energy can great results be attained, and, with them, the peace which God will give us after victorious combat."

On the 9th of August the Baden contingent of the German army approached Strasbourg, and summoned it to surrender. General Uhrich, the French commander, refused, and the next day issued the following proclamation:

GEN. UHRICH, THE HEROIC DEFENDER OF STRASBURG.

"Disturbing rumors and panics have been spread, either by accident or design, within the past few days in our brave city. Some individuals have dared to express the opinion that the place would surrender without a blow. We protest energetically, in the name of a population courageous and French, against these weak and criminal forebodings. The ramparts are armed with 400 cannon. The garrison consists of 11,000 men, without reckoning the stationary National Guard. If Strasbourg is attacked, Strasbourg will defend herself as long as there shall remain a soldier, a biscuit, or a cartridge. The well-affected may reassure themselves; as to others, they have but to withdraw.

"The General of Division, UHRICH.
"The Prefect of the Bas-Rhin, Baron PRON.
"Strasbourg, August 10."

On the 11th of August the three German armies forming the advance all stood upon French soil, and King Wilhelm addressed to the inhabitants of the departments then in possession of the German army the following proclamation:

"We, Wilhelm, King of Prussia, give notice to the inhabitants of the French departments in possession of the German army as follows: After the Emperor Napoleon had attacked by sea and by land the German nation, which desired, and still desires, to live at peace with the French people, I assumed the chief command over the German armies in order to repel this attack. In the progress of events I have had occasion to cross the French boundary. I make war with the French soldiers, and not with the citizens of France. These will, therefore, continue to enjoy a perfect security of their persons and their property just so long as they do not deprive me, by their own hostile acts against the German troops, of the right to extend to them my protection. The generals who command the different corps will establish by especial regulations, which shall be brought to the knowledge of the public, the measures which are to be taken against communities or against single persons, who set themselves in opposition to the usages of war. They will in similar manner fix every thing in regard to requisitions which shall be demanded by the necessities of the troops. They will also fix the rate of exchange between German and French currency, in order to make the single transactions between the troops and the people easy."

The defeat of Marshal MacMahon at Woerth, with the subsequent slight but disastrous engagements at Niederbronn and Reichshofen, was found to be even more appalling than was at first supposed. His losses, as ascertained some days later, were more than 9,000 killed and wounded, and 6,500 prisoners, besides a very considerable number of deserters. Making the best of this great yet inevitable misfortune, he issued, on the 9th of August, the following order of the day to his remnant of an army:

"Soldiers: In the battle of the 6th of August, fortune betrayed your courage, but you yielded your positions only after a heroic resistance which lasted not less than nine hours. You were 35,000 against 140,000, and were overwhelmed by force of numbers. Under these conditions defeat is glorious, and history will say that in the battle of Froschweiler the French showed the greatest valor. You have suffered heavy losses, but those of the enemy are much greater. Although you have not been successful, you see a cause for your misfortune which makes the Emperor satisfied with you, and the entire country recognize that you have worthily sustained the honor of the flag. Let us show that, though subjected to the severest tests, the First Corps, forgetting these, closes up its ranks, and, God aiding us, let us seize great and brilliant revenge."

The necessity for strong reënforcements compelled MacMahon to summon to his aid General De Failly (a portion of whose corps had already been with him at Woerth) and Generals Can robert and De Caen, both of whom were in southern Alsace. With all these troops, however, he could only gather from 50,000 to 60,000 men, so far had the real numbers of the French army-corps fallen below their nominal standard, and so numerous, even in this first stage of the war, were the deserters. The nominal strength of these four army-corps had been 200,000 men. Having obtained these reënforcements, MacMahon fell back to Nancy and Toul, his objective being Paris by way of Bar-le-Duc and Chalons, as he saw very clearly that, unless a strong force was interposed between Paris and the Prussian armies, they could not be checked in their victorious march toward the French capital; and the probability of their reaching that city was much greater than that of the French entering Berlin as conquerors, as the Emperor had promised them at the beginning of the war. It was necessary, moreover, that he should be in a position to receive the large reënforcements yet to be sent out from Paris, that he might attack the Prussians in flank, while Bazaine, who was now in chief command under the Emperor, and was gathering a large army in the neighborhood of Metz, should attack them in front. These plans, however, were destined to be suddenly and completely frustrated. The Crown-Prince of Prussia, who, after the battle of Woerth, ascertained what was the line upon which MacMahon was retreating, and had drawn his own army northward to Saar-union, to within reach of the other armies, commenced a relentless pursuit of the French general through Nancy and Toul, leaving to the German reserves the siege and reduction of the small fortified places on the route, and pressed on his rear through Commercy, Bar-le-Duc, and Chalons, not relinquishing the pursuit when MacMahon turned northward and attempted to create a diversion in favor of Bazaine.

Meanwhile, as we have already intimated, Bazaine, falling back from St. Avold, which had been for a time his headquarters, concentrates as large a force as possible in the vicinity of Metz, the strongest and best-provided of the French fortresses, but found, to his great annoyance and dismay when he reached the Moselle, that an infantry force, the advance of Prince Friedrich Karl's army, had secured an eligible location for crossing that river at Pont-à-Mousson, less than twenty miles south of Metz. With his large army, now numbering probably 150,000 or more troops, it would not answer for him to be shut up and besieged in Metz by the Prussian armies; yet he was in great peril of being caught there, for General Frossard, who came in with his corps from St. Avold on the 13th of August, reported himself pressed closely all the way by the Germans; the advance of von Steinmetz's army and the Second German Army (Prince Friedrich Karl's) were known to be coming in great force from the south. The Emperor and the Prince Imperial thought it necessary to leave Metz, and did so at 11 A. M. on Sunday, going, however, no farther than Longueville, near Metz, that day. He left the following address to the inhabitants of Metz, which was posted about the city after his departure:

"On quitting you to fight the invaders, I confide to your patriotism the defence of this great city. You will never allow the enemy to take possession of this bulwark of France, and I trust you will rival the army in loyalty and courage. I shall ever remember with gratitude the reception I have found within your walls, and I hope that in more joyous times I may be able to return to thank you for your noble conduct."

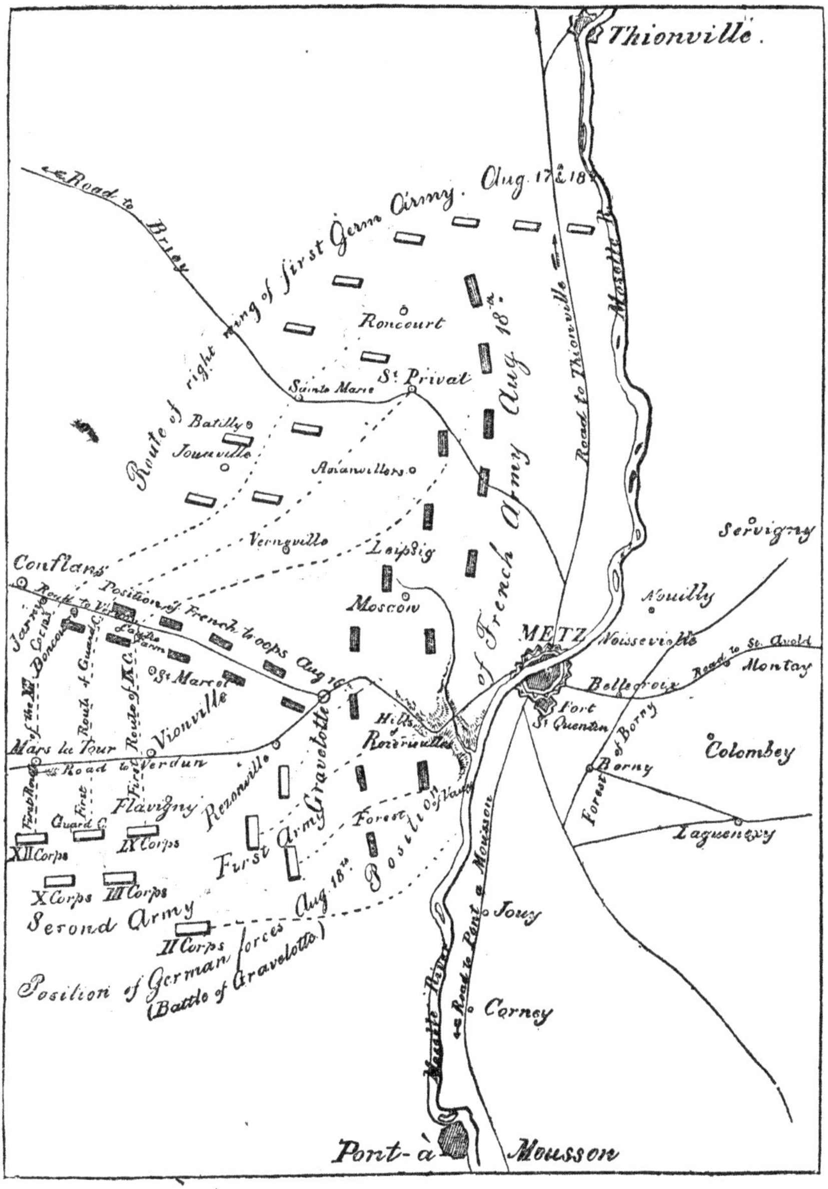

Thionville
Road to Briey
Route of right wing of first Germ Army. Aug. 17th & 18th
Roncourt
Sainte Marie
St. Privat
Batilly
Jouaville
Amanvillers
Verneville
Leipsig
Moscow
of French Army Aug 18th
Road to Thionville
Moselle R.
Conflans
Position of French troops Aug 16th
St Marcel
Vionville
Mars la Tour
Road to Verdun
Flavigny
Rezonville
Gravelotte
Hills of Rozerieulles
Forest
Position
First Army
Guard C.
IX Corps
XII Corps
X Corps
III Corps
Second Army
II Corps
Position of German forces Aug 18th
(Battle of Gravelotte)
Servigny
Nouilly
METZ
Noisseville
Road to St. Avold
Montay
Bellecroix
Fort St Quentin
Forest of Borny
Borny
Colombey
Laquenexy
Road to Pont a Mousson
Jouy
Corney
Moselle River
Pont-à-Mousson

This effort to withdraw Bazaine's army from Metz had been in spite of the attempted secrecy, observed by the Prussian commanders, and a reconnoissance in force ordered to prevent it. Bazaine was moving his advance across the Moselle, on the Verdun road, when the advance-guard of the First Army (von Steinmetz's) fell upon his rear-guard about 4 P. M., and compelled some of his divisions to face about to resist the attack. The First and Seventh Corps of the First Army soon came up to support the attack; and the Ninth Corps of the Second Army, having arrived from Pont-à-Mousson, joined in. The foregoing plan of the roads and villages west of Metz, and of the position of the Prussian and French forces, will materially aid our understanding of this and the battles of the following days.

The battle of Sunday, August 14th, was most severe on the east side of the Moselle, toward which the different corps of the First Army were rapidly marching to cross the river at Jouy, Coiney, and various other points between Metz and Pont-à-Mousson. Bazaine, desirous of making good his retreat upon Verdun, and finding that the Prussians were in large force in the woods around Borny, a small village east of the Moselle, at the junction of the Boulay, St. Avold, and Forbach roads, and in the villages to the northeast of that village, determined to repulse their attack; and when they opened fire upon the outworks of Metz, l'Admirault's corps, which was just starting for Verdun, together with the Third Corps, De Caen's, and the Imperial Guard, under General Bourbaki, and the garrison of Fort St. Quentin, advanced to the attack. The battle raged from a little after 4 P. M. to nearly 9 P. M. The French make no mention of their position at the beginning of the fight, but only speak of the German force as near Borny; but the Germans say that the French line at the beginning was Nouilly, Noisseville, Montay, and Colombey, and that they were forced back into the fortifications of Metz, and held there by the threatening position of the Second Army, which was across the Moselle, and commanded the road to Verdun by Mars-la-Tour. The accounts of the two parties are conflicting, but both agree that it was a very severe action, and that the losses were heaviest on the side of the Prussians, though they accomplished their object of detaining the French in Metz until they could bring their own troops across the Moselle, and flank and defeat all the efforts of the French general to retreat toward Paris.

The German account of the battle, which is official, but gives very few details, is as follows :

"The combats of the 14th, 16th, and 18th of August are closely connected with each other. After the defeat sustained by their advanced guard at Saarbruck on the 6th, and in consequence of the complete dissolution of their right wing under Marshal MacMahon, the bulk of the hostile army retreated on the line of the Moselle. The fortress of Thionville and the very important position of Metz, with its intrenched camp, gave extraordinary strength to this line. A direct attack upon it would have been difficult. The armies were, therefore, directed south of Metz toward the Moselle, in order to pass the river above the fortress, and so attack the enemy. The movement of great masses, which could only be carried on in a considerable breadth of country, had to be secured by special precautions. The First Army, consequently, undertook to cover this march.

" As the enemy for a time seemed disposed to await an attack on the east side of Metz, on the right bank of the Moselle, in a strong position on the French side, the nearest divisions of the Second Army were so approximated to the First Army as to be able promptly to support it. Meantime the other corps of the Second Army had already crossed the Moselle. The enemy consequently saw himself forced, in order not to lose his communications with Paris, to evacuate the right bank of the Moselle before Metz, as he could not venture to attempt an attack on our movement. The advanced guard of the First Army, pushing on toward him, promptly discovered this retreat, and in the encounter of the 14th of August threw itself on the French rear-guard, forcing it forward on the marching columns of their main army. The enemy was obliged to move round some of his divisions to support it, while on our side the entire First and Seventh Corps, and some detachments of the nearest (Ninth) Army Corps of the Second Army, joined in the engagement. The enemy was forced back and pursued till under shelter of the cannons of the Metz forts on the right bank of the Moselle. This combat had, moreover, this great advantage, that it delayed the enemy's retreat. This advantage it was possible to profit by."

Correspondents on both sides supply the following additional items respecting the battle:

" With all the caution used by the French in attempting to conduct the evacuation secretly, they could not escape the vigilant Germans. About 4 P. M. the preparations of the troops lying among the advanced works of Metz were so apparent, that two divisions were ordered to reconnoitre these troops. One division marched along the highway from St. Avold, the other by another road south of the former. The latter got into action first, and attacked so boldly that De Caen's corps, and parts of Frossard's, were forced to face about. The French occupied, in the beginning, Servigny, Noisseville, Montay, Colombey. On the right (German) wing the First Army-Corps advanced against Noisseville and Montay, and on the left wing the Seventh and half of the Ninth Corps were engaged. While the infantry were maintaining a heavy fight, the artillery of the First and

Thirteenth Divisions, fourteen batteries in all, succeeded in taking up a position in the general form of a horse-shoe on the hills north of Montay, and poured a concentric and well-delivered fire until nightfall upon the enemy's line, which proved very effective, in spite of the setting sun and an unfavorable wind. The French showed less skill in using their guns. The French were gradually driven backwards, and their positions repeatedly stormed. Toward evening General l'Admirault, determining, as a last resort, to make an offensive movement, attempted with his Fourth Corps to turn the right wing of his enemy toward Servigny; but General Manteuffel, bringing up his reserves, repulsed the attack. At 10 o'clock the Germans returned to their bivouacs. The French were held back for a day more, which invaluable time was put to good use by the troops hurrying over the Moselle at Pont-à-Mousson, where Prince Friedrich Karl was pushing northwestward toward the French line of retreat. Losses heavy on both sides. French accounts say that most of their men were wounded in the feet. Marshal Bazaine was said to be slightly wounded in the foot by a shell which killed his horse: 1,200 to 1,500 of their wounded were brought back in Metz. The Germans were thought to have lost 2,600 to 3,500.

"The regiments most closely engaged on the French side were the Sixty-ninth, Ninetieth, Forty-fourth, Sixtieth, Eightieth, Thirty-third, Fifty-fourth, Sixty-fifth, and Eighty-fifth of the line; the Eleventh and Fifteenth Foot Chasseurs; and the Eighth, Ninth, and Tenth batteries of the First Regiment of Artillery. Those which suffered most were the Forty-fourth and Ninetieth of the line, and the Fifteenth Foot Chasseurs. The colonel of the Forty-fourth was killed; the colonel of the Third Horse Chasseurs, and Generals Duplessis and Castanier, were wounded."

King Wilhelm sent the following despatches on the 15th:

"Yesterday evening victorious combat near Metz, by troops of the Seventh and First Army-Corps. Details still wanting. I am going at once to the battle-field.

"The advance-guard of the Seventh Corps attacked, last evening towards 5 o'clock, the retreating enemy, who took up a position and called reënforcements from the fortress. Parts of the Thirteenth and Fourteenth Divisions, and of the First Corps, supported the advance-guard. A very bloody fight spread along the whole line; the enemy was thrown back at all points, and the pursuit was carried as far as the glacis of the outworks. The neighborhood of the fortress permitted the enemy to cover his wounded to a great extent. After our wounded were cared for, the troops withdrew at daybreak into their old bivouacs. The troops are reported to have all of them fought with a wonderful energy and gayety not to be expected. I have seen many of them, and have thanked them from my heart. The joy was overpowering. I spoke with Generals Steinmetz, Zastrow, Manteuffel, and Göben."

The French official account is less extravagant than that of the correspondents, but greatly exaggerates the Prussian losses, while underrating its own.

"On taking command, Marshal Bazaine, seeing the country invaded on three sides by the armies of Prince Friedrich Karl, Prince Friedrich Wilhelm, and Marshal Steinmetz, contemplated uniting the scattered French troops at Metz, in order to be able to confront the enemy. One point in this movement was at Borny, a small village at the junction of the Boulay, St. Avold, and Forbach roads. There the enemy advanced, confident of triumph after his easy victory at Styring. While, therefore, on Sunday, August 14th, the enemy had decided to cross the Moselle and leave Metz behind him, a great movement was taking place in the French camp. General l'Admirault was preparing to turn Metz on the north, and thus separate himself from General De Caen, who would enter the city, when the enemy, who was well posted at Noisseville, Montay, and Coiney, had the boldness to open fire on us. The troops halted. The soldiers of l'Admirault, who had already left by the ravine of Valliere, returned and advanced toward the Prussians. In an instant the fire thus opened from Valliere to Grigy by way of Borny, being a length of nearly six miles. The Prussians never resist such an attack. The cannonade continued from 4 to 5 o'clock. It ceased then for an hour, to allow the infantry and mitrailleuses to do their work, and recommenced at 6.30, ceasing only when the enemy had entirely abandoned their positions. It was one of the most glorious feats of the war. The enemy left 8,000 dead on the field, while our loss was scarcely 1,000. General Picard, commander of one of the divisions of the Imperial Guard, told me, next day, that he had never seen any thing so terrible as the battle-field of Borny. Rows of men were lying in the order they stood; and the wounded were, in some cases, under the dead. This was the work of the French mitrailleuses. It must be said, however, that the Prussian steel-cannons did us considerable damage."

The Emperor sent the following despatch to Eugenie, dated at Longueville, on Sunday night, at 10 o'clock:

"The army began to cross to the left bank of the Moselle this morning. Our advance-guard had no knowledge of the presence of any force of the enemy. When half of our army had crossed over, the Prussians suddenly attacked in great force. After a fight of four hours, they were repulsed with great loss to them.

"NAPOLEON."

But, though boasting of his success in repulsing the enemy, Bazaine was too skilful a general not to be aware that it was a vital necessity of his position to be able to retreat to Verdun. After this severe battle, then, the whole night of the 14th was spent in moving his army across the Moselle, leaving General Changarnier with a strong garrison in Metz. An armistice of twenty-four hours was asked by the Germans, to bury their dead who had fallen the previous day in the battle of Borny, but their reconnoissances demonstrated the fact that all the French army except the garrison had left Metz, and been placed by Bazaine in *échelon* right and left from Rezonville, facing southwestward, with headquarters of the Emperor and Marshal Bazaine in Gravelotte. The Guards, Second, Third, and Fourth Corps of the French army, lay between Metz and Doncourt in two lines, facing southwest. The two roads leading to Verdun, the one by Mars-la-Tour, the other by Conflans, have their point of junction at Gravelotte. The possession of one or both these roads was indispensable to Bazaine, and he was prepared to fight fiercely and persistently for it.

He knew that the Second German Army (Prince Friedrich Karl's) had been, since the 13th, diligently and rapidly pushed forward from Pont-à-Mousson across the Moselle to Thiancourt, and thence to Mars-la-Tour, and that it was blocking the southernmost of these roads; but he was not probably aware that the left and centre had been, since Sunday, crossing the Moselle south of Metz, and were taking position east of the Second Army, but within supporting distance of it; nor was he aware of the other important fact, destined to turn the fortunes of the terrible battle of the 18th, that the right wing of the First Army, under the immediate command of von Steinmetz himself, was at this very time (the 15th and 16th of August) pontooning the Moselle north of Metz and between that city and Thionville, and would at a critical moment be hurled with crushing force on his right wing, effectually cutting him off from the Conflans road. For the present, however, he was simply concerned to regain possession of the Verdun road by Mars-la-Tour, and for this, on Tuesday, August 16th, he fought another desperate battle. The advance-guard of Prince Friedrich Karl, which had been hurrying forward by forced marches from the right bank of the Moselle, reached the southernmost Verdun road near Mars-la-Tour early on the morning of the 16th, and attacked the left wing of the French army. General von Alvensleben, with the Third Corps, opened the conflict, and a bloody battle, with divisions from all the corps under Bazaine's command, was gradually developed as the troops on each side came up. The Fifth German Division (General Stülpnagel) fought from 9 A. M. until 3 P. M. without supports. Then the Tenth Corps, the Seventeenth Division of the Ninth Corps, and the Hessian Twenty-fifth Division, one after the other, came up, and after six hours more the defeat of the French was complete. The positions they had occupied were in the hands of the Germans. They lost 2,000 prisoners, among whom were two generals, and seven guns. The victory was claimed by both sides; by Bazaine, because he had nearly held his position (he was driven back nearly to Gravelotte); by the Prussians, with more reason, because they had held possession of the road, and had inflicted on the French much heavier losses than they had sustained. It was clear, however, that the battle was indecisive, and that another must be fought before it could be determined which side should finally win.

The German official report was as follows:

"Two roads lead from Metz to Verdun, the direction which the French army had to take in case of a retreat upon Paris. Those corps of the Second Army which had already passed the Moselle were immediately directed against the southern road, the one most easily reached, in order, if possible, to arrest the enemy's flank-march on that side. This important task was brilliantly accomplished through a bloody and victorious battle. The Fifth Division (Stülpnagel) threw itself on the Frossard Corps, which covered the enemy's flank. The French army, with almost all its corps, was gradually engaged, while, on the Prussian side, the rest of the Third Army-Corps, the Tenth Army-Corps, a regiment of the Ninth Corps, and a brigade of the Eighth, took part. Prince Friedrich Karl assumed the command. The ground first won by us in a twelve hours' struggle was victoriously held, the south road from Metz to Verdun was gained and retained, and the enemy's retreat to Paris by this road cut off. The conduct of our troops was truly heroic. Our loss was very considerable, but that of the enemy infinitely greater, as could be seen by examination of the battle-field. Until the 19th it was impossible to bury the French dead, and the great number of corpses of the Imperial Guard evidenced the enormous losses of that *élite* force. In the French official account the strength of our troops is reckoned at double its actual numbers. The Emperor's proclamation on leaving Metz, as also other French official documents, leaves no doubt that the main army had the certainly quite natural intention of retreating to Verdun."

On the other hand, Bazaine reports:

" This morning the army of Prince Friedrich Karl directed a spirited attack against the left wing of our position. The Cavalry Division (Torton) and the Second Corps (Frossard) maintained a stout resistance to the attack. The corps, which were placed in *échelon* right and left from Rezonville, appeared gradually upon the battle-field, and took part in the combat, which continued until nightfall. The enemy had deployed heavy masses of men, and attempted several attacks, which were stoutly repulsed. Toward evening appeared a new army-corps, which attempted to cut off our left wing. We have everywhere maintained our position, and inflicted heavy losses upon the enemy; our losses are also great. At the moment when the battle raged at its height, a regiment of Uhlans attacked the general staff of the Marshal; twenty men of the escort were put *hors de combat*, the captain commanding killed. At 8 o'clock the enemy was repulsed on the whole line."

On the 17th Bazaine writes again:

"Yesterday, during the entire day, I gave battle between Vionville and Doncourt. The enemy was repulsed. We remained in our positions. I interrupted my movement for some hours in order to bring up ammunition. We have had Friedrich Karl and Steinmetz before us."

The following additional details of this battle were published in Paris:

"Prince Friedrich Karl attacked our right, and was firmly met. The corps of General Argand, at Rezonville, hastened into the action, which ceased only with night. The Prussians repeatedly attacked us, and were as often repulsed. Toward night a fresh corps sought to turn our position, but was beaten off. Our losses are serious. General Bataille is wounded. By 8 o'clock in the evening the enemy were repulsed along the entire line. He had 120,000 men engaged."

Vionville is nine miles west of Metz; Doncourt three miles north of Vionville. The French General Le Grand was killed; he was commander of a cavalry division, Fourth Corps. The

Emperor, after leaving Metz on the 14th, proceeded no further than Gravelotte, eight miles. Leaving that place on Monday, he passes, in advance of his escort, through Jarny, fifteen miles from Metz, on his way to Verdun. Hardly was he out of sight, when the town was in the hands of the German dragoons.

The flank-march by the north road, or by making a wide *détour* further north, still remained possible. Although such a retreat entailed on the French commander great dangers, it appeared possible that he would undertake it, as the only mode of escape from a highly unfavorable position, since otherwise the army was cut off from Paris and all its means of assistance. On the Prussian side, the 17th was turned to account in bringing forward for a final struggle the necessary corps, part of whom were already over the Moselle, while part had, in the night, thrown various bridges over it above Metz. At the same time the movements of the French forces were carefully watched by the German cavalry. King Wilhelm remained on the spot until, from the advanced hour of the day, no further movement of the enemy was to be expected.

On the 17th, Napoleon III, not deeming himself or the little Prince safe at Verdun, proceeded to Rheims.

On Thursday, the 18th, the final struggle of this week of battles occurred. The most complete and intelligible account of this fearful battle of Gravelotte, evidently compiled from official sources, is that of the *Army and Navy Journal* of September 24, 1870, which we append:

"At daybreak the First German Army, with the First, Seventh, and Eighth Corps, stood off the hills south of Rezonville. The Second Army, with the Third, Ninth, Tenth, Twelfth, and Guard Corps, were on the left flank south of Mars-la-Tour and Vionville. The southern branch of the Verdun road, west of Rezonville, was in the hands of the Germans. The northern

THE BATTLE OF GRAVELOTTE.

branch as far as Cautre was held by the French, whose line extended from Amanvillers, through Verneville and Gravelotte, to the Forest of Vaux. Towards 10 o'clock in the morning, after having already spent six hours in visiting the corps in position, the King, from the heights of Flavigny, ordered the Ninth Corps, in position there, to move toward the woods behind St. Marcel; while the Seventh and Eighth Corps marched against the Forest of Vaux, south of Gravelotte. The latter had orders to push the enemy very slowly, in order to give time to the Guards and Twelfth Corps to make a long *détour* on the left, by way of Jouaville, Batilly, and Ste. Marie. The Third and Tenth Corps were in reserve, and but few of their troops were in the fight, these being mostly artillery. The principal movement was that on the left. Preceded by Prussian and Saxon cavalry, the Second Army advanced, still maintaining communication on the right with the First Army. The Twelfth Corps took the direction by Mars-la-Tour and Jarny, while the Guards advanced between Mars-la-Tour and Vionville on Doncourt, and the Ninth Corps crossed the highway to the west of Rezonville, toward Cautre farm, north of St. Marcel. Their purpose was to gain the central and northern roads. They quickly found that the French were not retreating, and moved to the right, meeting at Ste. Marie and Roncourt resistance, which was overcome, and, after another struggle among the steep hills at St. Privat-la-Montagne, that place was gained. The right flank of this Second Army, holding the centre of the whole German line, had been earlier engaged with some advanced forces of the French, and toward noon the Ninth Corps was engaged at Verneville. The Guards and Twelfth Corps reached St. Privat about 4 P. M., and immediately moved south and east against Amanvillers. The fighting here was exceedingly severe. The Germans lay in a long curve, sweeping from St. Privat, where the Saxons fought on the extreme left, through

Ste. Marie and St. Ail (Guards), Verneville (Ninth Corps), Gravelotte (Eighth Corps), and Forest of Vaux (Seventh Corps), across the Moselle, on the right bank of which a brigade of the First Corps and artillery from the reserves were engaged. The French army fought with its back to Germany; the Germans had Paris in their rear. Bazaine's entire army was in line, including those troops which had been prepared for the Baltic expedition. On the left wing the flanking column, after meeting with resistance at every point, pushed its enemy back through Ste. Marie, Roncourt, St. Privat, St. Ail, Habonville, the wood of La Cusse, and Verneville, until, toward evening, two small outworks of Metz lying northeast of Gravelotte, and named *Leipsic* and *Moscou*, were reached. All three roads out of Metz were then firmly in the grasp of the Germans.

"The right wing had great difficulties to overcome. Early in the day its work was to press the French lightly in the Forest of Vaux. Back of this wood was the strongest part of the French position. It was covered by a deep road with sides fifty feet high, back of which was a plateau 325 to 600 feet in height. Behind this is the Rozieriulles hill, along the slopes of which the highway to Metz runs. This whole steep was covered with rifle-pits in three tiers. Behind these were the infantry; behind the infantry the artillery. The highway as it runs along this hill is only 5,000 yards in a straight line from Fort St. Quentin, one of the strong outworks of Metz. But the crest of the hill intervenes between them, and by the road the distance is nearly twice as great. The French soldiers, driven from this last position and crossing the ridge, would find themselves directly under the guns of their forts. When news of the successes on the left, and the evident abandonment of the retreat by the French, was brought to the King, he moved forward to a hill near Rezonville, and ordered more positive action on the right wing. The French, however, maintained their post with great determination. Driven from it at one time, they retook it by a counter-charge. The King, to whom news of the success had been sent arrived on the hill back of Gravelotte only to see his cavalry on the wrong side of the defile, on the opposite side of which the enemy stood. The fire of the artillery ceased; the troops had lost so heavily that the position seemed to be beyond their grasp. The King, however, ordered another attempt, and after an hour, during which night came on, the troops were re-formed. They were no sooner in motion, than the whole face of the hill revealed such rows of artillery and infantry delivering an extremely rapid and deadly fire, that General von Moltke sent an officer to recall the troops. Before he was out of sight the men appeared themselves, returning down the hillside, fully repulsed. Just then the Second Corps, which had been on the march since 2 o'clock in the morning, came up, and as soon as enough regiments showed themselves, they were sent to take the hill from which their comrades had so often returned in failure. Following the withdrawing storming party came the French in counter-attack. Their success was so great, that the German troops showed symptoms of serious disorder. Some parts of the line began a disorderly retreat, and the moment was critical. General von Moltke, who had anxiously awaited the coming of the Second Corps, rushed up, and himself gave them the word to advance. They sprang forward after him, and when the reënforcement was well up the hill, the repulsed troops were again sent forward, going through their terrible experience for the last time, as it proved, with great steadiness and spirit. This attack succeeded, and at 8.30 o'clock the last position of the French was in the hands of their enemy. During the night they withdrew completely into Metz. The losses in this battle, as in the encounters immediately preceding it, were immense. Even now they are not officially known, though an account from Paris says that Bazaine officially reported his wounded at Gravelotte at

18,000; but this probably includes the losses in all the battles west of Metz. Estimating the dead at 5,000, and adding the captured wounded, 3,000 (up to August 22d), the whole French loss would be 23,000. From 6,000 to 10,000 prisoners were taken in the battles east and west of Metz. On the German side, with the exception of prisoners, the losses must have been still greater; and for 18,000 killed and wounded that Bazaine lost, his enemy must have lost at least 25,000. An official report of the losses on the 16th of August has been published. It shows that there were 626 officers and 15,925 men placed *hors de combat*. Eighteen hundred and thirty-two horses were lost, not including those of several South German cavalry regiments."

The King's despatch from Rezonville says:

"The French army attacked to-day in a very strong position west of Metz, under my leadership, in nine hours' battle completely beaten, cut off from its communications with Paris, and thrown back on Metz."

He writes, on the 19th, from Rezonville:

"That was a new day of victory yesterday, the consequences of which are not yet to be estimated. Early yesterday the Twelfth Guards and Ninth Corps proceeded toward the northern road from Metz to Verdun as far as St. Marcel and Doncourt, followed by the Third and Tenth Corps; while the Seventh and Eighth, and finally the Second, remained opposite Metz. As the former swerved to the right, in thickly-wooded ground, toward Verneville and St. Privat, the latter began the attack upon Gravelotte, not heavily, in order to wait until the long flank-march upon the strong position, Amanvillers-Chatel, should be accomplished as far as the Metz highway. This column did not get into action until 4 o'clock with the Pivot Corps; the Ninth at 12 o'clock. The enemy put forth stout resistance in the woods, so that ground was gained only slowly. St. Privat was taken by the Guards, Verneville by the Ninth Corps; the Twelfth Corps and artillery of the Third then went into action. Gravelotte and the woods on both sides were taken and held by troops of the Seventh and Eighth Corps, and with great losses. In order to attack again the enemy, who had been driven back by the flank-attack, an advance beyond Gravelotte was undertaken at dusk, which came upon such a terrible fire from behind rifle-pits *en étage*, and artillery-fire, that the Second Corps, which just then came up, was forced to attack the enemy with the bayonet, and completely took and held the strong position. It was 8.30 o'clock before the firing gradually silenced itself in all quarters. By this last advance the historical shells of Königgrätz were not wanting near me, from which, *this* time, Minister von Roon removed me. All troops that I saw greeted me with enthusiastic hurrahs. They did wonders of bravery against an equally brave enemy, who defended every step, and often attempted offensive attacks, which were each time repulsed. What the fate of the enemy will now be, pushed into the intrenched, very strong position of the fortress of Metz, is still impossible to determine. I dread to ask about the losses, and to give names; for only too many acquaintances will be named, and often incorrectly. Your regiment (the Queen's) is said to have fought brilliantly. Waldersee is wounded severely, but not fatally, as I am told. I expected to bivouac here, but found, after some hours, a room where I rested on the royal ambulance which I had brought with me; and since I have not a particle of my baggage from Pont-à-Mousson, I have not been undressed for thirty hours. I thank God that he vouchsafed us the victory.

"Wilhelm."

In such a battle, extending over thirty or forty square miles, no eye-witness can see the whole, or can comprehend fully all the movements of the various corps and divisions. What one man could see, however, of this battle, which up to its date must be considered the severest of modern times, a correspondent of the New York *Tribune* has described with wonderful accuracy and life-likeness. Portions of his description are not necessary to our work, but those which portray the actual incidents of the battle we gladly transfer to our pages.

"The troops," says this correspondent, "had been passing through Pont-à-Mousson almost continually for several days previously; but now the tramp through every street and by-way made between midnight and dawn a perpetual roar. Hastily dressing, I ran out into the darkness and managed to get a seat on a wagon that was going in the direction of the front, now understood to be a mile or two beyond the village of Gorze, some twelve miles from Pont-à-Mousson. On our way we met a considerable batch of French prisoners, who were looked upon with curiosity by the continuous line of German soldiers with whom we advanced. The way was so blocked with wagons that I got out of my wagon and began to walk and run swiftly ahead. At Mouvient, on the Moselle, about half-way to Metz, I found vast bodies of cavalry—Uhlans and Hussars—crossing the river by a pontoon-bridge, and hurrying at the top of their speed towards Gorze. Quickening my own steps, I first heard the thunder of the cannonade, seemingly coming from the heart of a range of hills on the right. Passing through the village and ascending the high plain beyond, I found myself suddenly in a battle-field, strewn thickly, so far as my eye could reach, with dead bodies. In one or two parts of the field companies were still burying the dead, chiefly Prussians. The French, being necessarily buried last, were still lying in vast numbers on the ground. A few of those that I saw were not yet dead.

"As I hurried on, a splendid regiment of cavalry came up from behind me, and when they reached the brow of the hill they broke out with a wild hurrah, and dashed forward. A few more steps and I gained the summit, and saw the scene which had evoked their cry, and seemed to thrill even their horses.

"From the hill to which I had been directed by good authority to come, the entire sweep of the Prussian and French centres could be seen, and a considerable part of their wings. The spot where I stood was fearful. It was amid ghastly corpses, and the air was burdened with the stench of dead horses, of which there were great numbers. I was standing on the battle-field of the 16th—the Prussian side. On the left stretched, like a silver thread, the road to Verdun—to Paris also —for the possession of which this series of battles had begun. It was between the lines of poplars which stood against the horizon on my left; and on, as far as the eye could reach, toward Metz, with military regularity, strung on this road like beads, were the pretty villages, each with its church-tower, all of which are really only a hundred yards apart, although they have separate names—Mars-la-Tour, Flavigny, a little south of the road, Vionville, Rezonville, and Gravelotte, which is divided into Great and Little Gravelotte. On my right were the thickly-wooded hills behind which lies the most important village of the neighborhood, which I had just left—Gorze. So environed was the foreground of the battle, which should, one would say, be called the battle of Gravelotte, for it was mainly over and around that devoted little town that it raged. The area I have indicated is perhaps four miles square.

"I arrived just as the battle waxed warm. It was about noon of the 18th. The headquarters of the King of Prussia were then at the spot which I have described. The great representative men of Prussia, soldiers and statesmen, were standing on the ground watching the conflict just begun. Among them I recognized the King, Bismarck, General von Moltke, Prince Friedrich Karl, Prince Karl, Prince Adalbert, and Adjutant Kranski. Lieutenant-General Sheridan, of the United States Army, was also present. At the moment the French were making a most desperate effort to hold on to the last bit of the Verdun road—that between Rezonville and Gravelotte, or that part of Gravelotte which in some maps is called St. Marcel. The struggle was desperate but unavailing, for every one man in the French army had two to cope with, and their line was already beginning to waver. Soon it was plain that this wing —the French right—was withdrawing to a new position. This was swiftly taken up under cover of a continuous fire of their artillery from the heights beyond the village. The movement was made in good order, and the position, which was reached at 1.30 o'clock, would, I believe, have been pronounced impregnable by nine out of ten military men. When once this movement had been effected, the French retreating from the pressure of the Prussian artillery-fire, and the Prussians as rapidly advancing, the battle-field was no longer about Rezonville, but had been transferred and pushed forward to Gravelotte, the junction of the two branching roads to Verdun. The fields in front of that village were completely covered by the Prussian reserves, and interminable lines of soldiers were steadily marching onward, disappearing into the village, and emerging on the other side of it with flaming volleys.

" The second battle-field was less extensive than the first, and brought the opposing forces into fearfully close quarters. The peculiarity of it is that it consists of two heights intersected by a deep ravine. This woody ravine is over one hundred feet deep, and, at the top, three hundred yards wide. The side of the chasm next to Gravelotte, where the Prussians stood, is much lower than the other side, which gradually ascends to a great height. From their commanding eminence the French held their enemies fairly beneath them, and poured down upon them a scorching fire. The French guns were in position far up by the Metz road, hidden and covered among the trees. There was not an instant's cessation of the roar. Easily distinguishable amid all was the curious grunting roll of the mitrailleuse. The Prussian artillery was posted to the north and south of the village, the guns on the latter side being necessarily raised for an awkward half-vertical fire.

"The French stood their ground and died; the Prussians stood their ground and died—both by hundreds, I had almost said thousands. This, for an hour or two that seemed ages, so constant was the slaughter. The hill where I stood commanded chiefly the conflict behind the village and to the south of it. The Prussian reënforcements, coming up on their right, filed out of the Bois des Ognons; and it was at that point, as they marched on to the field, that one could perhaps get the best idea of the magnitude of the invading army now in the heart of France. There was no break whatever for four hours in the march of men out of that wood. It seemed almost as if all the killed and wounded revived and came back and marched forth again. Birnam Wood advancing to Dunsinane Hill was not a more ominous sight to Macbeth than these men of General Göben's army to Bazaine, shielded as they were by the woods till they were fairly within range and reach of their enemy's guns. So the French must have felt; for between 4 and 5 o'clock they concentrated upon that spot their heaviest fire, massing all available guns, and shelling the woods unremittingly. Their fire reached the Prussian lines and tore through them; and though the men were steady, it was a test to which no general cares to subject his troops long. They presently swerved a little from that line of advance, and there was no longer a continuous column of infantry pouring out of those woods.

"The attack of the Prussians in the centre was clearly checked. About 6 o'clock, however, a brigade of fresh infantry was again formed in the wood, and emerged from its cover Once out from under the trees, they advanced at double-quick. The French guns had not lost the range of the wood, nor of the ground in front. Seen at a distance through a powerful glass, the brigade was a huge serpent, bending with the undulations of the field. But it left a dark track behind it, and the glass resolved the dark track into falling and dying and dead men. Many of those who had fallen leaped up again, and ran forward a little way, striving still to go on with their comrades. Of those who went backward instead of forward there were few, though many fell as they painfully endeavored to follow the advance.

"Half an hour afterwards great numbers of troops began to march over the hill where I was standing, and moved forward toward the field where so hard a struggle had been so long protracted. These also were, I think, a portion of General Göben's troops, who had been directed upon a less dangerous route.

"The battle from this point on the Prussian left became so fierce that it was soon lost to us, or nearly lost, by reason of the smoke. Now and then the thick cloud would open a little and drift away on the wind, and then we could see the French sorely tried. To get a better view of this part of the field I went forward about half a mile, and from this new standpoint found myself not far from Malmaison. The French line on the hills was still unbroken, and to all appearances they were having the best of the battle. But this appearance was due, perhaps, to the fact that the French were more clearly visible in their broad height, and fighting with such singular obstinacy. They plainly silenced a Prussian battery now and then. But the Prussian line also was strengthened by degrees on this northern point. Infantry and artillery were brought up, and from far in the rear, away seemingly in the direction of Verneville, shot and shell began reaching the French ranks. These were the men and these were the guns of Steinmetz, who there and then effected his junction with the army of Prince Friedrich Karl, and completed the investment of Metz to the northwest.

"With reënforcements for the Prussians thus continually arriving on both sides of the field, the battle grew more and more obstinate. There could be no doubt that the French well understood the meaning of the movements of the Prussians, and of the gradual development of their line to the north.

"Steinmetz was able to extend his line gradually further and further until the French were outflanked, and began to be threatened, as it appeared, with an attack on the rear of their extreme right wing. So long as the smoke from the Prussian guns hovered only over their front, the French clung to their position. The distance from headquarters to where the Prussian flank-attack stretched forward was great, and, to add to the difficulty of clearly seeing the battle, the darkness was coming on. The puffs of smoke from the French guns, mingled with the flashes, brightening as the darkness increased, receded gradually. The pillars of cloud and flame from the north as gradually and steadily approached. With that advance the French fire every moment grew more slack. It was not far from 9 o'clock when the ground was yielded finally on the north, and the last shots fired on that terrible evening were heard in that direction.

"The King's face, as he stood gazing upon the battle-field, had something almost plaintive in it. He hardly said a word, but I noticed that his attention was divided between the exciting scenes in the distance, and the dismal scene nearer his feet, where they were just beginning what must yet be a long task—to bury the French who fell in Tuesday's battle. On them he gazed silently, and, I thought, sadly.

"Count Bismarck could not conceal his excitement and anxiety. If it had not been for the King, the Count would clearly have gone forward where the fighting was. His towering form was always a little in advance of the rest.

"When the French completely gave up their hold upon the road up to Gravelotte, the horses of the headquarters party were hastily called, the entire party mounting, and, with the King at their head, dashed down to a point not very far from the village. Then shouts and cheers arose, and followed them wherever they passed.

"A little after 4 o'clock a strange episode occurred. From the region where Steinmetz was supposed to be, a magnificent regiment of cavalry galloped out. They paused a moment at the point where the Conflans road joins that to Metz. Then they dashed up the road toward Metz. This road between Gravelotte and St. Hubert's is cut through the hill, and on each side of it rise cliffs from forty to sixty feet high, except at the point where it traverses the deep ravine behind the village. When it is remembered that at the time the culminating point to which that road ascends was held by the French, it will not be wondered at that only half that regiment survived. Their plunge into that deep cut on the hillside, where next day I saw so many of them and their horses lying, was of that brave, unhesitating, unfaltering kind which is so characteristic of German soldiers, among whom stragglers and deserters seem to be absolutely unknown.

"At a moment that seemed critical, there appeared on the field, occupying ground before held by a portion of the forces of Prince Friedrich Karl, a large body of troops. They moved into position under the eyes of the King, yet neither the King nor any of his staff could account for their appearance. They passed the point which in the morning had been the royal headquarters. Their march was begun at the time I have mentioned, and their advance did not cease till dark; but the mystery that hung over them was not dispelled. Whose was this new army? Whence did it come? The staff insisted that at the point whence it moved there were, or at any rate ought to be, no troops of the armies of either Steinmetz or of Prince Friedrich Karl. The rumor began and spread among the group of men who surrounded the King that this fresh, mysterious force was a part of the army of the Crown-Prince, and that a new junction had been effected. I know of no reason to suppose this true. Doubtless the staff soon cleared up the matter to their own satisfaction, but it happened that I was away in another part of the field before the riddle was solved.

"In any event, it cannot be doubted that the presence of that large body of men made itself felt upon the fortunes of the field. They were visible to the French as well as to us. Here was another example of the moral effect that may be and so often is exerted in battle by masses of men whose presence is known to the enemy, but who may not fire a shot in the actual conflict. From their line of march it is clear that the divisions were finally posted a little in the rear and on the left of the Prussian centre at the time when the attacks so long directed against the key of the French lines had ceased—in fact, had failed for the time. It was possible that the French, having suffered far less in holding their ground than the Prussians in attacking, might have advanced in their turn and have undertaken a vigorous offensive movement. If they had any such purpose, it is not unlikely that they abandoned it on sight of the Prussian reënforcements.

"Instead of advancing, the French now contented themselves with the mere occupation of the ground to which, earlier in the day, they had been driven back. At no time did they seriously strive to regain the westernmost line of hills which had been theirs in the morning. At no time did they recover, or seek to recover, by any vigorous forward movement, the junction of the roads at Gravelotte. From 7 to 8 o'clock the weight of the battle tended more and more to the north of the road. There was a lull, the meaning of which the French failed apparently to interpret. By 7 o'clock they may have believed themselves partly victorious. They were still, perhaps, in condition to renew on the morrow the struggle that had gone on all day for that fated road from Metz to Verdun. If they had not gained the road or the battle, they had not clearly lost the latter. Two hours later they had lost both.

"A little before 8 o'clock a large white house on the height beyond Gravelotte caught fire. It seemed through the gloom to be a church. Its spire grew into flames, and a vast, black cloud of smoke arose, contrasting strangely with the white smoke of the battle. More and more picturesque grew the whole field. As evening fell, the movements of the troops could be followed now by the lines of fire that ran flickering along the front of a regiment as it went into action. Tongues of fire pierced through and illuminated the smoke out of the cannons' mouths, and the fuses of the shells left long trains of fire like falling stars. No general likes fighting by night in ordinary circumstances, for chance takes then the place of skill; but the flanking movement on the French right had been resolved on by daylight, and it was the necessity of moving troops to a great distance over difficult ground which delayed its execution, and brought about what seemed a renewal of the battle after the day was done.

"To leave the French in their positions during the night would have been to imperil the plan on which the Prussian commander had resolved. So, from 8, or 8.30 to 9 o'clock, the decisive blow was struck. When the battle of Gravelotte had actually ended, we knew that the Prussians held the strong heights beyond the Forest of Vaux, which commanded the surrounding country to the limits of artillery-range from Metz; we knew that two great Prussian armies lay across the only road by which Bazaine could march to Paris for its relief, or for his own escape; we knew that a victory greater than that of Sunday, and more decisive than the triumph of Tuesday, had been won. We believed that the French army, which had fought as valiantly and as vainly as before, was now hopelessly shut up in its fortress.

"As I went back to the village of Gorze to pass the night, I turned at the last point to look upon the battle-field. It was a long, earth-bound cloud, with two vast fires of burning buildings at either end. The day had been beautiful so far as Nature was concerned, and the stars now looked down in splendor upon a work of agony and death such as no one could ever wish to see again."

Another correspondent who witnessed the battle, and also went over the battle-ground on the following day, after stating that the battle will rank with the bloodiest and most hardly-contested that have ever been fought in Europe, goes on to say:

"As I rode up the hill leading to the French position, I wondered not at the frightful files of corpses all around me, but that such a position could be taken at all. On the further side of the road the French had thrown up twelve small épaulements about breast-high; in eight of them they had placed mitrailleuses, for the empty cases were scattered all about. In one épaulement alone I counted forty-three empty cartridge-holders. Now, as each of these boxes contains twenty-five cartridges, 1,075 shots are fired by one during the day. Doubtless many more had actually been fired, for nearly every one did as I did, and carried off an empty case as a relic. The slope immediately beneath the French position, on the Verdun, was a frightful spectacle. Hundreds of Prussian corpses were strewed in quite a small space on the fatal slope. Where the Prussian battery had been placed (of which I spoke in my last), there were thirty horses lying almost touching one another, many with the drivers beside them, still grasping their whips. Most of the corpses were on their backs, with their hands clenched. This position was explained by the fact that most of the men had been shot grasping their muskets, and their hands clenched as they dropped their weapons and fell. Many corpses of Prussian officers lay by those of their men, with their white glove on their left hands, the right ones being bare, in order better to grasp the sword. In the hollow road itself the bodies of men and horses also lay thick; the corpses all along the sides of the road, for nearly 1,000 yards, made one continually unbroken row. A little lower down I found the tirailleur corpses. Many of these men had still their muskets in their hands, many forefingers being stiff on the trigger. On the left of the French position were two small cottages which had been a mark for the Prussian cannon, and their shells had made a complete ruin of the buildings. One roof was completely gone, and the whole front wall of the upper story of the other had been blown in. On the plateau behind the French earthworks all the ground was ploughed and torn by the Prussian shells, which, when they got the range, were admirably aimed. One third of its horses lay dead beside it. A shell had burst beneath one of the horses, and had blown him, the limber, and one of the gunners, all to pieces. All the French prisoners with whom I have spoken agree in asserting that it was the terrible accuracy of the Prussian artillery which forced them to yield their position. The farmhouse of La Villette once stormed and held by the Prussians, the earthworks on the Verdun road became untenable, as from the yard of La Villette the Prussian jaegers could shoot right into the twelve French earthworks. Seeing this, one could not help asking why so terrible a sacrifice of life was made by sending the infantry straight up the road at the French works. Perhaps it may have been thought necessary to make a moral impression on the French, and to show them that nothing would stop the Prussian infantry.

" It is admitted here that the mitrailleuses did much execution at close quarters. That the stories about their doing execution at 2,000 metres were pure invention, I now know; for, had they really shot that distance, I should, in all probability, not be writing this now, for I was within 1,500 yards of them, and never heard of any of their balls coming near us. All that did come were Chassepôts. After all the talk we had been treated to about their great superiority, one would have expected them to do better. But the fact is, the French soldiers do not do justice to their weapon, which is undoubtedly better than the needle-gun—a totally superannuated weapon, though it is made to do all it is capable of by the Germans, who never dream of drawing trigger until they feel sure of their aim. Their fire is, therefore, less rapid than that of the French, but far more deadly. Now, nothing so encourages young troops as to find that the 'swish,' 'swish' of balls is not followed by any very serious results. On the other hand, it is not at all encouraging to find that nearly every shot fired by the enemy tells. So much so was this the case on Thursday, that those who were at the 'taking' of Saarbruck by the 'infant Louis,' remarked that the French artillery-practice against the station was good, and in some cases excellent. But yesterday it is said to have been much inferior to what it was at Saarbruck, when they had greater opposition. I myself thought the Prussian artillery-practice slow; but when I got up on the top of the plateau occupied by the French, I saw how accurate it had been."

On the 19th the French army of Marshal Bazaine, which had, during the night, rested on its arms near the western outworks of Metz, withdrew sullenly into its fortifications, having lost in the three days' fighting, in killed, wounded, and prisoners, not far from 60,000 men. Their own reports acknowledge 12,000 dead and 6,000 unwounded prisoners; while the Germans have sent into Germany full twice that number, besides the many thousands of the wounded. The French name the battles of the 14th, 16th, and 18th of August respectively, Courcelles, Vionville, and Gravelotte. A general order of Marshal Bazaine, bearing date Gravelotte, August 16th, was found on the battle-field, which gives directions to the officers of the several army-corps for the marching of their troops to Verdun by the two roads *via* Conflans and Mars-la-Tour.

On the 19th the two German armies completely enveloped Metz, and its siege was formally commenced.

CHAPTER IX.

FROM Chalons, to which city he had betaken himself early in this week of battles, the Emperor, on the 17th of August, sent to Paris the following decree:

"The General Trochu is named Governor of Paris and Commandant-in-Chief of all the forces charged to provide for the defence of the capital.

"Done at Chalons.   NAPOLEON."

On the 18th General Trochu issued the following proclamation to the people of Paris:

"INHABITANTS OF PARIS: Amid the peril in which the country is, I am named Governor of Paris and Commandant-in-Chief of the forces charged to defend the capital in a state of siege. Paris seizes the part which belongs to it, and it wishes to be the centre of grand efforts, of grand sacrifices, and of grand examples. I come to join in them with all my heart. That will be the honor of my life, and the proud crowning of a career which, until this day, has remained unknown, for the most part, to you.

"I have faith the most complete in the success of our glorious enterprise; but it is upon one condition, the character of which is imperious, and without which our common efforts will be struck with impotence.

"I refer to good order; and I mean, by that, not merely

calmness in the street, but calmness at your firesides, calmness of your spirits, deference to the orders of the responsible authorities, resignation in presence of the trials inseparable from the situation, and, finally, the serenity, grave and collected, of a great military nation, which takes in its hand, with a firm resolution, amid solemn circumstances, the conduct of its destiny. And to establish the situation in that equilibrium so desirable, I do not turn to the powers which I hold by the state of siege and from the law. I demand it of your patriotism, and I will obtain it from your confidence, in showing myself, to the population of Paris, a confidence without limit.

"I appeal to all men of all parties, belonging to none myself. In the army no other party is known than that of the country.

"I appeal to their devotion. I demand of them to hold in bounds, by moral force, the hot spirits who do not know how to restrain themselves, and to do justice with their own hands to those men who are of no party, and who see in the public misfortune only an occasion to satisfy detestable appetites.

"And to accomplish my task, after which, I affirm, I will reënter into the obscurity from which I emerge, I adopt one of the old devices of the province of Brittany, where I was born: 'With the aid of God, for the fatherland!'

"At Paris. GENERAL TROCHU."

On the 19th, by imperial order, a Committee of Defence was formed in Paris, consisting of General Trochu, president; Marshal Vaillant, Admiral Rigault de Genouilly, Baron Jérôme David, General De La Tour, General Guiod, General d'Automarre d'Ervillé, and General Soumain. It possessed the fullest powers, and had a special executive committee that met daily in the War Office, receiving reports on the state of the defensive works, armament, munitions, and provisions in store, and all operations. These reports went subsequently to the Minister of

War, and thence to the Council. All the acts of the Corps Législatif were to take effect without imperial decrees confirming them or directing their execution.

On the 20th General Trochu published an address to the people, explaining how he desired to aid them. In this address he said:

"The idea of maintaining order by force of the bayonet and the sword in Paris, which is so agitated and given up to grief, fills me with horror and disgust. The maintenance of order by the ascendency of patriotism, freely expressed by the knowledge of the evident danger of the country, fills me with hope and serenity. But this problem is arduous, and I cannot solve it alone, but I can with the aid of those having such sentiments. That is what I term moral aid. The moment may arrive when malefactors, seeing us defending the city, will seek to pillage. Those the honest must seize. The error of all Governments I have ever known is to consider force the ultimate power. The only decisive power in the moment of danger is moral force."

On the 21st he issued the following appeal:

"*To the National Guard, to the Garde Mobile, to the Troops and Seamen in the Army of Paris, to all the Defenders of the Capital:*

"In the midst of events of the highest importance I have been appointed Governor. The honor is great, the perils also. I depend on your patriotism. Should Paris be subjected to a siege, never was there a more magnificent opportunity to prove to the world that long prosperity has not effeminated the country. You have before you the example of an army which has fought one against three. Their heroic struggle compels the admiration of all. Show by your conduct that you have the feeling of the profound responsibility resting upon you."

The German reserves, to the number of 200,000, were now called out to fill up the gaps in the regiments and occupy the territory which had been run over, so as to enable the soldiers of the line to go to the front. The bombardment of Strasbourg commenced on the 19th, and continued for several days. Vitry, a fortified town of some importance on the Marne, on the railroad from Chalons to Nancy, surrendered, and with it a large amount of arms, cannon, and ammunition. The French mined and destroyed at several places the railroad between Sedan and Thionville.

Since the 8th of August Marshal MacMahon had been engaged in collecting all the troops in Alsace and Lorraine which could be spared, and had received large reënforcements from Paris and elsewhere, till his army numbered somewhat more than 150,000 men. With this army he pushed on as rapidly as possible on the route to Paris as far as Chalons, the Crown-Prince of Prussia pursuing him, and often pressing him closely. Up to the 24th of August MacMahon remained at Chalons. The German cavalry had pushed on in advance, and some battalions of Uhlans (Lancers) had appeared around Epernay. The Third German Army, after the battle of Gravelotte, had been joined by the Guards, Fourth and Twelfth Corps, which were organized as a Fourth Army under the Crown-Prince of Saxony, and preparations were made for the immediate investment of Chalons.

On the 25th the German forces learned that, the night before, MacMahon had evacuated Chalons, and, instead of marching upon Epernay, had gone northwestward to Rheims, where the Emperor had preceded him on the 21st. The Emperor meantime had gone on to Rethel. The object of this movement was evidently to draw the German army northward, and aid Bazaine in raising the siege or environment of Metz. There were several strategical difficulties in the way of this movement,

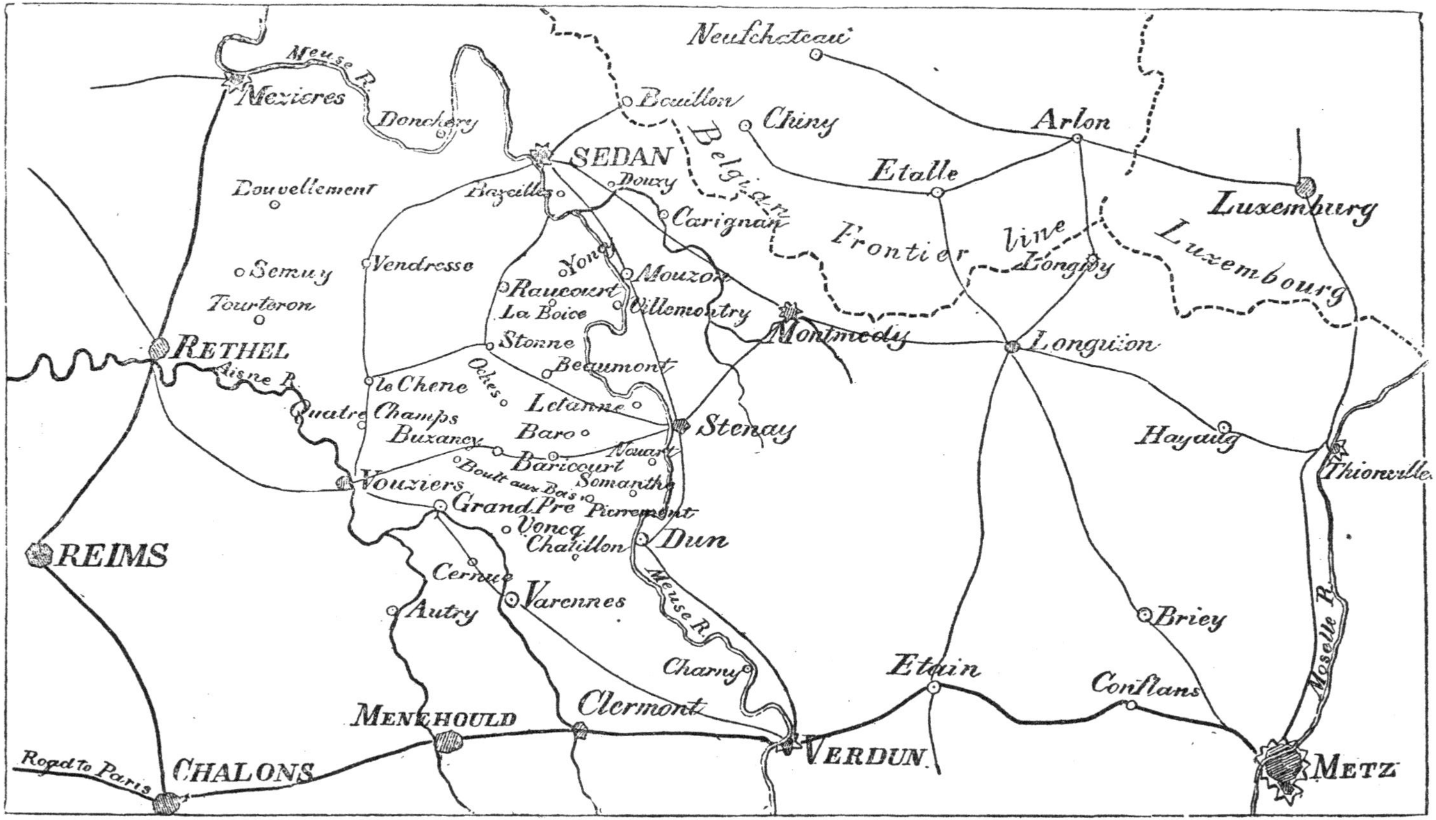
Meuse R.
Mezieres
Donchery
SEDAN
Bouillon
Neufchateau
Chiny
Arlon
Belgian
Etalle
Luxemburg
Douvellement
Bazeilles
Douzy
Carignan
Frontier line
Luxembourg
Semuy
Vendresse
Yonq
Mouzon
Longwy
Tourteron
Raucourt
La Boice
Villemontry
Montmedy
Longuion
RETHEL
Aisne R.
Stonne
Beaumont
le Chene
Oches
Letanne
Quatre Champs
Stenay
Buxancy
Baro
Hayaug
Baricourt
Nouart
Thionville
Vouziers
Boult aux Bois
Somanthe
Grand Pre
Pierremont
Voncq
Chatillon
Dun
REIMS
Cernue
Varennes
Meuse R.
Autry
Briey
Charny
Etain
Conflans
Moselle R.
Clermont
MENEHOULD
VERDUN
METZ
Road to Paris
CHALONS

which should have made a skilful commander hesitate long before attempting it. It required a very considerable detour, and it is not easy to take a large force rapidly over a long road,—especially when, as was the case here, it is much of it a forest, and traversed with difficulty,—when it is constantly pressed by a foe fully equal and possibly superior in numbers, and flushed with victory. Then, again, the route lay for a considerable portion of the way close to the Belgian frontier, the territory of a neutral; and their enemy, approaching them from the south, could easily force them over the line, where they would be disarmed and held as prisoners. The German forces around Metz, the First and Second Armies, were more than sufficient to hold Bazaine in check, and were being largely reënforced from the reserves, so that they could easily spare from 50,000 to 100,000 men to take the French in front, while the Third and Fourth Armies were pressing upon their flank. The opportunity was too tempting a one for the Germans not to avail themselves of it, and, conquering the French armies in detail, soon make themselves masters of France.

MacMahon and his army were making a rapid progress northward toward Rethel and Mézières, having passed the first-named point with part of his force on the 27th, while the remainder was marching in a line with it eastward toward the Meuse. The country is difficult; the Argonnes forest, better known as the forest of Ardennes, occupying at least one half the territory, and the country being hilly and broken.

The movement of the German armies to cut MacMahon off from a junction with Bazaine commenced on the 26th of August. At their commencement eight and a half army-corps lay in a long line, north and south. This front had to be changed for one at right angles to it—a task the difficulty of which was greatly increased by the fact that the line of march lay partly amid the forests of the Argonnes. The operations were so directed as not only to prevent MacMahon from reaching Metz, but also to cut him off from returning to Paris, thus compelling him to fight with the alternative of surrender, or of retreat to Belgium in case of defeat.

Within the next three days, notwithstanding these difficulties, the front of this great army had not only been changed, but they had pushed forward until their advance-guard, part of the Twelfth (Saxon) Corps, had reached Nouart, and the whole army were occupying a line nearly parallel with the Meuse, and extending from near Stenay westward beyond Vouziers. A skirmish took place at Nouart, seven miles southwest of Stenay, on the 29th of August, between the Saxon advance-guard and the head of the French column (Fifth Corps), which was attempting to reach the Meuse. The French troops were stopped and cut off from the road by which they were marching. Voncq was also stormed the same day by two dismounted squadrons of German hussars, and a large number of prisoners taken.

Pressed thus closely by his enemy, MacMahon had only the alternative of giving battle in this forest, and retreating into Belgium in case of defeat, or of crossing the Meuse if he could, and resting on Sedan. By this movement, though brought still nearer to the Belgian frontier, he would have a strong fortress to protect his right wing, and the advantage of a more open country to fight in. He chose the latter alternative, but found himself so hard pressed that he was obliged to accept the battle forced on him on the 30th, before he could cross the Meuse. MacMahon's army lay between the Ardennes mountains and the river Aisne, the left, formerly the right wing (since they had faced the other way in this movement), resting below Tourteron, while the right wing was attempting to cross the Meuse at Mouzon. The lines on which the various corps and divisions of the German armies moved, and their action through the day, are given as follows in their reports. (For the places, see plan on page 171.)

"According to the orders given the Third Army, the First Bavarian Corps, which on the 27th had been advanced past Vouziers, on the road to Stenay, as far as Bar and Buzancy, was to go *via* Sommauthe toward Beaumont. The Second Bavarian Corps followed behind the First. The Fifth Prussian Corps moved from Breguenay and Authe toward Pierremont and Oches, and formed, therefore, the left wing of the Third Army. The Würtemberg Division directed itself from Boult-aux-Bois, *via* Châtillon, against La Chêne. The Second Prussian Corps moved on the left of the Würtembergers, *via* Vouziers and Quatre Champs; and a side column of this corps occupied Voncq on the Aisne. The Sixth Corps was to extend itself from Vouziers southwesterly, or toward Chalons. The Fifth Cavalry Division marched toward Tourteron, the Fourth toward Châtillon, the Sixth toward Semuy, with advance troops toward Bouvellemont, cutting the road to Mézières. The Second Division of Cavalry moved toward Buzancy. Headquarters of the Crown-Prince were moved at 8.30 o'clock from Cernuc, *via* Grand Pre (where the King's quarters were), toward Breguenay, before which place three regiments and some artillery lay in two rows about half a mile long. Precisely at noon came the first shot from the hills before Oches, where some French artillery had posted itself, and was directed against the German artillery back of Buzancy, nearly 5,000 paces distant. There was, however, no attempt to make a stand, and the position was deserted so soon as German cavalry approached. The artillery retreated, following the chain of hills on which it lay, back to Stonne, its highest point. Although the ground here was very favorable, the retreat was soon continued toward Beaumont, where the French centre had been driven in after a sharp fight. The battle here was opened about midday by the Fourth Corps, which, making a sudden attack upon Beaumont, swept so suddenly upon the French, that a camp from which not an article had been removed fell into their hands. This corps was supported on the left by the First Bavarian Corps, placed in the Petit-Dieulet wood, where, being attacked on its left flank, a return attack was made, and the enemy thrown back on La Besace. On the right of the Fourth was the Twelfth Corps, operating against Letanne. Beaumont having been brilliantly seized, the Fourth and Twelfth Corps of the Fourth Army moved against the Givodeau wood and Villemontry, fighting at every step, and steadily extending its left wing, in order to occupy the hills which enclose Mouzon. From 6 to 8 o'clock a tremendous artillery and mitrailleur battle was kept up here, to which night alone put an end. The Fourth Corps then occupied the place. As the bridge here was the line of retreat for a great part of the French army, its crowded columns suffered terribly in crossing. Large quantities of baggage and material were also abandoned. Meanwhile, the western wing of the French army, formerly the right, now the left wing, crossed the river at Bazeilles. Part of the First Bavarian Corps having advanced in a northeasterly direction toward Voncq, driving back on its way a force that had been withdrawn without a fight from a strong position at Stonne, attacked them late in the day, and in its turn won guns and prisoners, and inflicted severe loss on the retreating columns. The German army bivouacked on the line Raucourt-Villemontry. The advantages gained during this day were, the winning of so much ground that the passes of the Ardennes remained entirely in German hands, and an approach to the frontier so close that the ground between it and the Meuse could be occupied as a base of operations. In addition, the number of guns and prisoners taken was enormous, amounting to more than thirty guns and 5,000 prisoners. The French appeared to have withdrawn toward Sedan, the main body having crossed the Meuse at Mouzon, under cover of heavy artillery-fire from the high right bank of the river. Mouzon is six miles north of Beaumont and ten miles southeast of Sedan. Bazeilles is about four miles southeast of Sedan."

The next day, August 31st, the King telegraphed to the Queen:

"We had yesterday a victorious action by the Fourth, Twelfth (Saxon), and First Bavarian Corps. MacMahon beaten and pushed back from Beaumont over the Meuse to Mouzon. Twelve guns, some thousands of prisoners, and a great deal of material, in our hands. Losses moderate. I return immediately to the battle-field in order to follow up the fruits of the victory. May God graciously help us further, as thus far. WILHELM."

This despatch shows that the Fourth Army, under the Crown-Prince of Saxony, which was moving between the Crown-Prince and MacMahon, had been reënforced from the Third Army.

This battle was of great importance to the German armies, as, although the greater part of MacMahon's army was not engaged in the fight, only De Failly's corps suffering largely, yet the whole French army was held back and prevented from concentrating so speedily as its commander had intended on the east side of the Meuse, and more time was given to the Germans to close around it, and, by hemming it in at Sedan, compel its surrender.

The 31st of August was mainly occupied by the Germans in bringing their forces across the Meuse, and by MacMahon in concentrating his forces around Sedan, most of them having, during the night of the 30th and the morning of the 31st, crossed at Bazeilles and Remilly. There was, however, some hard fighting by the Twelfth (Saxon) Corps from 5 A. M. to about 10 A. M., in the vicinity of Douzy. There was also a long artillery combat at Remilly between the First Bavarian Corps and the French, which resulted in the latter being driven back, and the former occupying the position ready for crossing.

On the morning of the 1st of September the two contending armies occupied the positions indicated in the annexed map.

As the German troops had been making forced marches and fighting for three days, and it was evident that MacMahon was in a trap from which he could not escape, it had been the purpose of the King of Prussia to give his troops a day of rest on the 1st of September, before dealing the finishing stroke to the French army; but the enthusiasm and ardor of the men were so great, and their desire to complete the work so earnest, that, late in the night of August 31st, the decision was made to move forward the ensuing day.

At midnight the necessary orders were issued by the Crown-Prince of Saxony, and the battle was to begin at 5 o'clock in the morning. His army occupied the right flank, the Twelfth Corps as advance-guard, behind them the Fourth, then the Guards, and, finally, the Fourth Cavalry Division. Those troops which remained west of the river were to cross at Douzy. On the left, and lying on the left bank of the Meuse, were the First and Second Bavarian Corps; their bridge was thrown over opposite Bazeilles. On the left flank the Eleventh Prussian Corps laid down its bridge, 1,000 paces below Donchery, and close by the Fifth Corps crossed; on the extreme left flank the Würtemberg troops crossed, at the village Dom-le-Mesnil. The Sixth Corps was in reserve between Attigny and Le Chêne. Opposed to these bodies were the French corps of MacMahon, Failly, Canrobert, the remains of General Douay's forces, and the newly-formed Twelfth Corps. Sedan was the centre of their position, and their lines extended from Givonne on the left, along the spurs of the Ardennes which lie behind the fortress, to the neighborhood of Mézières, upon which their right flank rested.

Map: Battle of Sedan, Morning of September 1st

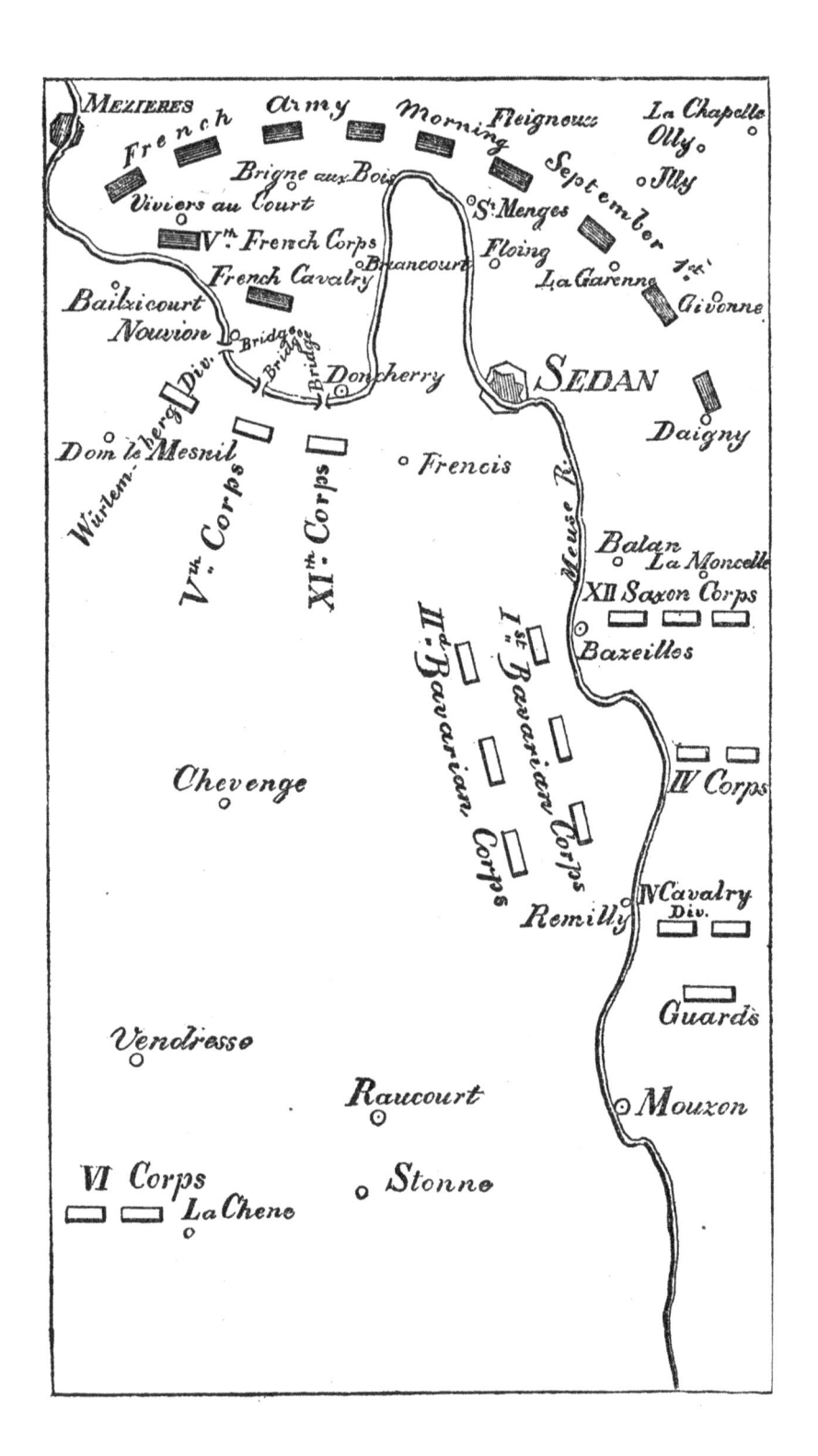

Labels visible on the map:
- Mezieres
- French Army Morning September 1st
- La Chapelle, Olly, Illy
- Brigne aux Bois, Fleigneux
- Viviers au Court, St Menges
- Vth French Corps, Floing
- French Cavalry, Brancourt, La Garenne, Givonne
- Bailxicourt, Nouvion, Bridge, Bridge
- Doncherry, SEDAN, Daigny
- Würtemberg Div., Dom le Mesnil
- Vth Corps, XIth Corps, Frenois
- Meuse R.
- Balan, La Moncelle, XII Saxon Corps, Bazeilles
- IId Bavarian Corps, 1st Bavarian Corps
- Chevenge
- IV Corps
- Remilly, IV Cavalry Div.
- Guards
- Vendresse
- Raucourt, Mouzon
- Stonne
- VI Corps, La Chene

Headquarters of the Crown-Prince were established on a hill near Château Donchery, from which not only the positions of all the German troops, but all the developments of the battle, could be plainly seen.

A thick fog overhung the country as the Fourth Army put itself in motion, a little after 5 o'clock, and at 6.30 steady artillery-fire was heard from behind Sedan, where the right wing had attacked the enemy on his left flank. His position here was very strong, lying in a wooded and hilly country by the villages Floing, Illy, La Chapelle, and Villers, and traversed by the valley in which lies the village of La Givonne. In spite of stout efforts on the part of the Germans, the conflict at length came to a standstill for an hour. During this time the Eleventh Corps pressed forward over the small hills which lie on the plain between Donchery and Sedan, and the Fifth Corps undertook the tactical march of the day, passing along the high hills northwest of the fortress to the rear of the enemy. Its object was to unite with the extreme right of the Fourth Army, and thus envelope the French. The Würtemberg troops, and, later, the Fourth Cavalry Division also, were to hold the plain against any sortie of the enemy—an event that could hardly have proven fortunate for him, as the river-crossings all lay in the hands of the Germans.

The Würtemberg troops were also charged with repulsing any movement made from Mézières. It was directed to cross at Nouvion, on the right bank, and take position near Viviers-au-Court on the road from Sedan to Mézières. Breaking camp at 6 o'clock in the morning, the river was crossed on a pontoon bridge which had been thrown across at daybreak, and at 9 o'clock Viviers-au-Court was reached. Here they were ordered to advance eastward, toward Brigne-aux-Bois in battle-order. In front of the latter place the Fifth and Eleventh Prussian Corps were met, who were in march toward St. Menges. At

10.30 o'clock the order was to take up position near Donchery While in this place, at 3 p. m., word came that a column from Mézières was marching in the direction of the pontoon bridge, and a detail of one regiment infantry, one squadron cavalry, and a field-battery, was sent to head it off, which was successfully done. Toward 5 p. m. the artillery was advanced to a point west of Sedan, for the purpose of bombarding the place.

To go back to the main operations: At 9.15 o'clock the Eleventh Corps had finished its extension in the ground west of Sedan, and begun a heavy fire from its batteries. At this signal the Saxon troops on the right flank, who had not before exhibited their full strength, attacked in force, and even at this early hour the French showed in some points a disposition to retreat. But the troops who resorted to this movement only fell into the hands of the flanking columns. West of Sedan, where the Eleventh Corps had posted strong batteries, the French made two cavalry attacks, which were conducted with great courage, and, by some regiments, as the Chasseurs d'Afrique, with the greatest valor. The infantry, however, showed less spirit, and the number of men taken without arms in their hands was considerable even at noon. In the meantime the Fifth Corps had accomplished its flanking march, falling in, toward the end of its movement, with those portions of the Fifth French Corps which had begun the retreat. The artillery, which, by the Emperor's orders, had been directed against this flanking corps, was quickly driven back, and the commander sent word that at the most only a few disordered bands could have found their way to the frontier.

The attention of the German leaders was now directed to Sedan itself and the ground near it, the only remaining refuge for an army that had retreated from so many fields. But even this line of retreat was rapidly cut off. The batteries of the right and left flanks approached each other rapidly. In this part of the field lay Bazeilles, a village which became the scene of one of the most terrible events of the war. Already, on August 31st, some houses had been fired by shells, because they harbored French soldiers, who endeavored to oppose the crossing of the river. During this day's battle some Bavarians advanced against the town, but met with so destructive a fire from some houses that these, too, had to be burned. The fight afterward extended through the streets, and, after several hours of very bloody work, the place was taken. Members of the Sanitary Corps advanced to bring off the wounded who were lying in the streets. The Germans report that these were received with a murderous fire, and six of them were wounded. Some troops then advanced to scour the town, and men, women, and children were driven from the houses with arms in their hands. But the French seemed determined to make a Saragossa of the place. No sooner had the soldiers passed by than the houses filled again, and firing from the windows was resumed. Several soldiers were shot, and orders were given for the destruction of the place. In the terrible scene which followed—soldiers, citizens, women, and children were burned to death; and for days afterward the place is said to have been noisome with the stench of half-roasted, half-putrid flesh. Scenes of dreadful cruelty occurred; and each side charges the other with dragging and throwing the living into the flames.

Continuing on, the Bavarians took the village Balan, and towards midday Villette was shelled from one of their batteries. The church-tower was immediately in flames; the French artillery withdrew; and the Eleventh and Twelfth Corps had now nothing in their way to Sedan. The French were hastening in dark masses to the fortress, and at the same time beyond the line of German troops thousands of prisoners were descending the hills to be collected in squads in the plain and transported to the rear. A little before 2 o'clock the junction of the right and left wings had been accomplished, and a double line of Germans stood around the town and its crowded refugees. In isolated positions a few troops still kept up the contest; but the great cannonade had ceased, and a pause began, during which the conquerors awaited the course of their enemy. No sign was made, and at 4.30 o'clock the batteries were ordered to open again. In a quarter of an hour a straw-magazine was in flames; and immediately after a white flag appeared upon the fortifications. The further history of this important event we will leave to be told by King Wilhelm, General von Moltke, and Count Bismarck, who have written accounts in every way remarkable, of the surrender, and the extraordinary occurrences which preceded and followed it.

The letter from the King says:

"VENDRESSE, September 3d, 1870.

"You now know from my three telegrams the entire extent of the great historical event that has occurred. It is like a dream, even when one has seen it develop hour by hour.

"When I remember that, after a great, fortunate war, I had nothing more glorious to expect during my reign, and now see this world-historic act completed, I bow myself before God, who alone, my Lord and my Helper, has chosen me to fulfil this work, and has ordained us to be instruments of His will. Only in this sense did I venture to undertake the work—that in humility I might praise God's guidance and mercy.

"Now for a picture of the battle and its consequences, in condensed terms:

"The army had arrived, on the evening of the 31st, and early on the 1st, in the positions before described, round about Sedan.* The Bavarians had the left wing at Bazeilles on the Meuse; near them the Saxons, toward Moncelles and Daigny; the Guards still on the march toward Givonne; the Fifth and

MACMAHON AT SEDAN.

Eleventh Corps toward St. Menges and Fleigneux. The Meuse makes here a sharp curve, and therefore from St. Menges to Donchery there was no corps placed, but in the latter town Würtembergers, who at the same time covered the rear against attacks from Mézières. The Cavalry Division of Count Stolberg was in the plain of Donchery as right wing; in the front toward Sedan, the rest of the Bavarians.

"The battle began at Bazeilles early on the 1st in spite of a thick fog, and a very heavy fight gradually spread, in which we were obliged to take house by house, which lasted nearly the whole day, and in which Schöler's Erfurt Division (from the reserve Fourth Corps) had to take part. Just as I arrived on the front before Sedan, at 8 o'clock, the great battery began its fire against the fortifications. A tremendous artillery battle now spread on all sides, continuing for hours, and during which ground was gradually won by our side. The villages named were taken.

"Very deep-cut ravines with woods made the advance of the infantry difficult, and favored the defence. The villages of Illy and Floing were taken, and the ring of fire drew itself gradually closer and closer around Sedan. It was a grand sight from our position on a commanding height behind the before-named battery, before and on the right of Frénois village, above St. Torcy.

"The determined resistance of the enemy began gradually to slacken, as we could discover by the disordered battalions which ran hastily back out of the woods and villages. The cavalry tried an attack against some battalions of our Fifth Corps, which maintained an excellent bearing; the cavalry rushed through the intervals between the battalions, then turned around and back by the same way; which was repeated three times by different regiments, so that the field was strewn with corpses and horses, all of which we could clearly see from our standpoint. I have not yet been able to ascertain the number of this brave regiment.

"Inasmuch as the retreat of the enemy lapsed in many places into flight, and every thing—infantry, cavalry, and artillery—crowded into the city and immediate neighborhood, but still no sign that the enemy proposed to withdraw himself by capitulation out of this dubious position showed itself, nothing remained but to order the bombardment of the city by the above-mentioned battery. After about twenty minutes it was already on fire in many places, which, with the numerous burning villages in the whole ring of battle, made a shuddering impression. I therefore ordered the fire to cease, and sent Lieutenant-Colonel von Bronsart of the general staff as flag of truce, to propose the capitulation of the army and fortress. He was immediately met by a Bavarian officer, who informed me that a French flag of truce had presented itself at the gate. Lieutenant-Colonel von Bronsart was admitted, and upon his inquiring for the general-in-chief he was unexpectedly led before the Emperor, who wished to give him at once a letter to me. When the Emperor asked what messages he had, and received for answer, 'To demand the surrender of army and fortress,' he replied that for that purpose he must apply to General de Wimpffen, who had just then taken command in place of the wounded Marshal MacMahon, and that he would also send his Adjutant-General Reille with the letter to me. It was 7 o'clock when Reille and Bronsart came to me. The latter came a little in advance, and from him we first learned with certainty that the Emperor was present. You can imagine the impression it made upon me, above all, and upon all! Reille sprang from the saddle, and handed me the letter of his Emperor, adding that besides that he had no message. Before I opened the letter I said to him, 'But I demand as the first condition that the army lay down its arms.' The letter began in this way:

'N'ayant pas pu mourir à la tête de mes troupes, je dépose mon épée à Votre Majesté'—(Not having been able to die at the head of my troops, I lay down my sword to your Majesty); confiding all the rest to me in secrecy.

"My reply was, that I complained of the style of our intercourse, and desired the sending of an authorized representative with whom the capitulation could be concluded. After I had given the letter to General Reille, I spoke some words with him as an old acquaintance, and so ended this act. I empowered Moltke as commissioner, and instructed Bismarck to remain behind, in case political questions came up; rode then to my wagon, and drove here, greeted everywhere on the road with stormy hurrahs from the advancing trains, while everywhere the popular hymns rose in chorus. It was thrilling! All had struck lights, so that one drove for a time in an improvised illumination. At 11 o'clock I was here, and drank with those around me to the health of the army which had fought out such a conclusion.

"Since I had received on the morning of the 2d no information from Moltke upon the terms of the capitulation which should have taken place in Donchery, I drove somewhat downcast toward the battle-field. At 8 o'clock in the morning I met Moltke, who came to me to obtain my acquiescence in the capitulation which he presented, and at the same time pointed out that the Emperor had left Sedan at 5 o'clock in the morning, and had also come to Donchery. Since he wished to speak to me, and there was a little castle in the park, I chose this for the meeting. At 10 o'clock I arrived on the height before Sedan. At 12 o'clock Moltke and Bismarck appeared with the completed terms of capitulation. At 1 o'clock I placed myself in motion with Fritz, accompanied by the staff cavalry escort. I alighted before the castle, where the Emperor came to meet me. The visit lasted a quarter of an hour. We were both very much moved at thus seeing each other again. All that I felt, after having seen Napoleon only three years before at the summit of his power, I cannot describe.

"After this meeting I rode from 2.30 to 7.30 o'clock through the entire army around Sedan.

"The reception by the troops, the sight of the decimated Guards—all that, I cannot describe to you to-day. I was profoundly moved by so many proofs of love and fidelity.

"Now, *lebe wohl.* With an agitated heart at the end of such a letter,

"WILHELM."

According to French papers, the terms of capitulation were:

"Between the undersigned, Chief of the General Staff of King Wilhelm, Commander-in-Chief of the German armies, and the General commanding the French army, both furnished with full powers from their Majesties, the King Wilhelm and the Emperor Napoleon, the following convention has been concluded:

"Article I. The French army placed under the orders of General Wimpffen, finding itself actually surrounded by the superior troops about Sedan, is prisoner of war.

"Article II. Considering the valorous defence of that French army, exemption for all the generals and officers, also for all the superior officials having the rank of officers, who give their parole of honor in writing not to carry arms against Germany, and not to act in any manner against her interests, up to the end of the present war. The officers and officials who accept these conditions retain their arms, and the effects which belong to them personally.

"Article III. All the arms, as well as the material of the army, consisting of flags, eagles, cannon, munitions, &c., shall be delivered at Sedan to a military commission appointed by the general-in-chief, to be sent immediately to the German commissioners.

"Article IV. The place of Sedan shall be placed in its present condition, and at the latest on the evening of the 2d, at the disposal of his Majesty the King Wilhelm.

"Article V. The officers who do not accept the engagement mentioned in Article II, as well as all the troops, disarmed, shall be conducted, ranged according to their regiments or corps, in military order. This measure will commence the 2d of September, and be finished the 3d. These detachments shall be conducted to the ground bounded by the Meuse near Iges, to be delivered to the German commissioners by their officers, who will then surrender their command to their under-officers. The surgeons shall without exception remain at the rear to attend the wounded.

"At Frenois, September 2, 1870.

"MOLTKE and DE WIMPFFEN."

The King's telegram announcing the success of his army was:

"Since 7.30 o'clock continuously advancing battle round about Sedan, Guards, Fourth, Fifth, Twelfth Corps, and Bavarian. Enemy almost entirely thrown back on the city.

"WILHELM."

The King also sent the following despatches from Sedan at 1.30 P. M.:

"The capitulation by which the entire army in Sedan [become] prisoners of war, is just now concluded with General Wimpffen, who takes command in the place of the wounded Marshal MacMahon. The Emperor has surrendered only himself to me, since he does not occupy the command, and hands over every thing to the regency in Paris. I shall determine his residence after I have seen him at a rendezvous which takes place immediately. What a change of fortune through God's guidance!

"WILHELM."

"What a thrilling moment, that of the meeting with Napoleon! He was bowed, but dignified and resigned. I have given him Wilhelmshöhe, near Cassel, for a residence. Our meeting took place in a little castle before the western glacis of Sedan. From there I rode through the army about Sedan. You can imagine the reception by the troops—indescribable! At dusk—7.30 o'clock—I had finished the five hours' ride, but returned here only at 1 o'clock. God help further!

"WILHELM."

On the 2d of September General von Moltke, the Chief of Staff of the Prussian army, issued the following order for carrying out the capitulation:

"HEADQUARTERS, FRÉNOIS, September 2, 1870.

"The French army lying in and about Sedan has capitulated. Officers will be liberated on their word of honor; the under-officers and common soldiers are prisoners of war. Arms and army material will be given up." (Here follows the text of the capitulation already given.) "The prisoners of war, whose number is not yet ascertained, will be assembled in the bend of the Meuse, near Villette and Iges, and afterward conducted away in *échelons*. The Eleventh and Twelfth Royal Bavarian Army-Corps, under the general command of General von der Tann, are appointed to the first guard. The supplying of the prisoners, for which, according to the promise of the

THE LAST CHARGE OF THE FRENCH AT SEDAN.

THE FIELD GUNS CAPTURED BY THE GERMANS AT SEDAN.

French general commanding, stores are to be brought from Mézières to near Donchery by railroad, will also be regulated by General von der Tann. That no difficulty in the approach of trains is laid in the way, is carefully to be observed. An infantry regiment from the Eleventh Corps will be placed in the fortress as garrison to-morrow after Sedan shall have been evacuated.

"The withdrawal of the prisoners in two lines by way of Stenay, Etain, and Gorze to Remilly, and Buzancy, Clermont, and St. Mihiel to Pont-à-Mousson, will be conducted by the army under his Royal Highness the Crown-Prince of Saxony and the royal commander-in-chief of the Third Army, according to the order of this morning. In order to avoid every doubt, it is to be remarked that the French officers captured yesterday in battle, and to-day before the close of the capitulation at 11 o'clock, are to be treated in accordance with the rules previously in force.

"Officers and officials who give their parole must themselves prepare the proper notification. Both classes must report as soon as possible to the quartermaster-general of the army. The horses to be delivered on the part of the French army shall, in accordance with the orders of his Majesty the King, be distributed for the benefit of all the active German forces, and the army commanders will be hereafter informed upon their respective quotas.

"The clearing up of the battle-field is the duty of the General of Dépôt-Inspection of the army of his Royal Highness the Crown-Prince of Saxony. The burial of the dead is to be hastened by means of the civil authorities.

"Von Moltke."

The following letter from Count von Bismarck describes his part in the negotiations:

"Donchery, September 2, 1870.

"After I had come here yesterday evening, according to your Majesty's order, to take part in the negotiations upon the capitulation, the latter were interrupted until about 1 o'clock at night by the granting of time for consideration, which General Wimpffen begged after General von Moltke had decidedly declared that no other condition than the laying down of the arms would be accepted, and that the bombardment would begin again at 9 o'clock the next morning if the capitulation were not concluded by that time. At 6 o'clock this morning General Reille was announced, who informed me that the Emperor desired to see me, and was already on the way here from Sedan. The General returned immediately in order to inform his Majesty that I followed him, and shortly after I found myself perhaps half-way between here and Sedan in the neighborhood of Frénois, in presence of the Emperor. His Majesty was in an open carriage with three superior officers, and an equal number in the saddle near by. Of the latter, Generals Castelnau, Reille, Vaubert, and Moskowa were personally known to me, the last-named appearing to be wounded in the foot. Arrived at the carriage, I dismounted from the horse, stepped to the side of the Emperor, and, standing on the carriage-step, inquired after the orders of his Majesty. The Emperor then expressed the wish to see your Royal Majesty, apparently under the impression that your Majesty was also in Donchery. After I replied that the headquarters of your Majesty were at present fifteen miles distant, in Vendresse, the Emperor inquired if your Majesty had fixed upon a place to which he should go at once, and afterward what my views thereupon were. I answered him that I had come here in full darkness, and the neighborhood was therefore unknown to me, and placed at his disposal the house occupied by me in Donchery, which I would immediately leave. The Emperor accepted this, and rode slowly toward Donchery, but drew up some hundred paces before the bridge leading over the Meuse into the city, in front of a laborer's house standing alone, and asked me if he could not descend there. I had the house inspected by Councillor of Legation Count Bohlen-Bismarck, who had meantime followed me. After he had reported that its interior was very bare and small, but that the house was free from wounded, the Emperor descended, and desired me to follow him within. Here, in a very small room, containing a table and two chairs, I had a conversation of about an hour with the Emperor. His Majesty expressed chiefly the wish to obtain more favorable terms of capitulation for the army. I declined absolutely to consider this subject with his Majesty, as this purely military question was to be settled between General von Moltke and General de Wimpffen. In return I asked the Emperor if his Majesty was inclined to negotiations for peace. The Emperor replied that, as prisoner, he was not now in a condition [to treat for peace]; and to my further question to whom, according to his views, the Government of France would now revert, his Majesty referred me to the existing Government in Paris. After explanation of this point, which was not to be decided with certainty from yesterday's letter of the Emperor to your Majesty, I perceived that the situation to-day, as yesterday, offered no other practical question than the military one; nor did I conceal this from the Emperor, but expressed the necessity which resulted therefrom to us of obtaining before all things, by the capitulation, a substantial means of securing the military results which we had won. I had already, yesterday evening, weighed the question in every direction with General von Moltke, whether it would be possible, without injury to German interests, to offer better terms than those fixed upon to the members of an army that had fought well. After due consideration, we were both forced to hold the negative of this question. When, therefore, General von Moltke, who meanwhile had approached from the city, went to your Majesty in order to lay before your Majesty the wish of the Emperor, this was done, as your Majesty knows, not with the purpose of supporting the same.

"The Emperor next went into the open air, and invited me to seat myself near him before the door of the house. His Majesty laid before me the question whether it were not possible to allow the French army to go over the Belgian frontier, in order to have it disarmed and disposed of there. I had also discussed this possibility with General von Moltke the evening before, and quoting the motives indicated above, I declined to go into the discussion of this method. In regard to the political situation, I took, for my part, no initiative, and the Emperor only in so far as he bewailed the misfortune of the war, and declared that he himself had not desired the war, but had been forced to it by the pressure of public opinion in France.

"From information received in the city, and especially through examination by the officers of the general staff, it was, in the meantime, between 9 and 10 o'clock, ascertained that Bellevue Castle, near Frénois, was suited to the reception of the Emperor, and also that it was not yet filled with wounded. I reported this to his Majesty, in the form that I pointed out Frénois as the place which I would submit to your Majesty for the interview, and therefore put it to the Emperor if his Majesty would go there at once, inasmuch as a stay in the small laborer's house was inconvenient, and the Emperor would perhaps require some rest. This his Majesty willingly entered into; and I escorted the Emperor, who was preceded by an escort of honor from your Majesty's body-guard of cuirassiers, to Bellevue Castle, where, meanwhile, the remainder of the suite and the equipages of the Emperor, whose arrival from the city appeared to have been considered uncertain until then, had gone. Also General de Wimpffen, with whom, in expectation of the return of General von Moltke, the discussion of the negotiations relative to a capitulation, which had been interrupted yesterday, were resumed by General von Podbielski, in presence of Lieutenant-Colonel von Verdy and the chief of staff of General de Wimpffen, which two officers were charged with the treaty. I took part only in the beginning, by laying down the political and legal conditions in accordance with the revelations furnished me by the Emperor himself, in asmuch as I immediately thereafter received, through Count von Nostitz, as messenger from General von Moltke, the information that your Majesty would not see the Emperor until after the close of the capitulation of the army—a notification by which the hope of receiving any other terms than those previously decided upon had to be given up. I then rode, with the intention of reporting to your Majesty the position of the affair, toward your Majesty at Chehery; met on the way General von Moltke with the text of the capitulation signed by your Majesty, which, after we had entered Frénois with him, was at once accepted without opposition, and signed. The bearing of General de Wimpffen, as well as that of the other French generals, the night before, was very dignified; and this brave officer could not restrain himself from expressing to me his deep pain that he should be just the one to be called, forty-eight hours after his arrival from Africa, and half a day after assuming the command, to place his name under a capitulation so ominous to French arms; nevertheless, the lack of provisions and munitions, and the absolute impossibility of any further defence, laid upon him the duty, as general, of restraining his personal feelings, since, in the existing situation, a further shedding of blood could alter nothing. The acquiescence in the dismissal of the officers upon their word of honor was recognized with great thankfulness, as an expression of your Majesty's intention not to trample upon the feelings of an army which had fought bravely, beyond the line which, in view of our political and military interests, was necessarily drawn.

General de Wimpffen has also subsequently given expression to this feeling, in a letter in which he spoke his thanks to General von Moltke for the considerate forms in which the negotiations have been carried on from his side.

"COUNT BISMARCK."

The severe wound received by Marshal MacMahon on the 31st of August prevented his presence in the final battle or the capitulation, and also prevented his rendering any report of the battle. General de Wimpffen, who was in command during the battle, issued an address to his soldiers after the capitulation, of which the following is a translation:

"SEDAN, September 3, 1870.

"SOLDIERS: On Thursday you fought against a force greatly superior in numbers, from daybreak until dark. You resisted the enemy with the utmost bravery. When you had fired your last cartridge, were worn out with fighting, and not being able to respond to the call of generals and officers to attempt to rejoin Marshal Bazaine on the road to Montmedy, you were forced to retreat on Sedan. In this desperate effort but 2,000 men could be got together, and your General deemed the attempt utterly hopeless and impracticable. Your General found, with deep regret, when the army was reunited within the walls of the town, that it had supplies neither of food nor ammunition; could neither leave the place nor defend it, means of existence being alike wanting for the population. I was therefore reduced to the sad alternative of treating with the enemy. I sent, yesterday, to the Prussian headquarters, with full powers from the Emperor, but could not at first bring myself to accept the conditions imposed by the enemy. This morning, however, menaced by a bombardment to which we could not reply, I decided to make a fresh attempt to get honorable terms. I have obtained conditions by which we are saved much of the possible annoying and insulting formalities which the usages of war generally impose.

"Under the circumstances in which we find ourselves, it only remains for us, officers and soldiers, to accept with resignation the consequences of this surrender. We have at least the consolation of knowing a useless massacre has been avoided, and we yield only under circumstances against which no army could fight, namely, want of food and ammunition. Now, soldiers, in conclusion, let me say, that you are still able to render brilliant services to your country, without being needlessly slaughtered.

"DE WIMPFFEN,
"*General Commanding-in-Chief.*"

A member of General de Wimpffen's staff soon after the battle published an account of the General's part in it, reflecting very severely on the management of the whole matter by the Emperor, asserting that he refused to De Wimpffen the opportunity of making an escape with the greater part of the army, and, when he sought to resign, compelled him to continue in the command and capitulate in consequence of his own blunders. To these charges the Emperor's adjutant-generals replied, and, though admitting his offer of resignation, demonstrated the impossibility and folly of his attempting to escape with any considerable portion of his force.

But though there are no official reports of the battle and surrender by French officers, there are not wanting graphic and unusually accurate descriptions of both by French correspondents. One of these, from the pen of a French officer, a correspondent of the *Tribune*, we append, as perhaps the best account extant from a French standpoint:

"I pass over all that has happened since I wrote you from

Mézières, to come at once to the events of August 31st and September 1st—the latter the saddest day the French arms have ever witnessed.

"Early in the morning of the 31st orders were given to bring into Sedan all the wagon-trains and oxen which had been left outside the glacis. By this time the streets were blocked up by troops of every kind, which had entered the town during the night. I tried to ride down to the Porte de Paris, where the train was stationed, to carry the orders. I was obliged to get off my horse and make my way as best I could between the horses and caissons, which choked up every street and square of the town. As I reached the Porte de Paris, I met the wagon-train entering as fast as possible, followed closely by the rushing oxen, and intermingled with the weeping and terror-stricken peasantry of the neighborhood flying into the town for protection. They little knew that it was about the worst place they could have chosen. The gates on that side were immediately afterward closed, while the troops slowly filed out through the opposite gate toward Douzy, where all MacMahon's forces were posted, expecting to be again attacked by the Prussians, who had closely followed up the French army.

"About 10 o'clock that morning cannonading was heard six or seven miles away, toward the village of Bazeille. I went up on the rampart overlooking the country in that direction. Thence I could see the Prussian position, and, with my field-glass, could watch the firing; but I could not see the French lines, which were hid from me by trees about a mile from the town. I therefore, at noon, walked out of the town at the Porte de Balan, and ascended, on my left, the rising ground which is close by the town. Not more than half a mile from the gate I passed through regiments of reserve infantry. Their arms were piled and the fires smoking, the soup not having long been eaten. I continued ascending, and everywhere passed reserve corps of infantry and artillery. I got higher and higher, from hillock to hillock, till I reached a battery of reserve, the guns of which were unlimbered and placed facing the rear of the French left. This battery was so pointed as to fire over the crest of the rising ground on which I stood. About a quarter of a mile distant, in front of a little churchyard, stood also several officers of the different corps which were stationed on my right and left, all being of the reserve.

"From the point I had now reached a charming prospect was within view. The French line of battle extended right in front, spreading on the slope of the ground which forms one side of this basin of the Meuse. In front of the centre of the French lines, and lower down in the vale, was the village of Bazeille, which was then beginning to burn, the Prussian shells having set fire to it. Parallel almost to the front of the French positions ran the Meuse, crossed by a bridge a little to the left of Bazeille. The French right was upon a knot of wooded ground held by tirailleurs, the wooded ground extending nearly to the grounds of Sedan. The left was lost to my sight behind the inequalities of the ground toward the road to Bouillon. As far as I could see, on the right and left and in front of me, were massed regiments of all arms; but toward the left, on the second line, was a very large force of heavy cavalry—dragoons and cuirassiers.

"The sun was shining brightly, and every thing was plainly visible. The glittering of weapons, the bright and showy colors of the French uniforms, the white smoke curling under the blue sky, or lingering like vapor beneath the trees, the lurid flames rising from the burning village of Bazeille, all seen from a commanding position, formed a spectacle such as one has but rarely the opportunity to witness. The principal Prussian batteries were directly opposite the French centre, on a plateau or table-land which terminated abruptly, and made it a very strong posision.

"For some time cannonading continued on both sides. At 2 o'clock a force of Prussian infantry advanced across the bridge in the village of Donzy, and immediately there began a very sharp *fusillade*, lasting, however, not more than ten minutes. I think the French must have lost ground in that encounter, although I could not see it, because of some trees that intervened; but a battery of six mitrailleuses advanced and opened fire through the trees. Six volleys came all at once. The Prussians fell hurriedly back, leaving whole ranks behind, which had gone down like those leaden soldiers which children play with.

"At about 4.30 o'clock the firing had ceased everywhere. The village, which had been blazing all day, was still smoking. The French remained in the same position. Though the day had apparently been without result, its description is a necessary prelude to the bitter story of the morrow. At 5.30 o'clock I returned to the town.

"The Emperor, who had arrived during the night, had issued a proclamation which was posted on the walls, saying that he had confided the command of the armies to the generals whom public opinion had seemed to select as most capable of leading them, and that he himself intended to fight as an officer, forgetting for a while his position as a sovereign.

"The next morning—Thursday, September 1st—I returned, as soon as the gates of the town were opened, to my post of observation on the elevated ground where the battery was still placed. The French positions did not seem to me much altered, but the right was now on the other side of Sedan. At 7 o'clock the cannonade began in earnest, some slight firing having taken place earlier. The Prussian batteries facing us appeared to me much more numerous; indeed, it seemed to me there were batteries everywhere. They roared from every point of the Prussian line, which then stretched nearly parallel in front of the French. I could follow the falling of their shells, which exploded as they touched the ground, and fell with wonderful precision. I noticed, also, how quickly they changed and corrected their fire. As soon as a French corps took up a position, it was instantly assailed by shells. The first would perhaps fall a few feet short or beyond, but the second or third was sure to find its way to the troops and do its awful work among them. The French shells, on the contrary, exploded generally before they reached the ground, and the smoke of the explosion formed innumerable little clouds at different heights, some at such an elevation that the shell could do no harm, I should think, to the enemy.

"I noticed some inexplicable movements. A few squadrons of Prussian cavalry made as if they would charge a French force which was toward the left. Immediately two regiments of French cavalry charged in turn upon the Prussian squadrons, which fell back and fled. But at the same moment a Prussian corps of infantry opened a murderous fire upon those too eager French cavalry regiments, and they came back sadly shattered from their rash pursuit. About 9 o'clock I could not help fancying that the Prussians were extending farther to the left; for, on asking whether certain new batteries were French, I was told they were Prussian. The Prussian line was evidently curling around us.

"I have learned since that the Crown-Prince had crossed the Meuse during the night about five leagues from Sedan, and that this had not been known to MacMahon. A large force of Bavarians must also have arrived after the commencement of the battle, for it was Bavarian troops who began pounding us from the left. At 10.30 o'clock the advance of the Prussians was perceptible on both wings at the same time. Some French infantry which was close to the town on the east side gave way, as it seemed to me, rather quickly. Soon afterward shells were coming from behind my left, and it became evident that the French position had been turned, and that a fresh German corps had taken a position in our rear.

"The reserves were now necessarily directed against these points. The battery near which I stood was already in action, and I thought it quite time to beat a retreat. The place was becoming as dangerous as any in the field. Among the guns close to me, the Prussian shells began falling with their usual beautiful precision; so I got on the other side of the slope, and made my way toward the town.

"As the road to Bouillon, which crossed the field of battle, was wholly closed to me now, I also perceived that I should be shut up in that circle which the Prussians had been drawing about the army and the town, and which was ultimately completed. I made my way as fast as I could, by the safest paths. When I reached the suburb before the Porte de Balan, I found it encumbered with soldiers of all corps, hastening, as I was, into the town. It was a defeat, evidently, yet it was not 11 o'clock, and the battle was destined to continue at various points for some time longer, though continuing without any real hope of victory.

"To one entering the town as I did, there was no longer any battle to describe. It was first a retreat, and too soon a rout. I thought myself lucky to get away from the field as I did; for, an hour afterward, the rout of those forces that had been near by me was complete. Already soldiers were crushing against each other in the struggle to get inside the town. Dismounted cavalry were trying to make their way, some even by the ramparts, leaping down from the counterscarp, others forcing their way in by the postern gates. From a nook of the ramparts, where I rested a moment, I saw also cuirassiers jumping—horses and all—into the moat, the horses breaking their legs and ribs. Men were scrambling over each other. There were officers of all ranks—colonels, and even generals, in uniforms which it was impossible to mistake—mixed in this shameful *mêlée*. Behind all came guns, with their heavy carriages and powerful horses, forcing their way into the throng, maiming and crushing the fugitives on foot.

"To add to the confusion and horror, the Prussian batteries had by this time advanced within range, and the Prussian shells began falling among the struggling masses of men. On the ramparts were the National Guards manning the guns of the town, and replying with more or less effect to the nearest Prussian batteries. It was a scene horrible enough to have suited the fancy of Gustave Doré himself. I could form but one idea of our unhappy army—that it was at the bottom of a seething caldron.

"I hurried back as best I could to my hotel, following the narrow streets, where the shells were least likely to reach the ground. Wherever there was a square or open place, I came upon the bodies of horses and men quite dead or still quivering, mown to pieces by bursting shells. Reaching my hotel, I found the street in which it stood choked, like the rest, with wagons, guns, horses, and men. Most luckily, at this moment the Prussian fire did not enfilade this street; for a train of caissons filled with powder blocked the whole way, itself unable to move backward or forward. There was every chance that these caissons would explode, the town being then on fire in two places; and I began to think Sedan was a place more uncomfortable than even the battle-field over which a victorious enemy was swiftly advancing.

"From friends whom I found at the hotel I learned that the Emperor, who had started early in the morning for the field of battle, had returned about the same time that I did, and passed through the streets with his staff. One of my friends was near him on the Place Turenne, when a shell fell under the Emperor's horse, and, bursting, killed the horse of a general who was behind him. He himself was untouched, and turned around and smiled; though my friend thought he saw tears in his eyes. which he wiped away with his glove. Indeed, he had cause enough for tears on that fatal 1st of September.

"Meantime, shells began to fall in the direction of our street and hotel. We all stood under the vaulted stone entrance, as the safest shelter we could find. I trembled on account of the caissons still standing in the street, and filling all the space from end to end. It was at this time when we waited, watching painfully for the shell which would have sent us all together into another world, that General de Wimpffen came past, making a vain effort to rally and inspirit his flying troops. He shouted, '*Vive la France! En avant!*' But there was no response. He cried out that Bazaine was taking the Prussians in the rear. News which had been current all the morning at intervals, coming now from the mouth of General de Wimpffen, seemed to be believed, and a few thousand men were rallied, and followed him out of the town. People began to have hope, and for one brief moment we believed the day might yet be saved. Need I say that this intelligence was a patriotic falsehood of brave General de Wimpffen? Mad with anguish, and in direct opposition to the Emperor's orders, he had resolved to rally what men he could, and make a stand. He could not have known that he was bound in the grasp of at least 300,000 men.

"The bugle and the trumpet ring out on all sides. A few thousand men hearken to the sound. My friend Rene de Guiroye, of the Chasseurs d'Afrique, whom I have just met, after losing sight of him for ten or twelve years, got on horseback again and joined the General. The sortie took place thus: They went out at the Porte de Balan. The houses of the suburb are already full of Prussians, who fire on the French out of every window. The church, especially, is strongly garrisoned, and its heavy doors are closed. The General sent off

De Guiroye to bring two pieces of cannon. These soon arrived, and with them the door of the church was blown in, and 200 Prussians were captured and brought back with the French, who, in spite of all efforts, were themselves soon obliged to retire into the town. It was the last incident of the battle—the last struggle.

"While this took place at the Porte de Balan, the Prussian shelling went on, and the shells began to fall into the hotel. Shocking scenes followed. A boy, the son of a tradesman around the corner of the street, came in crying, and asking for a surgeon. His father's leg had been shot off. A woman in front of the house met the same fate. The doctor who went to the tradesman found him dead; and, returning, attempted to carry the woman to an ambulance. He had scarcely made a step, when she was shot dead in his arms. Those of us who stand in the gateway and witness such scenes have got beyond the feeling of personal fear. Any one of us, I will venture to say, would give his life to spare France on this dreadful day. Yet we stand pale and shuddering at the sight of the fate which befals the poor people of the town.

"I care not to dwell upon horrors, which, nevertheless, I shall never be able to forget. I can mention more than one brave officer who did not fear to own that he shrank from the sight of what had become a mere massacre. Those who were safely out of the way as prisoners, whether officers or men, needed no pity. When, after a time, it became clear that there was no sign of Bazaine, the hopes of the French again departed. A sullen sort of fight still went on. The guns of the town answered the Prussians. An aid-de-camp of the Emperor went by on foot, and I heard him ask the officers near by to help him in putting an end to the fire. Such being the Emperor's wish, at length the white flag was hoisted on the citadel. The cannonade ceased suddenly about 4.30 o'clock. Eager as we were to know the cause, we cannot leave the house, for the street is impassable, and we have to be content with learning the mere fact of the surrender. As night drew on, the crowd a little diminished, and by some effort it was possible to make one's way about the town. The spectacle it offered was more horrible than war. Dead were lying everywhere; civilians and soldiers mingled in the slaughter. In one suburb I counted more than fifty bodies of peasants and bourgeois—a few women among them, and one child. The ground was strewn with splinters of shells. Starving soldiers were cutting up the dead horses to cook and eat, for provision had again failed us, as every thing has failed since this campaign began. I was glad to get away from the sight of our disasters, and lose their remembrance in a few hours of sleep.

"The next day we were told that the Emperor had gone to the King's headquarters to treat for a surrender. At 11 o'clock his household and carriages left the town, and we knew that he was a prisoner, and the Empire no more. About the same hour there was posted in the streets a proclamation from General de Wimpffen, saying that, notwithstanding prodigies of courage, the army, having no more ammunition, found itself unable to respond to the summons of its chiefs and force its way to Montmedy. That being surrounded, he had made the best conditions he could—conditions such as would inflict no humiliation on the army.

"These conditions prove to be the surrender of the whole army, not less than 100,000 men, as prisoners of war, with all their arms, baggage, horses, standards, and guns. The officers who sign an engagement not to serve against Prussia during the war may return to their homes, the remainder to be sent to German towns in Germany. Many officers refuse to sign, preferring to share the captivity of their men.

"On Saturday the whole force laid down their arms. Not a few soldiers, in their rage, broke rather than give up their arms, and the streets were littered with fragments of all kinds of weapons broken: swords, rifles, pistols, lancers, helmets, cuirasses, even mitrailleuses covered the ground; and in one place, where the Meuse runs through the town, the heaps of such fragments choked the stream and rose above the surface. The mud of the streets was black with gunpowder. The horses had been tied to the houses and gun-carriages, but nobody remembered to feed or water them, and in the frenzy of hunger and thirst they broke loose and ran wild through the town. Whoever liked might have a horse—even officers' horses, which were private property —for the trouble of catching them.

"When the Prussians came into the town they were very sore and angry at the sight of all this destruction and waste. What must have pleased them still less, was the state in which they found the military chest. As soon as the surrender was resolved on, the French officers were told to make out the best accounts they could, present them, and receive payment. Naturally, the statements thus brought in soon proved sufficient to empty the treasury. I know of officers who demanded and received payment for horses that were not killed and baggage which had not been lost. Demoralization showed itself in every way. Even the standards were burned or buried—an act of bad faith, not to be palliated even by the rage of a beaten army.

"Their rage is greater against no one than General de Failly. He had a room in the hotel where I was staying. On Friday a great multitude of soldiers gathered before the house, the doors of which were closed, demanding General de Failly with such shouts and menaces that the landlord thought it prudent to hurry him out of a back window. The soldiers, could they have reached him, would have torn him to pieces. Since then I have heard the report that he was shot by one of his own men; but no such event had happened on Saturday, and could not well happen later.

"It was a relief on Saturday when the Prussians came in and occupied the town, and restored order. I am sorry to have to acknowledge that all through the campaign the French have acted much more like a conquering army, in a hostile country, than the Prussians. All the annoyance I have experienced personally came from my own countrymen—from the peasants, who, above all, saw a spy in every stranger. When I fell into the hands of the Prussians, I found them courtesy itself. On leaving Sedan, and thence to the frontier, in passing through the Prussian posts, I was stopped often. I had but to say, 'I am the correspondent of an American journal,' and I was at once sent kindly forward. On the back of my French military pass the Prussian Staff had endorsed a Prussian safe-conduct. Often I was not obliged even to show my papers—my word was taken; and, once out of Sedan, I was speedily through.

"When I left Sedan on Sunday morning things were rapidly getting in order. The streets were cleared of dead horses and men. The indescribable filth of the town was swept into the river. The shops were opening again. Discipline had taken the place of disorder. I saw enough of Prussian organization and energy to change, if the grievous defeat of a noble army had not already changed, the opinion I have so often expressed, that ultimate victory for France was sure.

"I have followed MacMahon from the day when I found him reorganizing his army at Châlons to the fatal day at Sedan, when he surrendered the last organized force in France, save the remnant of that which is shut up in Metz. Certainly, when I was at the camp of Châlons, and then at Rheims, I had observed that the number of stragglers was enormous, and I continually met soldiers who did not know where their regiments were. I had seen men and officers disabled by wounds which French soldiers of other days would have despised; I had remarked how untidy and careless the men were allowed to be about their dress and equipments. These things, slight, but significant to a military eye, had caused me, no doubt, some misgivings as to the rapidity of the success we had a right to expect. I saw, also, how prone French officers were to avoid the fatigues of long marches and the discomfort of bivouacs. I remember how often I have traversed the French lines at dead of night and at early dawn, and never heard a challenge, never came across a French vedette, never have fallen in with a party of scouts. On the other hand, I have seen officers spend the time that ought to have been given to their men, in cafés or in poor village inns. Often even officers of the staff seemed to neglect their duties for paltry amusements, showing themselves ignorant, sometimes, even of the name of the Department in which they were; so that I have known a French General obliged to ask his way from peasants at the meeting of two roads. I struggled long against all this kind of evidence, but the end is only too clear. Painful it is to me, but I am bound to declare my belief that any further effort France may make can only cause useless bloodshed; and that a means of escape from her peril must now be sought otherwise than by force of arms."

Not less vivid and graphic are the descriptions of the battle and surrender from correspondents who were in the Prussian headquarters and on the field during the whole of that terrible day. One of these descriptions, from the same pen that furnished to the *Tribune* the glowing description of the battle of Gravelotte, is deserving of a place. We give portions of it:

"On the evening of Wednesday, from 5 to 8 o'clock, I was at the Crown-Prince's quarters at Chemery, a village some thirteen miles from Sedan to the south-southwest on the main road. At 5.30 we saw that there was a great movement among the troops encamped all around us, and we thought, at first, that the

King was riding through the bivouacs; but soon the 37th regiment came pouring through the village, their band playing '*Die wacht am Rhein*' as they marched along with a swinging stride. I saw at once, by the men's faces, that something extraordinary was going on. It was soon plain that the troops were in the lightest possible marching order. All their knapsacks were left behind, and they were carrying nothing but cloaks, slung around their shoulders, except that one or two *bon vivants* had retained their camp-kettles. But if the camp-kettles were left behind, the cartouche-cases were there—hanging heavily in front of the men's belts, unbalanced, as they ought to be, by the knapsacks. Soon I learned that the whole Prussian corps—those lent from Prince Friedrich Karl's army, the Second Army, and the Crown-Prince's—were making a forced march to the left, in the direction of Donchery and Mézières, in order to shut in MacMahon's army in the west, and so drive them against the Belgian frontier. I learned from the officers of the Crown-Prince's staff, that at the same time, while we were watching regiment after regiment pass through Chemery, the Saxons and the Guards, 80,000 strong, on the Prussian right, under Prince Albert of Saxony, were also marching rapidly to close on the doomed French army on the right bank of the Meuse, which they had crossed at Remilly on Tuesday, the 30th, in the direction of La Chapelle, a small village of 930 inhabitants, on the road from Sedan to Bouillon, in Belgium, and the last village before crossing the frontier.

"Any thing more splendid than the men's marching it would be impossible to imagine. I saw men lame in both feet hobbling along in the ranks, kind comrades, less footsore, carrying their needle-guns. Those who were actually incapable of putting one foot before another, had pressed peasants' wagons and every available conveyance into service, and were following in the rear, so as to be ready for the great battle, which all felt sure would come off on the morrow. The Bavarians, who, it is generally believed, do not march so well as they fight, were in the centre, between us at Chemery and Sedan, encamped around the woods of La Marfee, famous for a great battle in 1641, during the wars of the League. When I had seen the last regiment dash through—for the pace at which they went can really not be called 'marching,' in the ordinary sense,—I rode off, about a quarter past eight in the evening, for Vendresse, where the King's headquarters were, and where I hoped to find house-room for man and beast, especially the latter, as being far the most important on the eve of a great battle.

"When I got within about half a mile of Vendresse, going at a steady trot, a sharp 'Halt' rang out through the clear air. I brought my horse to a stand-still, knowing that Prussian sentries are not to be trifled with. As I pulled up, twenty yards off, I heard the clicks of their locks as they brought their weapons to full cock and covered me. My reply being satisfactory, I jogged on into Vendresse, and my mare and myself had soon forgotten sentinels, forced marches, and coming battles, one of us on the straw, the other on the floor.

"At 7 o'clock on Thursday morning my servant came to wake me, saying that the King's horses were harnessing, and that His Majesty would leave in half an hour for the battlefield; and as a cannonade had already been heard near Sedan, I jumped up, seized crusts of bread, wine, cigars, &c., and crammed them into my holster, taking my breakfast on the way.

"Just as I got to my horse, King Wilhelm drove out in an open carriage with four horses, for Chevange, about three and a half miles south of Sedan. Much against my will, I was compelled to allow the King's staff to precede me on the road to the scene of action, where I arrived myself soon after 9 o'clock. It was impossible to ride fast, all the roads being blocked with artillery, ammunition wagons, ambulances, &c. As I rode on to the crest of the hill which rises sharply about 600 or 700 feet above the little hamlet of Chevange, nestled in a grove below, a most glorious panorama burst on my view. As General Forsyth, of the United States Army, remarked to me later in the day, it would have been worth the coming, merely to see so splendid a scene, without 'battle's magnificently stern array.' In the lovely valley below us, from the knoll on which I stood with the King and his staff, we could see not only the whole Valley of the Meuse (or Maas, as the Germans love to call the river that Louis XIV stole from them), but also beyond the great woods of Bois de Loup and Francheval, into Belgium, and as far as the hilly forest of Numo, on the other side of the frontier. Right at our feet lay the little town of Sedan, famous for its fortifications by Vauban, and as the birthplace of Turenne, the great Marshal. It is known, also, as the place where sedan chairs originated. As we were only about two and a quarter miles from the town, we could easily distinguish its principal edifices without the aid of our field-glasses. On the left was a pretty church, its Gothic spire of sandstone offering a conspicuous target for the Prussian guns, had General Moltke thought fit to bombard the town. To the right, on the southeast of the church, was a large barrack, with the fortifications of the citadel. Behind it and beyond this to the southeast again was the old chateau of Sedan, with picturesque, round-turreted towers of the sixteenth century, very useless, even against four-pounder Krupp field-pieces. This building, I believe, is now an arsenal. Beyond this was the citadel—the heart of Sedan, on a rising hill above the Meuse to the southeast, but completely commanded by the hills on both sides the river, which runs in front of the citadel.

"The French had flooded the low meadows in the valley before coming to the railway bridge at Bazeille, in order to stop the Germans from advancing on the town in that direction.

With their usual stupidity (for one can find no other word for it), the French had failed to mine the bridge at Bazeille, and it was of immense service to the Prussians throughout the battle. The Prussians actually threw up earthworks on the iron bridge itself to protect it from the French, who more than once attempted early in the day to storm the bridge, in the hope of breaking the Bavarian communication between the right and left banks of the Meuse. This they were unable to do; and although their cannon-shot have almost demolished the parapet, the bridge itself was never materially damaged.

"On the projecting spurs of the hill, crowned by the woods of La Marfee, of which I have already spoken, the Bavarians had posted two batteries of six-pounder rifled breech-loading steel Krupp guns, which kept up a duello till the very end of the day with the siege-guns of Sedan across the Meuse. Still further to the right flank, or rather to the east (for our line was a circular one—a crescent at first, with Sedan in the centre, like the star on the Turkish standard), was an undulating plain above the village of Bazeille. Terminating about a mile and a half from Sedan, at the woods near Rubecourt, midway—that is to say, in a line from Bazeille north—there is a ravine watered by a tiny brook, which was the scene of the most desperate struggle and of the most frightful slaughter of the whole battle. This stream, whose name I have forgotten, if it ever had one, runs right behind the town of Sedan.

"From the woods of Fleigreuse on the north, behind the town rises a hill dotted with cottages and fruit-laden orchards, and crowned by the wood of La Givonne, which runs down to the valley of which I have just spoken. Between this wood and the town were several French camps, their white shelter-tents standing out clear among the dark fruit-trees. In these camps one could see throughout the day huge masses of troops which were never used. Even during the height of the battle they stood as idle as Fitz-John Porter's at the second battle of Bull-Run. We imagined that they must have been undisciplined Gardes Mobiles, whom the French Generals dared not bring out against their enemy.

"To the Prussian left of these French camps, separated from them by a wooded ravine, was a long bare hill, something like one of the hills on Long Island. This hill, on which was some of the hardest fighting of the day, formed one of the keys of the position of the French army. When once its crests were covered with Prussian artillery, the whole town of Sedan was completely at the mercy of the German guns, as they were not only above the town, but the town was almost within musket-range of them.

"Still further to the left lay the village of Illy, set on fire early in the day by the French shells. South of this the broken railway-bridge, blown up by the French to protect their right, was a conspicuous object.

"Right above the railway-bridge, on the line to Mézières, was the wooded hill crowded by the new and most hideous 'chateau,' as he calls it, of one Monsieur Pave. It was here the Crown-Prince and his staff stood during the day, having a rather more extensive but less central view, and therefore less desirable than ours, where stood the King, Count Bismarck, von Roon, the War Minister, General Moltke, and Generals Sheridan and Forsyth—to say nothing of your correspondent.

"Having thus endeavored to give some faint idea of the scene of what is, in all probability, the decisive battle of the war, I will next give an account of the position of the different corps at the commencement of the action, premising that all the movements were of the simplest possible nature, the object of the Prussian Generals being merely to close the crescent of troops with which they began into a circle, by effecting a junction between the Saxon corps on their right and the Prussian corps on their left. This junction took place about noon, near the little village of Olley, on the Bazeille ravine, behind Sedan, of which I have already spoken. Once their terrible circle formed and well soldered together, it grew steadily smaller and smaller, until at last the fortifications of Sedan itself were entered.

" On the extreme right were the Saxons—one corps d'armée, with King Wilhelm's Guards; also a corps d'armée in reserve behind them. The Guards had suffered terribly at Gravelotte, where they met the Imperial Guard; and the King would not allow them to be again so cruelly decimated. Justice compels me to state that this arrangement was very far, indeed, from being pleasing to the Guards themselves, who are ever anxious to be in the forefront of the battle.

" The Guards and Saxons, then about 75,000 strong, were all day on the right bank of the Meuse, between Rubecourt and La Chapelle, at which latter village Prince Albert of Saxony, who was in command of the two corps which have been formed into a little extra army by themselves, passed the night of Thursday.

" The ground from Rubecourt to the Meuse was occupied by the First Bavarian Corps. The Second Bavarian Corps extended their front from near the Bazeille railway-bridge to a point on the high road from Donchery to Sedan, not far from the little village of Torcy. Below the hill on which the Crown-Prince was placed, the ground from Torcy to Illy, through the large village of Floing, was held by the First and Third Prussian Corps, belonging to the army of Prince Friedrich Karl, and temporarily attached to the army of the Crown-Prince.

" This was the position of the troops about 9 o'clock on Thursday morning, September 1, and no great advance took place till later than that, for the artillery had at first all the work to do. Still further to the left, near Donchery, there were 20,000 Würtembergers ready to cut off the French from Mézières, in case of their making a push for that fortress.

"The number of the Prussian troops engaged was estimated by General Moltke at 240,000, and that of the French at 120,000. We know that MacMahon had with him on Tuesday 120,000 men, that is, four corps; his own, that lately commanded by General de Failly, now under General Le Brun; that of Felix Douay, brother of General Abel Douay, killed at Weissenburg; and a fourth corps, principally composed of Garde Mobile, the name of whose commander has escaped me. MacMahon, although wounded, commanded in chief on the French side.

"It is almost needless to say that the real commander-in-chief of the Prussians on that day was von Moltke, with the Crown-Prince and Prince Albert of Saxony, immediately next in command.

"There were a few stray cannon-shots fired, merely to obtain the range, as soon as it was light; but the real battle did not begin until 6 o'clock, becoming a sharp artillery-fight at 9, when the batteries had each got within easy range, and the shells began to do serious mischief. At 11.55 the musketry-fire in the valley behind Sedan, which had opened about 11.25, became exceedingly lively—being one continuous rattle, only broken by the loud growling of the mitrailleuses, which played with deadly effect upon the Saxon and Bavarian columns. General Sheridan, by whose side I was standing at the time, told me that he did not remember ever to have heard such a well-sustained fire of small-arms. It made itself heard above the roar of the batteries at our feet.

"At 12 o'clock precisely the Prussian battery of six guns, on the slope above the broken railway-bridge over the Meuse, near La Villette, had silenced two batteries of French guns at the foot of the bare hill already mentioned, near the village of Floing. At 12.10 the French infantry, no longer supported by their artillery, were compelled to retire to Floing, and soon afterward the junction between the Saxons and Prussians behind Sedan was announced to us by General von Roon, eagerly peering through a large telescope, as being safely completed.

"From this moment the result of the battle could no longer be doubtful. The French were completely surrounded and brought to bay. At 12.25 we were all astonished to see clouds of retreating French infantry on the hill between Floing and Sedan, a Prussian battery in front of St. Menges making accurate practice with percussion shells among the receding ranks. The whole hill, for a quarter of an hour, was literally covered with Frenchmen running rapidly.

"Less than half an hour afterward—at 12.50—General von Roon called our attention to another French column in full retreat to the right of Sedan, on the road leading from Bazeille to the La Givonne wood. They never halted until they came to a red-roofed house on the outskirts of Sedan itself. Almost at the same moment General Sheridan, who was using my operaglass, asked me to look at a third French column moving up a broad, grass-covered road through the La Givonne wood, immediately above Sedan, doubtless to support the troops who were defending the important Bazeille ravine to the northeast of the town.

"At 1 o'clock the French batteries on the edge of the wood toward Torcy and above it opened a vigorous fire on the advancing Prussian columns of the Third Corps, whose evident intention it was to storm the hill northwest of La Givonne, and so gain the key of the position on that side. At 1.05 yet another French battery near the wood opened on the Prussian columns, which were compelled to keep shifting their ground till ready for their final rush at the hills, in order to avoid offering so good a mark to the French shells. Shortly afterward we saw the first Prussian skirmishers on the crest of the La Givonne hills, above Torcy. They did not seem to be in strength, and General Sheridan, standing behind me, exclaimed, 'Ah! the beggars are too weak; they can never hold that position against all those French.'

"The General's prophecy soon proved correct, for the French advanced at least six to one; and the Prussians were forced to retreat down the hill to seek reënforcements from the columns which were hurrying to their support. In five minutes they came back again, this time in greater force, but still terribly inferior to those huge French masses.

"'Good heavens! The French cuirassiers are going to charge them,' cried General Sheridan; and sure enough, the regiment of cuirassiers, their helmets and breast-plates flashing in the September sun, formed in sections of squadrons and dashed down on the scattered Prussian skirmishers, without deigning to form a line. Squares are never used by the Prussians, and the infantry received the cuirassiers with a crushing 'quick-fire'—*schnellfeuer*—at about a hundred yards' distance, loading and firing with extreme rapidity, and shooting with unfailing precision into the dense French squadrons. The effect was startling. Over went horses and men in numbers, in masses, in hundreds; and the regiment of proud French cuirassiers went hurriedly back in disorder; went back faster than it came; went back scarcely a regiment in strength, and not at all a regiment in form. Its comely array was suddenly changed into shapeless and helpless crowds of flying men.

"The moment the cuirassiers turned back the brave Prussians actually dashed forward in hot pursuit at double-quick, infantry evidently pursuing flying cavalry. Such a thing has not often been recorded in the annals of war. I know not when an example to compare precisely with this has occurred. There was no more striking episode in the battle.

"When the French infantry saw their cavalry thus fleeing before foot-soldiers, they in their turn came forward and attacked the Prussians. The Prussians waited quietly, patiently enduring a rapid and telling fire from the Chassepôts, until their enemies had drawn so near as to be within a hundred yards of them Then to the fire of the Chassepôts they returned a fire as rapid from their needle-guns; and the French infantry could no more endure this Prussian fire than the cavalry, to whose rescue they had come. The infantry fled in its turn, and followed the cavalry to the place whence they came, that is, behind a ridge, about 500 yards on the way to Sedan, where the Prussian fire could no longer reach them.

"The great object of the Prussians was gained, since they were not driven from the crest of the hill they fought to hold. Holding it thus against cavalry, the Prussians persuaded themselves that it was possible to establish artillery on this hill.

"'There will be a devil of a fight for that crest before it is won or lost,' said Sheridan, straining his eyes through his field-glass at the hill, which was not three miles from us. The full sun was shining upon that hill; we, gazing upon it, had the sun behind us.

"At 1.30 French cavalry—this time, I presume, a regiment of *carabiniers*—made another dash at the Prussians, who, on their part, were receiving reënforcements every moment; but the *carabiniers* met with the same fate as their brethren in iron jackets, and were sent to the right-about with heavy loss. The Prussians took advantage of their flight to advance their line about 200 yards nearer the line which the French infantry held.

"This body of adventurous Prussians split into two portions, the two parts leaving a break of a hundred yards in their line. We were not long in perceiving the object of this movement, for the little white puffs from the crest behind the skirmishers, followed by a commotion in the dense French masses, show us that these '*diables de Prussians*' have contrived, Heaven only knows how, to get two four-pounders up the steep ground, and have opened fire on the French. Something must at this point have been very much mismanaged with the French infantry; for, instead of attacking the Prussians, whom they still outnumbered by at least two to one, they remained in column on the hill; and, though seeing their only hope of retrieving the day vanishing from before their eyes, still they did not stir. Then the French cavalry tried to do a little Balaklava business—tried, but without the success of the immortal six hundred, who took the guns on which they charged. The cuirassiers came down once more, this time riding straight for the two field-pieces; but before they came within 200 yards of the guns, the Prussians formed line, as if on parade, and, waiting till those furious French horsemen had ridden to a point not fifty yards away, they fired. The volley seemed to us to empty the saddles of almost the whole of the leading squadron. The dead so strewed the ground as to block the path of the squadron following, and close before them the direct and dangerous road they had meant to follow. Their dash at the guns became a halt.

"When once this last effort of the French horse had been made and had failed—failed, though pushed gallantly so far as men and horses could go—the French infantry fell swiftly back toward Sedan. It fell back because it saw that the chance of its carrying that fiercely-contested hill was gone, and saw, also, that the Prussians holding the hill were crowning it with guns, so that their own line could not much longer be held facing it. In an instant, as the French retired, the whole slope of the ground was covered by swarms of Prussian *tirailleurs*, who seemed to rise out of the ground, and push forward by help of every slight roughness or depression in the surface of the hill. As fast as the French went back these active enemies followed. After the last desperate charge of the French cavalry, General Sheridan remarked to me that he never saw any thing so reckless, so utterly foolish, as that last charge. 'It was sheer murder.'

"The Prussians, after the French infantry fell back, advanced rapidly—so rapidly that the retreating squadrons of French cavalry, being too closely pressed, turned suddenly round and charged desperately once again. But it was all no use. The days of breaking squares are over. The thin blue line soon stopped the Gallic onset.

"It struck me as most extraordinary that at this point the French had neither artillery nor mitrailleuses, especially the latter, on the field to cover their infantry. The position was a most important one, and certainly worth straining every nerve to defend. One thing was clear enough, that the French infantry, after once meeting the Prussians, declined to try conclusions with them again, and that the cavalry were seeking to encourage them by their example. About 2 o'clock still other re-enforcements came to the Prussians over this long-disputed hill between Torcy and Sedan to support the regiments already established there.

"All the time that this great conflict was going on under Fritz's eyes, another was fought not less severe and as murderous for the Bavarians as the one I have attempted to describe was for the French. If there was a want of mitrailleuses on the hill above Torcy, there was certainly no lack of them in the Bazeille ravine. On that side there was, for more than an hour, one continuous roar of musketry and mitrailleuses. Two Bavarian officers told me that the loss in their regiments was terrific, and that it was the mitrailleuses which made the havoc.

"At 2.05 in the afternoon the French totally abandoned the hill between Torcy and Sedan, and fell back on the faubourg of Caval, just outside the ramparts of the town. 'Now the battle is lost for the French,' said General Sheridan, to the delight of the Prussian officers. One would almost have imagined that the French had heard his words—they had hardly been uttered when there came a lull in the firing all along the line, or rather circle, as such it had now become.

"Count Bismarck chose that moment to come and have a talk with his English and American friends. I was anxious to know what the Federal Chancellor had done about the neutrality of Belgium, now threatened, and my curiosity was soon gratified. 'I have told the Belgian Minister of War,' said Count Bismarck, 'that, so long as the Belgian troops do their utmost to disarm any number of French soldiers who may cross the frontier, I will strictly respect the neutrality of Belgium; but if, on the contrary, the Belgians, either through negligence or inability, do not disarm and capture every man in French uniform who sets his foot in their country, we shall at once follow the enemy into neutral territory with our troops, considering that the French have been the first to violate the Belgian soil. I have been down to have a look at the Belgian troops near the frontier,' added Count Bismarck, 'and I confess they do not inspire me with a very high opinion of their martial ardor or discipline. When they have their great-coats on, one can see a great deal of paletot, but hardly any soldier.'

"I asked His Excellency where he thought the Emperor was: 'In Sedan?' 'Oh, no!' was the reply; 'Napoleon is not very wise, but he is not so foolish as to put himself in Sedan just now.' For once in his life Count Bismarck was wrong.

"At 2.45 the King came to the place where I was standing. He remarked that he thought the French were about to try to break out just beneath us, in front of the Second Bavarian Corps. At 3.50 General Sheridan told me that Napoleon and Louis were in Sedan.

"At 3.20 the Bavarians below us not only contrived to get themselves inside the fortifications of Sedan, but to maintain themselves there, working their way forward from house to house. About 4 o'clock there was a great fight for the possession of the ridge above Bazeille. That carried, Sedan was swept on all sides by the Prussian cannon. This point of vantage was carried at 4.40. When carried there could no longer be a shade of doubt as to the ultimate fate of Sedan.

"About 5 o'clock there was again a sudden suspension of the cannonade along the whole line. Many were the speculations as to the cause, but nobody seemed to divine the truth. You must judge of our surprise when, five minutes later, we saw a French officer, escorted by two Uhlans, coming at a handsome trot up the steep bridle-path from Sedan to our post, one of the Uhlans carrying a white duster on a faggot-stick as a flag of truce. The messenger turned out to be a French colonel, come to ask for terms of surrender. After a very short consultation between the King and General von Moltke, the messenger was told by the General that, in a matter so important as the surrender of at least 80,000 men, and an important fortress, it was necessary to send an officer of high rank. 'You are, therefore,' said the General, 'to return to Sedan and tell the Governor of the town to report himself immediately to the King of Prussia. If he does not arrive within an hour, our guns will again open fire. You may tell the commandant that there is no use of his trying to obtain any other terms than unconditional surrender.' The *parlementaire* rode back with this message. When he was fairly out of ear-shot his mission was most eagerly canvassed.

"At 6.30 there arose a sudden cry among the members of the King's staff, '*Der Kaiser ist da!*' and then came a loud hurrah. Soon we began to look anxiously for the arrival of the second flag of truce. In ten minutes more General Reilly rode up with a letter for the King of Prussia.

"As soon as the French General was in sight, the slender escort of cuirassiers and dragoons we had with us was drawn up in line, two deep. Behind the King, in front of the escort, was the staff; and ten yards in front of them again, stood His Majesty, King Wilhelm of Prussia, ready to receive General Reilly. That officer, as we soon learned, was the bearer of an autograph letter from the Emperor Napoleon to **King** Wilhelm. The Emperor of the French wrote: 'As I cannot die at the head of my army, I lay my sword at the feet of your Majesty'—[' *Ne pouvant pas mourir à la tête de mon armée, je viens mettre mon épée aux pieds de votre Majesté*'].

"Why Napoleon III could not die, as did thousands of his soldiers, sword in hand, with his face to the foe, is not so clear.

"On receipt of this most astounding letter, there was a brief consultation between the King, the Crown-Prince, who had come over from his hill on the arrival of the flag of truce, Count Bismarck, General von Moltke, and General von Roon. After a few minutes' conversation, the King sat down on a rush-bottomed chair, and wrote a note (on another chair held as a table by two aides-de-camp) to the Emperor, asking him to come next morning to the King of Prussia's headquarters at Vendresse.

"While the King was writing this note Count Bismarck came up to Generals Sheridan and Forsyth, and myself, and heartily shook our hands. 'Let me congratulate you most sincerely, Count,' said General Sheridan. 'I can only compare the surrender of Napoleon to that of General Lee at Appomattox Court-House.'

"When it came my turn to grasp the Chancellor's hand, I could not help saying, after I had warmly congratulated him, 'You cannot but feel a pride, Count Bismarck, in having contributed so largely to the winning of to-day's victory.' 'Oh! no, my dear sir,' was the mild answer; 'I am no strategist, and have nothing to do with the winning of battles. What I am proud of is, that the Bavarians, the Saxons, and the Wurtembergers have not only been on our side, but have had so large a share—the largest share—in the glory of the day; that they are with us, and not against us. *That* is my doing. I don't think the French will say now that the South Germans will not fight for our common Fatherland.'

"I asked His Excellency whether Louis was taken with his papa, and was told that no one knew; and I think that no one much cared where that little man was.

"When the King had written his letter, he himself handed it to General Reilly, who stood bareheaded to receive it—the Italian and Crimean medals glittering on his breast in the fading sunlight. Queen Victoria's image and superscription have not often been seen on the uniforms of men surrendering without conditions.

"At 7.40 General Reilly left for the beleaguered town, escorted by the Uhlans. The duster which had served as a flag of truce was offered to me as a souvenir of that memorable day; but it had a strong resemblance to other dusters, and I declined the proffered relic.

"As soon as General Reilly was gone I was most anxious to be off to the Belgian frontier, in the hope of getting messages through; but Count Bismarck's aid-de-camp assured me that it was physically impossible to go that night, and that I must wait till morning, and even then must be careful not to fall into the hands of stray French soldiers, who were known to be dispersed in all directions along the Belgian frontier, and to be little better than bandits. So I slept at the village of Chevange, a mile behind our post, after a little hunting for quarters, actually getting a bed.

"Next morning early I started for Belgium. As I rode along I suddenly came first on a knot of Uhlans; then on two lackeys in the green and gold Imperial livery. Directly behind them came His Majesty Napoleon III, in his travelling carriage, on his way to report himself a prisoner at King Wilhelm's headquarters at Vendresse, a little dirty village some eight miles from Sedan."

CHAPTER X.

WHILE this desperate fighting, terminating in an inevitable, if not an inglorious, surrender, was going on around Sedan, Marshal Bazaine, for whose benefit and release MacMahon had perilled and lost his army, attempted to break out of Metz by a sortie from the northeast. Why he selected this point, which would, if successful, have carried him still farther away from MacMahon's army, does not exactly appear; possibly because he may have believed the German investing force weakest at that point.

The sortie was commenced on the morning of August 31st, at which time the army of Marshal MacMahon was not less than seventy miles distant, and the railroad connections broken and in the hands of the Prussians. The German force on the east side of the Moselle besieging, or rather isolating, Metz, belonged to the Second Army, and that corps, consisting almost entirely of East-Prussian line-troops and Landwehr, was under the special command of General von Manteuffel. This corps lay in almost a semicircle from Malvoy and Olgy, eight or nine miles north of Metz, to the river Sille, three miles south of the city.

The fighting commenced between 9 and 10 o'clock in the morning of August 31st, the French troops massing heavily, and hurling themselves on the German left wing just at Colombey and Bellecroix, villages nearly due east from Metz. They were vigorously supported by the fire from Fort Bellecroix and Fort St. Julien, as well as from some batteries hitherto masked. There was a feint of attacking the German right wing lying between Malvoy and Charly, but it was only a feint. About 3

GENERAL MANTEUFFEL.

P. M. the French, under command of General Lebœuf in person, made a most determined and resolute attack upon the German centre at Servigny, Retonfay, and Noisseville, supported by concealed batteries and the forts. The fighting was of the most desperate and obstinate character. Servigny, Noisseville, Retonfay, and Poixe were each taken and retaken several times, much of the fighting on the German side being done with the bayonet. The battle did not cease till 11 P. M., and the troops on both sides rested on their arms.

Fighting was resumed the next morning at 4 A. M., although the whole field was covered with a thick fog. The ground about the village of Noisseville was again fought over obstinately, the village itself being captured and lost three times by each party. On the left flank, Flanville and Corney were captured by the Germans; and on the right, after desperate fighting, the French were driven southward and into Metz, being pushed into and through the Grimont wood, and Grimont itself, under the guns of Fort St. Julien. Once more the French centre advanced against Servigny, and its right flank took and retook, but finally lost, Mercy le Haut; but their attacks were delivered with less force than at first, and finally ceased about midday, September 1st. The loss on the German side was about 3,000, officers and men; on the French side, considerably heavier. The full reports of these battles have not yet, we believe, been published, but we subjoin the despatches of two of the German generals.

From Malaincourt General Stichle (chief of staff to Prince Friedrich Karl) telegraphed on the 2d of September:

"From the morning of August 31st to midday of September 1st Marshal Bazaine has almost unceasingly attempted, with several corps from Metz, to break through toward the north. General Manteuffel, under chief command of Prince Friedrich Karl, has repulsed all these attempts in glorious battles, which may be united under the name of Battle of Noisseville. The enemy was again thrown back into the fortress. The First and Ninth Corps, Kummer's Division (line and Landwehr), and the Twenty-eighth Infantry Brigade, took part in the battle. The principal fighting took place at Servigny, Noisseville, and Retonfay. Night-surprises were repulsed with East-Prussian bayonets and clubbed muskets. Our losses not yet ascertained, but not very large proportionally; those of the enemy heavy."

General Manteuffel telegraphed:

"Since yesterday morning Marshal Bazaine has been in battle day and night with his entire army, against the First Army-Corps and Kummer's Division; and yesterday night and to-day he has been everywhere driven back. The French have fought with the greatest courage, but have to give way to the East-Prussians. Prince Friedrich Karl, the commander-in-chief of the blockading troops, has yesterday and to-day expressed his recognition and his good wishes for both victories. The Fourth Landwehr Division took a distinguished part in to-day's victory.

"VON MANTEUFFEL."

The French troops, finding all their efforts to break through the cordon of troops which surrounded them unavailing, withdrew, in the afternoon of September 1st, within their fortified lines.

Strasbourg, Laon, Toul, and Pfalzburg still held out, and these, with Metz, detained nearly 200,000 German troops to isolate and besiege them. There was, however, no lack of German soldiers, notwithstanding the terrible slaughter of the battles already fought. On the 4th of September the King of Prussia, at the head of the First, Third, and Fourth Armies— a force of not less than 300,000 men—was marching toward

Paris. Subsequent reënforcements brought up the entire German armies in France to above 700,000 men, notwithstanding all losses.

While this surrender was going on at Sedan, and the attempted sortie at Metz was proving unsuccessful, what was the condition of affairs at Paris? There had not been wanting indications of the speedy downfall of the Empire. Even as early as the battle of Woerth, on the 6th of August, the Ollivier Ministry had tried in vain to repress the bold questioning and the daring and inconvenient interpellation of the Radicals in the Corps Législatif; and after the downfall of that Cabinet, the Palikao Ministry found themselves compelled to allow the Radical members a share in the Committee of Defence. Denunciations of the Emperor's policy and generalship had become alarmingly frequent, and, though the Palikao Ministry had persistently deceived the people, representing nearly every defeat as either a victory, or, at most, a drawn battle, and on the very day of the surrender, and at least an hour after the preliminaries of the capitulation had been agreed upon, had published a despatch from the Emperor, saying, "All goes wonderfully well; our plans all succeed," yet there was a restlessness and impatience which betokened the coming storm. And a fearful storm it proved.

"The commotion," says an eye-witness, "commenced on Saturday, September 3d. The news of the Emperor's surrender, and the capitulation of MacMahon's army, were made known to the Empress at 7 o'clock in the evening. She immediately retired into her apartment, and refused to receive even intimate friends. Toward 9 o'clock the broad facts were known to a few persons only, but a general uneasiness prevailed, and angry groups assembled. At 11 o'clock on Sunday, while the Mobiles, on their way to camp at Saint Maur, accompanied by a small crowd, were proceeding up the Boulevards toward the Bastille, they sung the Marseillaise, and some shouted, '*La Déchéance!*' —'The Overthrow' (of the Empire). This cry had been already heard in other localities.

"Opposite the guard-house of the Police Sergeants, on the Boulevard Bonne Novelle, the police charged a crowd with drawn swords and revolvers, killing a Garde Mobile, a National Guard, and injuring several people. The mob turned upon the police and drove them back. The news of this act excited great indignation, and cries of 'Down with the Police Sergeants!' were heard everywhere. The crowd had also assembled in the Place de la Concorde and about the Chamber of Deputies. This crowd was also charged by the police, and many individuals were hurt. The bridge was barred to the public, and paraded by the police and troops till midnight.

"At the sitting of the Chamber, at noon, Count de Palikao made the following official statement of the disaster to Mac-Mahon's army, and the capture of the Emperor:

"'FRENCHMEN: France has encountered a great misfortune! After three days' heroic fighting by MacMahon against 300,000 enemies, 40,000 men were made prisoners. General Wimpffen, who had assumed the chief command of the army in the place of the severely-wounded Marshal MacMahon, subscribed the capitulation. This terrible misfortune shall not shake our courage. Paris is to-day in a state of defence. The military forces of the land are organizing themselves, and within a few days a new army will stand under the walls of Paris. Another army is forming on the banks of the Loire. Your patriotism, your unanimity, your energy, will save France. The Emperor was made prisoner in this battle. The Government unites with the great bodies of state. They will take every measure which the gravity of the occasion demands.'

"Jules Favre demanded a vote of *déchéance*, but the Chamber adjourned till next day at 12 o'clock. The news was not generally known till after 9 o'clock on Sunday morning, when the Ministerial statement appeared on the walls and in the morning papers. Soon immense excitement was apparent everywhere. By noon the Place de la Concorde was crowded, and the passage of the bridge interrupted to the public by the Police Sergeants, gendarmerie on horseback, and the troops on the bridge and around the Chamber. Popular Deputies were recognized, and met with acclamations and cries of '*La Déchéance!*' and '*Vive la République!*' As the day wore on the crowds augmented. On the passage of companies of National Guards, the people shouted, '*Vive National Garde!*' '*Vive la République!*' and the Guards reciprocated.

"At 2 P. M. the gates of the Tuileries garden were closed, and had remained so since morning, watched by the Zouaves and other detachments of the Imperial Guard. The people on the outside were trying to shake the gates on the side of the Place de la Concorde. At 2.20 o'clock a rush was made by a part of the crowd, headed by some of the National Guard. The Police Sergeants and gendarmerie made an armed demonstration of resistance, but suddenly yielded, and the crowd rushed by, shouting, '*La Déchéance!*' and '*Vive la République!*' People fraternized with the gendarmes and troops, and these with the National Guard. There was no resisting the masses who followed, and soon they surrounded the Chamber, and finally invaded it. At 3 o'clock shouting and commotion in front of the Chamber were heard. I saw the crowd from the Place de la Concorde. A procession marched slowly along the quay. The members of the Left recognized that they were being escorted to the Hôtel de Ville. Then came a rush of the mob from the other side of the bridge, the National Guards, the Mobiles, and the troops shouting, '*La Déchéance!*' and '*Vive la République!*'

"It becomes known that the Emperor is deposed by the Chamber, and that the Republic is declared. The people rush upon the Police Sergeants and disarm them. One National Guard has his head gashed with a sword, and is led away. The Police Sergeants get off the best way they can. The people assail the gates of the Tuileries. The Guards, after a menace, consent to a parley. The men clamber up and wrench off the eagles from the gates. The gates are presently opened, and the people flock in, going toward the palace. The flag is still flying from the top of the central pavilion. The crowd approaches the private garden. There is a detachment of troops there. The officer is summoned to open the gates. He refuses, but says he can let his men be replaced by the National Guard. This is done, and the officer saves his honor. The people walk in, and immediately invade the interior of the palace. The flag is torn and handed down. The Empress has left. The Mobiles and people amuse themselves looking at the albums and the Prince Imperial's playthings. They notice that the draperies of the windows are partly removed. The people write with chalk, 'Death to Thieves.' They respect property. The whole palace is visited, but nothing removed.

"Meanwhile, in the morning, at an earlier hour, the Deputies were returning to appoint a committee to consider the three proposals submitted by Palikao, Thiers, and Favre. These were as follows. That of Jules Favre, presented the previous day, was:

"'Article I. Louis Napoleon Bonaparte and his dynasty are declared incapable of the powers which the Constitution has conferred upon them.

"'Article II. A Commission of Government will be nominated by the Corps Législatif, composed of . . . , which will be invested with all the powers of Government, and which has for its express mission to resist invasion to the uttermost, and to chase the enemy from the country.

"'Article III. M. the General Trochu is retained in the functions of Governor-General of the city of Paris.'

"This was signed by twenty-eight members. The sitting adjourned at midnight.

"Meeting again at noon, the Minister of War, Count Palikao, read the following proposition for a law:

"'Article I. A Council of Government and of National Defence is instituted. This Council is composed of five members. Each member of the Council is named by a majority absolute of the Corps Législatif.

"'Article II. The Ministers are named subject to the approval of the members of the Council.

"'Article III. The General, Count Palikao, is named Lieutenant-General of this Council.

"'Done in the Council of the Ministers the 4th September, 1870, for the Emperor, and in virtue of the powers which he has confided to us.

"'Eugenie.'

"M. Thiers then read the following proposal, signed by forty-five or forty-six members:

"'In view of the circumstances, the Chamber names a Commission of Government and of National Defence. A constituent assembly will be convoked as soon as the circumstances permit it.'

"The Minister of War announced that the Government was perfectly willing to consult the country. It is agreed to discuss the three propositions together. The Chamber adjourned for a short time. A company of National Guards having charge of the gates shouted, '*La Déchéance!*' and, as the Deputies passed, some few Nationals mounted the steps of the Palace of the Corps Législatif, and signalled their comrades from the Pont de la Concorde. Presently the latter rushed forward, followed by the crowd, all classes intermixed, and shouting '*Vive la République!*' Once inside the palace-gates, the people spread themselves all over the building, except the hall where the sessions of the Deputies are held. The next hall was occupied by troops, who fraternized with the people.

"Crémieux addresses the people. They demand the withdrawal of the troops. Palikao appears, and promises that the troops shall be removed. Schneider, president of the Corps Législatif, led by two officers, crosses the courtyard, pale, haggard, and with tears in his eyes. He disappears into the hall where the sessions are held. Attempts are made to force its doors. General Mottcrouge orders the National Guards to defend the entry. There are loud cries of '*Déchéance!*' and '*Vive la République!*' The Deputies of the Left pass out and receive acclamation. Gambetta recommends calmness, and says, 'The majority must proclaim the *Déchéance*.'

"In one of the galleries somebody begins a speech. A few Deputies of the Right enter, but suddenly, as if panic-stricken, they retreat precipitately. Schneider now appears. He attempts to speak; grows foggy; becomes unnerved; puts on his hat and leaves the chair. At this moment a small side-door under the galleries opens, and about thirty push through. A National Guard causes them to withdraw, and closes the door, locking it. On the tribune there are shouts and gesticulations. Every body speaks at once.

"Another party of citizens forces its way in. The president's cry of 'Order!' is drowned by shouts of '*Vive la République!*' Palikao endeavors to obtain a hearing, and, failing, puts on his hat and quits the Chambers. The president tries unsuccessfully to allay the uproar, two Deputies going to his assistance, and all three very violently gesticulating. The Deputies of the Left address the people, striving to quell the tumult. Then Gambetta appeals to them to preserve order, and to await the arrival of the Representatives, as they will bring in the question of *Déchéance*.

"It is now 3 o'clock. Suddenly a crowd of people rush into the hall. The Deputies try to keep them back, but the hall is entirely invaded. The president puts on his hat and leaves the hall, declaring the session closed. As he quits his seat, National Guards and people come crowding in. There are general cries of ' *Vive la République!* ' The Deputies of the Left mix with the people, and all cry, ' To the Hôtel de Ville! ' Gambetta and other Republican leaders leave the Chambers and go in procession down the Pont de la Concorde, followed by the crowd.

"Meanwhile, outside the Chambers men climb up to the statue of Law, over the portal, and destroy the eagle which adorns the baton in the hands of the image. Then it is itself destroyed—the head first, then the arms. Gambetta and the procession pass down the Quai des Tuileries. Soldiers applaud and shout with the crowd. A lieutenant-colonel cries, ' *Vive la République!* ' The procession stops and fraternizes. The Turcos and the Spahis at the barracks of the Quai d'Orsay wave their turbans. The flag over the pavilion of the Tuileries is hauled down. In front of the Préfecture there are cries of ' Down with Pietri! ' The Préfecture is closely shut.

"Arrived in front of the Hôtel de Ville, the crowd forces its way in. Jules Favre and Jules Ferry go to the further end of the great hall. Two Gardes Mobiles, with drawn swords, clamber up the ornamental chimney and seat themselves in the lap of a marble nymph. Gambetta, Crémieux, and Kératry press in and take a place beside Favre, followed by Picard, Etienne

Arago, Glais-Bizoin, Schoelcher, and others. Gambetta, Crémieux, and Kératry are by themselves at the Mayor's table.

"Amid the tumult, Gambetta declares the Republic a fact, and that Emmanuel Arago is appointed Mayor of Paris. The people shout approval. The Bureau is constituted. Kératry is appointed Prefect of Police. The Bureau retires to constitute a Provisional Government and Ministry. At 4 o'clock the Bureau returns, and Gambetta declares the Provisional Government, constituted under the title of Government for the National Defence, consisting of Arago, Crémieux, Favre, Simon, Gambetta, Ferry, Glais-Bizoin, and Garnier-Pagés. The people shout Rochefort's name. It is added amid acclamation. The members of Government again retire. There is a discussion whether the tri-color or the red flag is to be adopted. Schoelcher says 'tri-color,' and it is adopted.

"The Rochefort episode was as follows: A hundred of Rochefort's constituents met, by appointment, at 3 P. M., at the Great Market Hall. At a given signal the leader raised a cane with a flag attached to it, and, with a shout, 'To Sainte Pélagie!' ascended. The group was joined by other men who up to that time had been lurking in the immediate vicinity, making in all about 300 when they reached the prison. There were three marines acting as sentries outside. One of them made believe to lower his bayonet. It was raised by his comrade. The crowd took the guns and broke them, but fraternized with the marines. There was no opposition from the wardens. Rochefort's cell-doors were burst in, and he was taken out.

"There was no coach at the door. A lady passing in one got out of it, and made Rochefort get in. He was driven to the Hôtel de Ville, arriving there at 5 o'clock, and was carried in triumph to the throne-room, where, amid the shouts and congratulations of friends, he learns that he is a member of the new Republican Government."

The first act of the new Republican Government was to issue the following address:

"To the Army: When a general has compromised his command, it is withdrawn from him. When a Government has placed the weal of the fatherland in danger by its mistakes, it is set aside. That is what France has just done. In displacing a dynasty which is responsible for our misfortunes, it has at one stroke completed a great act of justice in the eyes of the world. France has executed the judgment which had long been secretly expected of her by all. France has at the same time performed an act of salvation. The nation has for its preservation only the necessity of raising itself, and, besides that, to hold to two things: its determination, which is unconquerable; and its heroism, which has not its equal, and which has aroused the astonishment of the world during undeserved disasters. Soldiers, in the terrible crisis through which we are hastening, we have seized the helm, but with it we have not in any way sought party ends. We find ourselves not at the helm, but in battle. We are the Government of no party, but we are a Government of the National Defence. We have only one object, only one desire: the good of the fatherland by the army and the nation, which gathers around the glorious symbol which eighty years ago drove back Europe. To-day, as then, the name Republic means: Thorough concord between army and people for the defence of the fatherland.

"General Trochu,	Garnier-Pagés,
Emmanuel Arago,	Glais-Bizoin,
Crémieux,	Pelletan,
Jules Favre,	E. Picard,
Jules Ferry,	Rochefort,
Gambetta,	Jules Simon."

Jules Favre, as Minister of Foreign Affairs, notwithstanding the gloomy outlook in regard to the war, issued the following circular, which bears the appearance of expressing a courage and resolution which he could hardly have felt:

"The policy of France is peace, leaving Germany the master of her own destinies. The King of Prussia had said that he made war against the dynasty, and not against France; yet the dynasty is gone, and France is free, yet is this impious war continued. Will the King face this responsibility before the world and before history? France yields not one foot of soil, not a stone of a fortress. A shameless peace means the extermination of our cause and that of Europe. We are undismayed. The army is resolute and provided. Three hundred thousand combatants can hold Paris to the last. They can hold the city for three months, and conquer. If crushed, France will arise and avenge it. Let Europe know that the Ministry have no other aim or ambition than peace; but, war proving inevitable, we will continue the struggle, confident of the triumph of justice."

One of the first things which engaged the attention of the new Government, as being more pressing even than the reorganization of labor—the favorite hobby of French Republicans—was the necessity of some negotiations for peace. They had, unfortunately, committed themselves, at the outset, to the position that they would not relinquish a foot of territory or a stone of any fortress. Thus hampered, M. Jules Favre, while soliciting the good offices of the neutral powers to aid in his efforts for peace, sought and obtained an interview with the Prussian Premier, von Bismarck. He was met at once by a serious preliminary difficulty: on the supposition that he and Bismarck might agree upon some terms for peace, who was to guarantee their fulfilment? The Provisional Government was merely the rule of a few self-chosen persons, who had taken advantage of the confusion of the period to place themselves in power. They had no vote of the people to sustain them in their position, not even the sanction of the popular voice in the cities of France. They were wholly irresponsible—much more so, even, than the imperial dynasty they had assumed to displace. M. Favre urged that, if they could agree upon terms, they might be submitted to a popular vote within four or six weeks; but Bismarck replied, that this was asking too much; that, if their treaty should be rejected, and the Germans had remained inactive while waiting for the decision, they would be greatly worse off than to go on as they were now doing; they would, in fact, be thereby relinquishing almost the entire results of their victories thus far. He insisted, as the necessary condition of an armistice looking to peace-negotiations, that they must have material guarantees of the good faith of France, and named, among these, the possession of Metz and Strasbourg—both of which must soon capitulate at all events—and the temporary occupation of some one of the forts of the outer cordon around Paris. As M. Favre did not dare to accept these propositions, the interview terminated; Count von Bismarck intimating that any treaty of peace must include the surrender of the two fortresses of Metz and Strasbourg, and perhaps some other territory, together with a considerable money indemnity.

On M. Favre's return, the propositions of Count von Bismarck were indignantly rejected by his colleagues, and M. Favre was rebuked by them for even listening to them; and on the 24th of September the following was issued from Tours, to which city, since Paris was placed in a state of siege, the Government had migrated:

"*Proclamation to France:* Before the siege of Paris, Jules Favre desired to see Count von Bismarck, to know the intentions of the enemy. The following is the declaration of the enemy : Prussia wishes to continue the war in order to reduce France to a second-rate power. Prussia demands Alsace and Lorraine as far as Metz, by right of conquest. Prussia, before consenting to an armistice, demands the rendition of Strasbourg, Toul, and Mont Valerien. Paris is exasperated, and will rather bury herself beneath her ruins. To so insolent pretensions we can respond but by resistance to the last extremity. France accepts the struggle, and counts upon her children.

"CRÉMIEUX,
GLAIS-BIZOIN,
FOURICHON."

Meanwhile, von Bismarck addressed to each of the North-German representatives abroad the following Circular :

"MEAUX, Friday, September 16, 1870.

"Your Excellency is familiar with the Circular which M. Jules Favre has addressed to the foreign representatives of France in the name of the men at present holding power in Paris, and who call themselves '*Le Gouvernement de la Défense National.*' I have learned simultaneously that M. Thiers has entered upon a confidential mission to the foreign courts; and I may presume that he will endeavor, on the one side, to create a belief in the love for peace of the present Parisian Government, and, on the other side, will request the intervention of the neutral powers in favor of a peace which shall deprive Germany of the fruits of her victories, and for the purpose of preventing every basis of peace which would make the next attack of France on Germany more difficult.

"We cannot believe in the sincerity of the desire of the present Parisian Government to make peace so long as it continues, by its language and its acts at home, to excite the passions of the people and to increase the hatred and bitterness of a population stung by the sufferings of war, and to repudiate in advance every basis acceptable to Germany as unacceptable by France. By such a course it becomes impossible to make peace. The people should be prepared by calm words, and in terms corresponding to the gravity of the situation.

"If we are to believe that negotiations with us for peace are honestly intended, the demand that we should conclude an armistice without any guarantees for our conditions of peace could be meant seriously only on the supposition that we lack military or political judgment, or are indifferent to the interests of Germany. Moreover, the hope entertained by the present rulers in Paris of a diplomatic or material intervention of the neutral powers in favor of France, prevents the French nation from seeing the necessity of peace. When the French nation become convinced that, as they have wantonly conjured up the war alone, and Germany has had to fight it out alone, they must also settle their account with Germany alone, they will soon put an end to their resistance, now surely unavailing.

"It would be an act of cruelty to the French Government by the neutral powers to permit the Parisian Government to nourish among the people hopes of intervention that cannot be realized, and thereby lengthen the contest.

"We are far from any inclination to mix in the internal affairs of France. It is immaterial to us what kind of a Government the French people shall formally establish for themselves. The Government of the Emperor Napoleon has hitherto been the only one recognized by us. Our conditions of peace, with whatever Government legislating for the purpose we may have to negotiate with, are wholly independent of the question how or by whom the French nation is governed. They are prescribed to us by the nature of things, and by the law of self defence against a violent and hostile neighbor.

"The unanimous voice of the German Governments and the German people demands that Germany shall be protected by better boundaries than we have hitherto had against the dangers and violence we have experienced from all French Governments for centuries. So long as France remains in possession of Strasbourg and Metz, so long is its offensive strategically stronger than our defensive, so far as all South Germany and North Germany on the left bank of the Rhine are concerned. Strasbourg in the possession of France, is a gate wide open for attack on South Germany. In the hands of Germany, Strasbourg and Metz obtain a defensive character.

"In more than twenty wars we have never been the aggressors of France; and we demand of the latter nothing else than our safety in our own land, so often threatened by it. France, on the other hand, will regard any peace that may be made now as an armistice only, and, in order to avenge the present defeat, will attack us in the same quarrelsome and wanton manner as this year, as soon as it feels strong enough in its own resources or in foreign alliances.

"In rendering it difficult for France, from whose initiative alone hitherto the disturbances of Europe have resulted, to resume the offensive, we at the same time act in the interest of Europe, which is that of peace. From Germany no disturbance of the European peace is to be feared. Although France had been trying to force the war upon us for four years, we, by our care, and by restraining the feelings of our national self-respect, so incessantly outraged by France, had prevented its occurrence. We mean now, for our future safety, to demand the price of our mighty efforts. We shall demand only that which we must have for our defence. Nobody will be able to accuse us of want of moderation, if we insist upon this just and equitable demand.

"Your Excellency will make these views your own, and advocate them in discussions.   BISMARCK."

STRASBURG CATHEDRAL WITH NEIGHBORING BUILDINGS IN FLAMES.

During this period of ineffectual negotiation the Germans were by no means inactive. The First, Third, and Fourth Armies, largely reënforced, pressed on toward Paris, and on the 20th of September the investment of Paris was complete. On the 23d, Toul surrendered, and Strasbourg followed on the 27th of September. The garrison of Toul was very small (only about 2,350), but the fortifications were of such strength that they had endured a long siege. The amount of war-material surrendered was large. The garrison of Strasbourg numbered 17,000 men and 451 officers, aside from the large population of the city.

The events of the 1st and 2d of September, followed by the revolution of the 4th of September, seemed to have so confused and stunned the minds of the French leaders and people as to render them incapable of any judicious action. Even General Trochu, the only one of their leaders who had any clear idea of their difficulties and dangers, confined his efforts to fortifying Paris, regardless of the fact that, with a population of two millions in the city, and an army of 430,000 cut off by the siege from any active movements, a capitulation must be inevitable within a short period—not more, certainly, than ten or twelve weeks—and that capitulation would involve the surrender of this great army, and the virtual annihilation of the entire French military power. Of the entire armed force which France had been able to put into the field, or could in any emergency bring into service, estimating it in round numbers at 1,000,000 men—though that number was never under arms at once during the war—not less than 150,000 were *hors de combat* from sickness, wounds, or death on the field of battle. 60,000 men had been taken prisoners previous to the surrender at Sedan; over 100,000 were made prisoners there; nearly 30,000 at Metz, in the battles of August 31st and September 1st, and the subsequent capitulations of Toul, Strasbourg, &c. More than 200,000 more were shut up in Metz and eventually surrendered; and these 430,000 being withdrawn from active service, there would be left, in the event of their surrender, but a mere handful of troops to defend France against the invader. It seems never to have occurred to these leaders that 150,000, or 200,000 men at the utmost, could defend Paris better than twice that number, and that, with fewer mouths to feed, they could protract the siege proportionally longer; while their armies in the field might inflict such damage upon the enemy as to compel him to raise the siege of the capital. But the greatest misfortune which afflicted France during the whole of this war was the want of honest, capable, and efficient leaders. The people were brave and patriotic, though, except the regular army, they were unskilled in the use of arms; but their leaders, when not traitors—as some of them undoubtedly were—lacked knowledge of military affairs, and capacity for the important and responsible positions in which they were placed. The siege of Paris illustrated this most painfully. With two millions of people shut up in that great city, the accumulated supplies dealt out by weight and measure, and their enemy carefully guarding every avenue by which further supplies could reach them, the great mass of the population seem to have been turbulent and troublesome, improvident, and insensible to the dangers which threatened them. Crime was rampant, riots frequent, and the sorties to drive back the foe and raise the siege infrequent and ineffective. At the same time, their tendency to boasting and exaggeration seemed constantly to increase. Every little sortie, however badly conducted or speedily repulsed, was magnified into a wonderful victory. They had slain 15,000, 20,000, or 30,000 Prussians, with a loss of only a hundred or two themselves;—the Prussians had become disgusted, and were about to abandon the siege; indeed, they had already abandoned it, and the way was now open to all parts of France;—the German leaders were wounded or killed in these sanguinary battles, or had died of typhoid fever, or become maniacs from remorse;—von Moltke, Prince Friedrich Karl, the Crown-Prince of Prussia, the Crown-Prince of Saxony, the Duke of Mecklenburg-Schwerin, and General Manteuffel, were all reported as dead, and the King of Prussia had gone back to Berlin in a straight-jacket, under the care of Count von Bismarck. If it had been only idle, sensational papers which had propagated these silly stories it would have been bad enough, for the immense crop of falsehoods would have indicated that the people were ready to be deceived; but it was their leaders—such men as Gambetta, Crémieux, Glais-Bizoin, and Ferry—who reiterated these falsehoods, and, in default of any foundation upon which to base them, fabricated, in their proclamations, the details of conflicts and victories which were entirely fictitious.

The sympathy of the friends of free and liberal government were at first heartily with the newly-proclaimed French Republic; they hoped to see a sound Government of the people, for the people, spring from the corruption, rottenness, and decay of the Empire; but a Government founded upon falsehood, and maintaining its hold upon the people solely by the grossest misrepresentations, whatever may be the motive of those falsehoods, soon loses its hold on the confidence or sympathy of right-thinking men of all nations. For the people they may feel the tenderest concern; for their leaders, their only emotion can be that of disgust.

When the German armies were about closing around the doomed city, a part of the Provisional Government removed to Tours, and there exercised their functions. At first it was only Crémieux, Glais-Bizoin, and Fourichon who thus attempted to govern from Tours. Keratry subsequently joined them, and Gambetta, after remaining awhile in Paris, finally escaped from that city in a balloon. Trochu, Favre, Ferry, Rochefort, and one or two more less prominent, remained in Paris. The Tours section postponed the election of a Constituent Assembly indefinitely, and, while making the most frantic appeals to the European powers to intervene and secure peace, constantly proclaimed that they would not give up one foot of territory or one stone of a fortress.

Great efforts were made to raise an army in the south of France, to be called the Army of the Loire. Only undisciplined and raw recruits were available, with few exceptions, for this army, but it was expected to do great things. General Bourbaki, who, by an adroit manœuvre, had succeeded in getting out of Metz before its surrender, was to have command of it, and its numbers were variously stated at from 100,000 to 150,000 men. At length, in the last days of October, General Bourbaki assumed command; but, finding that it had at no time mustered over 60,000 men, and that these were the rawest of recruits and constantly deserting, he offered to resign, but was not allowed to do so. Garibaldi, the Italian hero, was called to command one of the armies of the Republic, and, though crippled and suffering from the still unhealed wounds of Mentana, he came, only to find that all his efforts would be neutralized by the jealousies of Gambetta and his associates, and that not more than 5,000 men—not a quarter of them well equipped—could be allowed to gather around his standard. The *Franc-tireurs*, a class of guerillas or brigands, formed themselves into bands of considerable numbers, and occasionally raided on the German lines; but finding that, under the wholesome though rigid regulations of King Wilhelm, they were liable to be marched immediately to execution when caught, they very generally preferred the safer if less honorable plan of plundering their own countrymen.

There were, indeed, occasional sorties of some magnitude both from Paris and Metz; but these seldom rose to the dignity of battles, and were invariably unsuccessful, though one or two of them inflicted considerable loss upon the Germans, but a much

THE SHARPSHOOTERS OF THE VOSGES LYING IN AMBUSCADE AND
ATTACKING A GERMAN CONVOY.

greater one on themselves. The most noteworthy of these at Paris was one of the 19th of September, and another early in October. Neither seem to have been in any respect a success for the French, though both were vaunted as such. The affair of the 19th of September originated in an attack made by General Ducrôt, who, in violation of his parole of honor given at Gravelotte, had taken a command again in the French army, upon the Germans who were occupying the woods of Meudon, Clamart, Chatenay, Fontenai, and Choisy, a line of six miles on the south of Paris. Ducrôt had about 40,000 men, and occupied a strong position at Villejuif, and the heights of Chatillon and Clamart; but, attacking rashly, and without knowing what force was in his front, he threw himself against the corps of Vogel de Falkenstein, over 100,000 strong; and though a part of his troops fought well, others were panic-stricken, and, in the end, he was soundly whipped, and lost his fortified position—a serious disaster to the French cause. Subsequent to this, there were three or four successive sorties made in the same direction by the French, but their only result was that, after considerable severe fighting and heavy losses, the Germans each time gained some ground they had not previously held.

The Germans were meanwhile overrunning and capturing other cities of France. Epinal, Etampes, Angerville, Orleans, a large and important city on the Loire, the granary of France, Gien, and later Dijon, were taken and held by their troops, and Tours, Lyons, and Marseilles threatened.

The new troops raised outside of Paris after its isolation were raw recruits, a small proportion (the Gardes Mobiles) capable, with sufficient training and good officers, of making very superior troops, but, under the circumstances, entirely unable to cope with the thoroughly-trained German soldiers, commanded as they were by the best military talent of the century. The greater part of the French levy, whether known as National Guards

Partisans, *Franc-tireurs*, or by other titles, were utterly incapable, and either ran or surrendered after the first fire. Knowing nothing of the use of fire-arms (since Napoleon III had prohibited their use, except in the regular army), they had no confidence in themselves, and could not be made to fight, except where the objects of their assault were unarmed.

The contempt naturally felt by the German soldiers for such foes is well illustrated by an official report of a commission sent by the King of Prussia to ascertain the exact state of affairs in the eastern and central provinces of France, made at Versailles, October 10th, 1870:

"Recent events throw light upon the forces at the disposal of the French Government over and above those enclosed in Paris, Metz, and some other fortresses. Several marches southwest of Strasbourg the *corps d'armée*, under the command of General von Werder, fell in with a body of troops whose composition proved that the production of fresh regular forces need be no longer feared in France. It had been organized some weeks since at Langres, and belonged to the Southern Army. The recruits had come from the Haute-Marne, Saône, and Yonne, Côte d'Or, and the country near Dijon. If at all capable of playing a part in the war, it ought to have marched north, and endeavored to relieve Strasbourg while there was time; but consisting chiefly of Mobiles, it could not venture on so independent a step, and contented itself with troubling our southern communications between Alsace and Paris. Its greatest exploit was an attempt to surprise Nancy, which, however, was so easily foiled by one Landwehr battalion that we could not even boast of having had an engagement. Such were the troops General von Werder (with General von Dagenfeld under him as chief of the Baden Division) attacked near Epinal. He put 2,000 *hors de combat*, ourselves losing less than one eighth of this number. This has probably disposed of the Southern branch of the French army fo a little while.

"Further west the Bavarian First Corps, reënforced by one Prussian division of infantry and two Prussian cavalry divisions, under the command of General von der Tann, assumed an energetic offensive against the hosts congregating on the Loire. Some time ago, when we had completed the investment of Paris, two Prussian cavalry divisions, among them Prince Albrecht's, had been despatched to patrol the country south of the capital, in the direction of Etampes, Pithiviers, and Orleans. They had had many skirmishes with Francs-Tireurs, who abounded in that neighborhood, and though unable to resist our attack in any one single instance, yet clung to their hiding-places in the woods, and were apparently intent upon organizing a guerilla war. These Francs-Tireurs came from the Seine and the Southern Departments.

"When our cavalry had penetrated as far as the forest of Orleans, the Crown-Prince ordered General von der Tann, who had his headquarters at Longjumeau, to proceed in the direction of that city, and further on to Tours, the seat of the Provisional Government. With General von der Tann's Corps marched the Twenty-second Division of the Eleventh Prussian Corps, as also our two cavalry divisions. This force arrived on the 7th at Arpajon, and on the 8th reached Etampes, by Etréchy. At Etampes the van were engaged by the enemy, who, seemingly showing fight, caused our troops to prepare for battle. Our infantry marched through a ravine in the direction of Angerville, with cavalry on both sides. Had the enemy remained in their former position we should have outflanked and might have seriously injured them by this movement; but on getting near Angerville, where the defile widens into a vast plateau, we found the French had retreated on learning the approach of a considerable force. Only the village of Monnerville, south of Etampes and Angerville, was still occupied by a small rear-guard. On this occasion we became acquainted with a new description of troops called Partisans, forming a sort of body-guard to the Government at Tours. In the account-books they had with them their pay and other emoluments from the Republican authorities were accurately stated. They were mostly men above 40, or youngsters between 16 and 18, those between these two extremes having been previously drafted into the Mobiles. Directly we got to Etampes and Angerville the Partisans remaining in those towns were either taken prisoners or ran away. They were, indeed, unable to defend themselves, being totally ignorant of every thing military, and, moreover, armed with Minié rifles, which cannot compete with modern weapons. In reply to our questions, they said they knew nothing of the service, and altogether represented their situation as pitiable. The peasants would not give them any thing to eat, nor even direct them how to find their way across the country. The fear of the Germans was so universal in those parts that every body shunned intercourse with the indigenous troops. The costume of the Partisans consists in a short black coat, black trowsers, gaiters, and a red sash round the waist. They wear hats with broad brims, those of the captains being about four times as large as those worn by the privates. The Commander-in-Chief of the body taken prisoners at Angerville was a private gentleman from Nantes. Most of them had the words *Partisans de Gers* on their hats. The Department de Gers being 400 miles south of Paris, and only 150 miles north of the Pyrenees, their presence in the Orleannois would seem to prove that the central Departments are already drained of most of the people that can be induced to join.

"Since then Orleans has been taken by General von der Tann. It is one of the wealthiest cities in France. The region north of it, the so-called Beauce, is certainly the most fertile district we have as yet entered. It provides Paris with enormous quantities of excellent wheat, ground by the steam and water mills in the province. It also abounds in oats (which will be a great acquisition for our cavalry), and produces grapes and every variety of fruit in such plenty that, in addition to supplying Paris, its choice articles are exported to foreign countries. The possession of the Beauce will sensibly diminish the number of our provision trains from Germany.

"The occupation of Orleans is also important from a strategical point of view. Situate on the right bank of the Loire, and being the point of junction for the Central Railway and the lines from Nantes, Bordeaux, and Toulouse, it protects our army from attack from the south, and all but prevents our enemies in the North holding communications with the South. By blowing up a single arch of the two magnificent bridges over the Loire, each of which has cost 2,000,000f., we render it difficult for a Southern enemy to penetrate North, the next two bridges at Jargeau and Beaugency not being strong enough for artillery to pass over. Gien, higher up the river, is already ours, and the Sologne, which is the name of the country lower down, beyond Blois, is so barren and destitute of roads that it serves as a natural safeguard from that side. Orleans is known for the pacific disposition of its inhabitants, and has large barracks and other buildings which will be useful should the campaign be prolonged."

An added difficulty which the French Provisional Government had to encounter, was found in the diversity of opinion among the people, and the want of cordiality which existed toward them in many parts of France. In Marseilles and Lyons, the Red Republicans were largely in the majority, and organized a provisional government of their own, whose object was to proclaim the doctrines of the Revolution of 1791. "Down with the aristocrats!" was their cry; and these ruffians were disposed to seize the reins of government, and rule *révolutionnairement*. A fear of the German troops, and a disposition to conciliate them by good treatment and ready surrender, prevailed very widely among the smaller towns and villages of France, and it was not easy to raise volunteers for the army in any section to which they had penetrated.

The tract, sixty or seventy miles in width, and extending from the Rhine to Paris, over which the conquering armies had passed, was thoroughly stripped of food for man and beast, and the horrors of famine were felt throughout the whole district early in October.

On the 29th of October Metz was surrendered by Marshal Bazaine, although it was said there was provision sufficient for the army for four months longer. Yet, as a capitulation must come sooner or later, and there was no hope of the raising of the siege, it was perhaps humane and wise to give up before starvation came. By this capitulation an army and garrison of 173,000 soldiers, and over 20,000 sick and wounded, were surrendered, the details being as follows :

"67 infantry regiments; 13 battalions of Foot Chasseurs; 18 fort and dépôt battalions; 36 cavalry regiments, namely: 10 of Cuirassiers, 1 of Guides, 11 of Dragoons, 2 of Lancers, 3 of Hussars, 6 of Chasseurs, and 3 of Chasseurs d'Afrique; also, 6 dépôt squadrons; 115 field batteries; 17 batteries of mitrailleuses; 69 eagles belonging to infantry, 2 of which were captured at Mars-la-Tour, and 36 eagles belonging to cavalry.

"Including the garrison surrendered, the army originally comprised 221 battalions of infantry and 162 squadrons of horse. The original numerical strength was 210,000 infantry, 21,450 cavalry, 690 guns, and 102 mitrailleuses.

"Besides the foregoing, there were three marshals—Bazaine, Canrobert, and Lebœuf; three corps commanders—Frossard, De Caen, and l'Admirault; 40 division generals; 100 brigadier-generals; of sound prisoners, 90,000 sent to North Germany, and 50,000 sent South; the sick and wounded being distributed in the same proportion."

Thirty-five thousand had perished in the siege and the sorties made by the besieged, not including those who were slain in the three battles of August 14th, 16th, and 18th.

The intelligence of this surrender was received at Tours by the Provisional Government with great rage and indignation. Marshal Bazaine was denounced as a traitor, and the resolve to continue the resistance unflinchingly was duly promulgated in the following proclamation:

"FRENCH REPUBLIC.
"LIBERTY—EQUALITY—FRATERNITY.
"PROCLAMATION TO THE FRENCH PEOPLE.

"FRENCHMEN: Raise your spirits and resolution to the fearful height of the perils which have broken upon the country. It still depends on us to mount above misfortune, and show the world how great a people may be who are resolved not to perish, and whose courage increases in the midst of calamity.

"Metz has capitulated. A General, upon whom France counted, even after Mexico, has just taken away (*vient d'enlever*) from the country, in its danger, more than a hundred thousand of its defenders. Marshal Bazaine has betrayed us. He has made himself the agent of the Man of Sedan and the accomplice of the invader; and, regardless of the honor of the army of which he had charge, he has surrendered, without even making a last effort, a hundred and twenty thousand fighting men, twenty thousand wounded, guns, cannon, colors, and the strongest citadel of France—Metz-Virgen; but for him, to the contamination of the foreigner, such a crime is above even the punishments of Justice!

"Meanwhile, Frenchmen, measure the depths of the abyss into which the Empire has precipitated you. For twenty years France submitted to this corrupting power, which extinguished in her the springs of greatness and of life. The army of France, stripped of its national character, became, without knowing it, an instrument of tyranny and of servitude, and is swallowed up, in spite of the heroism of the soldiers, by the treason of their chiefs.

"In the disasters of the country in less than five months, 250,000 men have been delivered over to the enemy—a sinister sequel to the military *coup de main* of December.

"It is time for us to reassert ourselves, citizens; and, under the ægis of the Republic which we have determined not to allow to capitulate, within or without, to seek, in the extremity even of our misfortune, the renovation of our political and social morality and manhood.

"However tried by disaster, let us be found neither panic-stricken nor hesitating. Let it be seen that we are ready for the last sacrifices; and, in the face of enemies whom every thing favors, let us swear never to give up so long as there remains an inch of sacred soil under the soles of our feet. Let us hold firmly the glorious banner of the French Revolution. Our cause is that of Justice and of Right. Europe sees it; Europe feels it. In the presence of so many unmerited misfortunes, Europe, of her own accord, receiving from us neither invitation nor encouragement, is moved, and begins to act. No illusion is now left. Let us no longer languish or grow weak, and let us prove by our acts that we can ourselves maintain honor, independence, integrity—all that makes a country proud and free.

"Long live the Republic, one and indivisible!

"Crémieux,
Glais-Bizoin,
Gambetta."

This proclamation had the merit of being more truthful than those which had preceded it, but it did not come up to the full measure of the misfortunes of France. At this very time over three hundred thousand French soldiers were prisoners in Germany; one hundred and fifty thousand more had perished by sickness, or had fallen on the field of battle; the regular army, except a few regiments on garrison duty, or who had but just returned from Algeria, was completely destroyed; the more than four hundred thousand troops shut up in Paris were composed of National Guards, Guard Mobiles, and other raw recruits, not only wholly undisciplined, but completely ignorant of the use of fire-arms, having been forbidden to possess them during the whole of Louis Napoleon's administration. The armies which Gambetta was trying to raise and arm in the provinces were equally undisciplined and ignorant. There were no generals of known reputation left except Trochu and Ducrot, who were both in Paris, and Bourbaki in the Army of the Loire, whose fidelity to the Provisional Government was probably unjustly doubted. The energy and executive ability which Gambetta had displayed, and which had enabled him to improvise large armies, was very creditable to him under the circumstances in which he was placed; but if he permitted himself any moments of sound reflection, he must have seen that his task was a hopeless one. The errors already committed in the defense of Paris rendered its surrender at no very distant day inevitable; and the irregular and undisciplined troops he had collected and could collect were not only incompetent to compel the raising of the siege of Paris, but were unable to withstand the thoroughly trained and disciplined German troops whenever they met in anything like equal numbers. There was nothing to hope for in the future, except a peace made on terms which would be more severe and distressing with each added day of resistance. Meanwhile the winter months were drawing on, and the crops, unusually scanty as they were, had been in many sections either harvested, or seized by the invading forces; the French peasantry, never too provident, and living almost from hand to mouth, were famishing, and looked forward in grim despair to a winter of famine and death.

Already, too, were the hoarse mutterings of another revolution heard from various quarters, and the Provisional Government found its authority denied, and its orders unheeded in Southern France.

Yet the pride and conceit of the French leaders and of the French people was unsubdued. Though almost everywhere defeated, they insisted that every reverse was a victory, or, at the most, but a blessing in disguise; and until they were sufficiently humbled to own their weakness, there seemed no hope of their relief.

Alas, poor France! how bitterly dost thou suffer for all thy sins in the past! The blood of thousands of martyrs slain by thy kings; the terrible disorder and anarchy of thy great Revolution; the greed and vain-glory which led thee to crave and take, whenever thou hadst the opportunity, the lands and spoil of other nations; the insane love of glory which has made thee willing to plunge into war on the slightest pretexts, and thus rendered thee the terror of all thy neighbors; and, above all, the licentiousness and corruption which have eaten out thy life, and rendered thee seemingly only fit for destruction—all these thy crimes rise up in judgment against thee, and cry for vengeance on thy head. But if thou wilt be wise, there is still hope for thee. When thou hast passed through the furnace, and thy dross is thoroughly purged from thee, there shall arise a new France, purer and better than the old, and take its place among the sisterhood of nations, a regenerated and truly great people.

CHAPTER XI.

IN continuing our narrative of the events of the war after the surrender of Metz, we must confine ourselves mainly to two topics: the siege of Paris, with its sorties and final surrender; and the efforts made in the provinces to compel the raising of the siege of Paris, and also to defeat the Germans in other parts of France. Though distinct from each other, these two topics were so connected that they can only be considered properly together.

We have already detailed the approach of the German armies to Paris, their partial investment of the city on the 15th of September, and the more complete beleaguering of it by the close of the month; but one or two items in relation to this investment are worthy of notice, though ante-dating the capitulation of Metz.

The German armies first deployed, about the middle of September, before the northeastern defences of Paris. This part of the line of investment was established without serious opposition, greatly to the surprise of the Germans, who anticipated resistance at the passage of the Seine. Trochu's troops were certainly unfit at this time to be trusted in battle, and could not have prevented the investment, though they might have retarded it under a skilful general, without jeopardy to themselves. If it was wise, however, not to oppose the passage of the Seine with such troops, it was madness to attempt, as Trochu did four days later, the reoccupation of the elevated country south of Paris. The extension of the German line from the Seine to Versailles in front of the southern line of forts, brought on an engagement (September 19th) known to the French as the Battle of Chatillon, and to the Germans as that of Sceaux. Lying between the two towns thus named, and commanding the country round, and the French forts in its front, is a range of hills known as the Heights of Sceaux; and it was for the possession of this position that the battle was fought. General Trochu, with apparently culpable negligence, had failed to seize and fortify this important position.

He had declared his intention to remain strictly on the defensive, until he could arm, organize, and discipline the immense mass of *Gardes Mobiles*, marines, and volunteers who had crowded into Paris for its defence. He doubtless had also some indefinite hope of aid coming from the army which had already begun to form on the Loire at Orleans; but dependence on this force, or on his own unskilled soldiery, was, as events proved, mistaken confidence. But after resolving that nothing remained to him but to hold the defensive, Trochu was weak enough to be overruled by the advice of subordinates and the wishes of his associates in the Government, and consented to make an effort to retake the Heights, which he had permitted the Germans to seize without opposition. If it was folly not to have secured them before the approach of the Germans, it was insanity to attempt to recapture them with a single corps of half-drilled, untried troops. The unwisely-ordered attack was badly directed and tardily conducted; the troops displayed great gallantry, but they also displayed their want of discipline, and their efforts naturally resulted in positive repulse.

The movements of the Germans in strengthening their lines south and west of the city more than once induced Trochu to make reconnoissances, which in one or two instances resulted in brief yet serious engagements. On September 30th two columns, operating from Chatillon and St. Cloud, advanced to develop changes which had been made in the investing line in front of

NEW MITRAILLEUR, EMPLOYED BY VON DER TANN, AT ORLEANS.

these positions, but they had hardly deployed before overwhelming numbers of Germans were advancing from their bivouacks to meet them. The French were driven back at both points, and, being flanked on their right by the overlapping lines of the Germans, suffered severe losses. The only result of the affair was to reveal precisely what the French did not wish assured them—that the Germans were daily transferring forces from the east to the west side of Paris, and preparing to bombard the city on its weakest front. By these movements, masked by the Heights of Sceaux and their own strongly maintained lines, the Germans finally disposed their great forces around the city in the order named on our map, which illustrates the operations of the siege.

The Saxon Corps, a brave body of troops, but weakened by their heavy losses in the battles around Metz, were first in order on the north-northeast of the city, overlooking La Briche, St. Denis, and the Fort de L'Est. Next in order, northeast of the city, were the Prussian Guards, the finest corps of the Prussian Army, having in their front the Fort of Aubervilliers; next, at the east and southeast, lay the Würtemburg Division, the troops which distinguished themselves at Sedan. Between these and the city were the strong forts of Romainville, Denois, Rosny, and Nogent. South of the city, and to the south-southeast, lay the small Fifteenth Prussian Corps, the Sixth Prussian, and the Second Bavarian Corps, and along the front of this line bristled some of the strongest forts of the Parisian defences—Charenton, Ivry, Bicetre, Montrouge, Vanvres, and Issy. At the southwest and west the Eleventh and Fifth Prussian Corps held strongly fortified lines, having the great fortress of Mont St. Valerien, occupying a neck of land formed by a bend of the Seine, in their front; while the Fourth Prussian Corps extended from the opposite bank of the Seine to Pierrefitte, where it joined the Saxon Corps.

The circle thus completed about Paris was never broken; but it must not be supposed that the whole army was stretched out along the positions we have named. From the five or six pickets who watched from the entrenched posts nearest the enemy the every movement of the besieged, to the last cantonment of the corps in the rear, fully five miles of ground intervened. The picket posts were all shell-proof earthworks, hardly larger than the "gopher holes" of our own troops, but much more elaborately built. Behind each of these posts their reserves of a company were posted in farm-houses; behind these a regiment in some convenient hamlet or chateau; behind these, again, a brigade cantoned in the comfortable dwellings of the nearest village; further still to the rear a division lived in camps, or chateaus, or towns; and, last of all, distant, yet not so far away that it could not promptly deploy to aid the advance when attacked, were the corps in possession of the larger cities, as Versailles, St. Germain, &c. This disposition gave the Germans every facility for concentrating immense numbers on any threatened point to repulse the sorties of the French. The system on which the Germans conducted the siege was different in many respects from that in vogue during our own war. The advanced posts, where small bodies of men kept vigilant lookout on the proceedings of the French in the city and forts, were strongly entrenched with the design of being held until supports could come up. In their immediate rear larger forces were posted in camps, or stationed in convenient farm-houses, villas, and chateaus; while divisions and corps, still further to the rear, were cantoned in the numerous villages and towns which form suburban Paris. With houses to live in, warm beds and rich linen to rest upon, wine in the cellars, fruit on the trees, and vegetables from near and distant gardens of the occupied departments, the besiegers had little to dread from delay, and could afford to wait until famine forced capitulation. Strong as this line was known to be, the French did not despair of breaking through it; and while the Germans prepared for the bombardment, their enemy made two or three fruitless efforts to raise the siege and escape. The most of these were made against Trochu's judgment, and, badly supported and worse directed, failed ignominiously. The first of any note, made on October 28th against Le Bourget, on the north of Paris, appears to have been permitted as a sort of concession to a corps of Paris volunteers, led by noted Communists. It is significant of the condition of Paris at this time, that, on its failure and the repulse of their corps with heavy loss, Communists of Paris invaded the Hotel de Ville, captured Trochu and the members of the Government, proclaimed a new Republic, and for several hours were in possession of the Government. A corps of Mobiles happily arriving, thrust the new leaders out, and restored the Committee of National Defense, else France would have been again revolutionized by a Paris mob.

But while this siege was thus daily enclosing more firmly in its iron gripe the doomed city, what was doing in the provinces in the way of effort to compel the German King to raise the siege? Justice requires the acknowledgment that their exertions were great; and if success had been possible with their undisciplined troops, the great obstacles in the way of organization, and the scarcity of able and efficient generals, they would have gone far toward achieving it. After the failure of M. Favre's efforts to obtain an armistice and negotiate a treaty of peace on terms which he and his associates considered admissible, no further efforts were made in that direction for some months, and all the energies of the fiery, but not always wise, Gambetta, were turned toward the organization of new armies, and, as his proclamations phrased it, hurling back the invader. We have already mentioned his escape with Fourichon, Cremieux, and Glais-Bizoin from Paris in a balloon, and the establishment of one branch of the Government at Tours. He had no sooner arrived there than he undertook the work of rallying and organizing and training forces for the purpose of taking the field against the Germans. He inspired the people with his own enthusiasm, and, by sheer force of personal character and energy, he brought comparative order out of chaos, and organized three great armies, great in numbers, but still fatally and necessarily lacking in that discipline which was indispensable for success. Camps were established at Lille and Rouen in the north, at Conlie in the west, and at Orleans, Bordeaux, and Lyons in the south; and to these flocked the recruits who had not, undirected and unwisely, huddled in Paris. The formation of the most distant of those camps was not interrupted by the Germans, whose main forces were still engaged before Metz and Paris; but General von Moltke seems early to have contemplated a dispersal of the forces which were concentrating, with more daring than discretion, at Orleans, only forty miles in the rear of his position south of Paris. A small army, detached from the investing force at Versailles, under General von der Tann, advanced upon Orleans on October 10th, surprising the French advance at Artenay on that day, and driving the main body of the Army of the Loire out of Orleans on the following day. Beyond Orleans, von der Tann durst not venture, and the result of the expedition was simply to push the recruiting French a little further south. At the same time, von der Tann's right became exposed to attack from the troops forming at Conlie, behind Le Mans, and thus he was placed on the defensive, in a position which demanded his utmost vigilance. He was glad to remain quiet until a month later, when the surrender of Metz gave him promise of large reënforcements from the disengaged army of Prince Friedrich Karl. No sooner had this event occurred (October 26th), than von Moltke resolved on the dispersal of the French armies in the provinces. Von Steinmetz's old army, recruited to 75,000

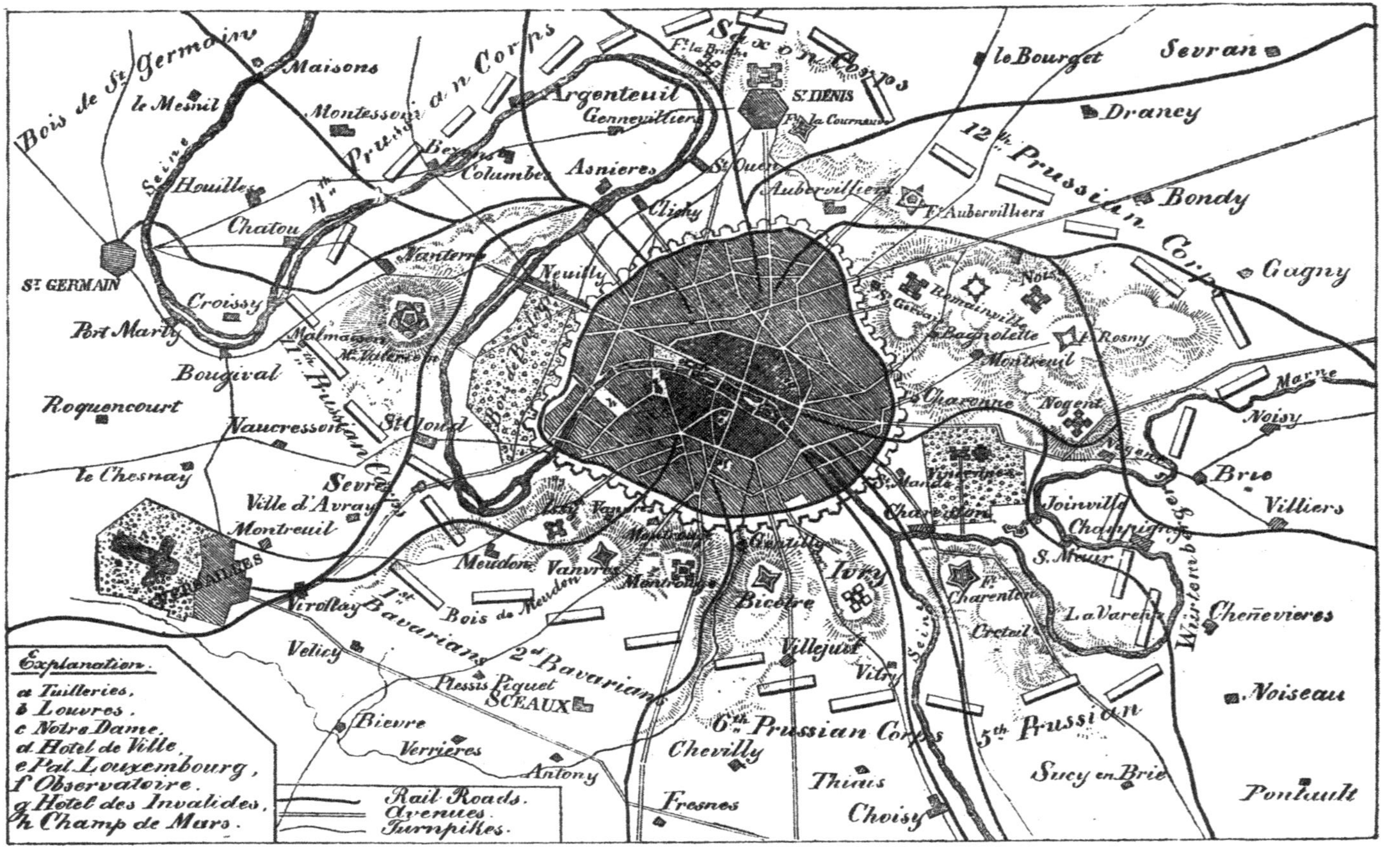

PARIS AND ITS DEFENSES, SHOWING ALSO THE LOCATION OF THE GERMAN ARMIES.

or 80,000 men, was given to General Manteuffel, and directed against the camps about Lille and Rouen, and the fortified positions in the north. Prince Friedrich Karl, with the old Second Army, was pushed westward, with orders to disperse d'Aurelles de Paladines below Orleans, and Chanzy at Conlie or Le Mans. Von Werder was already forcing the advance-guard of the Lyons Army further southward, and debouching from the Vosges into the Saone Valley.

The French Minister of War at Tours no sooner heard of the surrender of Metz, than he resolved (after absurdly stopping in his rage to outlaw Bazaine and set a price on his head) to throw the Army of the Loire in overwhelming force on von der Tann before Prince Friedrich Karl could come up, hoping to crush him, and perhaps reach the rear of the investing line about Paris. Some sort of unity of action appears to have been secured by communication with Trochu by carrier-pigeons, but all plans failed. Chanzy and d'Aurelles were hastily concentrated for the attack, the former making also a flank movement from Le Mans to the rear of von der Tann's position at Artenay. But the German was too well aware of the danger menacing him to relax in vigilance. Constant reconnoissances of his cavalry warned him of the French movement; and, though forced to abandon Orleans on November 9–10, he did not yield without a struggle, which delayed the French advance, and hastened the approach of Prince Friedrich Karl from Metz.

Anything like victory had been so unusual with the French in the progress of the war hitherto, that their success in driving von der Tann out of Orleans almost crazed them. The German General had yielded, not without a stubborn resistance, to a force more than three times that of his own army, and by his resistance had effected a delay which enured to the benefit of the German army subsequently; but the losses he sustained were far less than the French journals, with their extraordinary talent for exaggeration, represented. Such announcements as the following, in a battle where the entire loss in killed, wounded, and prisoners could not have exceeded 2,000, and by the defeated party was stated at but half that number, are even more absurd than some of the glowing despatches of our own war:

"The Prussians have lost over 10,000 men in killed and wounded, and 1,800 prisoners, in the battles around Orleans, and are retreating toward Chartres and Etampes. A large number of guns, thrown away by the enemy, have been picked up, and distributed among the National Guards at Orleans. The entire Army of the Loire is advancing."

The last item, like much of the rest of the despatch, was entirely false. The entire Army of the Loire were not advancing, and, with their knowledge of the speedy approach of the army of Prince Friedrich Karl, did not dare to advance.

In justice to General d'Aurelles de Paladines, who, in consequence of this victory, was exalted from comparative obscurity into one of the greatest commanders of modern times, it should be said that he was not so much disposed to over-estimate his success. His despatch to Minister Gambetta was as follows:

"We have taken possession of the city of Orleans, after a fight which has lasted two days. Our aggregate losses in killed and wounded do not reach 2,000, while those of the enemy are much larger.

"We have made more than 1,000 prisoners thus far, and are continually adding to them as we follow up the fleeing enemy. Among the property captured are two cannon of the Prussian model, twenty ammunition-wagons, and a great number of vans and provision-wagons. The hottest of the fight took place around Coulmier, on Wednesday, the 9th. Notwithstanding the bad weather and other unfavorable circumstances, the *élan* displayed by the troops was remarkable."

His congratulatory order to his officers is in still better taste

"The action of yesterday was a glorious one for our army. Every position of the enemy was vigorously carried, and the enemy is now retreating. I have informed the Government of your conduct, and am instructed to return to you their thanks for your victory. Amid the disasters in which France is plunged, her eyes are upon you, and she counts upon your courage. Let us all make every effort, in order that this hope may not be mistaken.

"D'Aurelles de Paladines,
"*Commander-in-Chief.*
"General Headquarters, *November* 10, 1870."

M. Gambetta, with that rashness which often leads impulsive and energetic men to jump at conclusions, decided that in General d'Aurelles de Paladines he had found the commanding officer he had sought amid the number whom he had been obliged to reject, and gave him full control of his newly-organized and not thoroughly-disciplined Army of the Loire. The other armies of the provinces were commanded by General Bourbaki, the only one of Napoleon's old generals, except Ducrot, who was in Paris, who was not a prisoner. General Chanzy was at this time second in command to General d'Aurelles. He was another new man, but apparently a good officer, if his troops and his subordinate officers could have been depended upon. In the north of France another army, likewise raw recruits, was put under the command of General Faidherbe, an officer of considerable ability, who had been for some years Governor of the French colony of Senegal, on the west coast of Africa.

The German General von der Tann fell back from Orleans to Toury, and subsequently to Angerville, in the direction from whence he expected reënforcements from the army of Prince Friedrich Karl; but he showed no panic and no disposition to avoid attacks.

Meanwhile, M. Gambetta had issued a proclamation to the army, announcing that the Government expected the deliverance of the capital from its valor. But, greatly to his surprise, General d'Aurelles de Paladines did not follow up his success so promptly as had been expected. Day after day he remained near Orleans in a state of inactivity which the Government could not account for. He saw, more clearly than the Minister of War did or could, that his success had been merely temporary, and in some sense accidental, and that a forward movement, until Orleans had been put in a state of complete defense, would, with his imperfectly-trained and not very steady troops, imperil what he had gained. During these two or three weeks, then, he had been exerting himself to the utmost to put the city into such a condition of defense that it might be able to repel any attacks of a considerably superior force. He had formed an entrenched camp before the city, and fortified it with ninety-five naval guns manned by seamen from Cherbourg. Behind this defense he believed his army might hold its ground under any circumstances, while drawing reserves and supplies from the country behind the Loire.

But while he was making these preparations for defense, as early as the middle of November, General von Voight Rhetz, commander of the Tenth German Corps, part of the army of Prince Friedrich Karl, had arrived at Tonnere with 20,000 men; and the Duke of Mecklenburg, with the right wing of the German army on the Loire, no longer regarding the French general, marched westward, occupied Dreux after a short engagement, marched across the Department of the Eure et Loire, and then through the Orne and the Sarthe as far as Bellême. Notwithstanding the weakened condition of General von der Tann, who remained behind, General d'Aurelles still remained in his position before Orleans, instead of striking at him before the German reënforcements could come up.

The Duke of Mecklenburg, in his march westward, had only encountered a feeble resistance from small bodies of ill-organized troops raised in the west. When, at last, toward the end of November, General d'Aurelles was ready to move, his army of the Loire formed a semi-circle around Orleans from the Forest of Cercottes, which it occupied, to the environs of Meung. His extreme left, the Seventeenth Corps, under command of General de Sonis, was at first stationed at Chateaudun, an advanced and dangerous position, so far from the remainder of the army that it was in danger of being cut off. This position it was found necessary to abandon, and draw his lines closer to Orleans. The Sixteenth Corps, under command of General de Chanzy, lay next, on the left; the centre, with the headquarters, was occupied by the Fifteenth Corps, under General Martin de Pallieres; on the right lay the Twentieth Corps, commanded by General Crouzat, who had been summoned in great haste from Chagny. The extreme right was formed by the Eighteenth Corps, which at first was stationed at Gien, but took up a position at the extremity of the Forest, and in front of Montargis. The German right was commanded by the Duke of Mecklenburg, the centre by General von der Tann, and the left by Prince Friedrich Karl, who, when he arrived on the field of battle, ranked both the other commanders. The plans for the whole movement, it is hardly necessary to say, had been projected by that consummate strategist, General von Moltke.

On the 28th of November, General d'Aurelles attacked the Tenth Prussian Army Corps and First Cavalry Division, forming the extreme left wing of the German Army, at Beaune de

Rolande, and had very nearly overthrown them, when the arrival of Prince Friedrich Karl, who took command in person changed the fortunes of the day. Beaune de Rolande is twenty seven miles northeast of Orleans and sixteen miles northwest of Montargis. The French loss in this engagement, in killed, wounded, and prisoners, was not far from 7,000. General d'Aurelles was slightly wounded. The German loss did not exceed 1,000 men. The object of General d'Aurelles in giving battle at this point, so far from Orleans, was undoubtedly to furnish moral aid, and, if possible, substantial assistance, to the sortie which, under General Trochu's direction, General Ducrot was then making from Paris. Beaune de Rolande is only about twenty-two miles, or one good day's march, from Fontainebleau, which was to be the point of junction; and if the commander of the Army of the Loire could succeed in breaking through Prince Friedrich Karl's lines, and Ducrot could force his way through the ranks of the besiegers of Paris, there would be some hope of raising the siege of the capital. It was unfortunate for General d'Aurelles that he could succeed in bringing only a part of his force into action at Beaune de Rolande—only the Twentieth Corps being in full force, and some brigades or divisions from the Fifteenth and Sixteenth. The result, though not regarded as a serious defeat at the time, proved a very serious disaster subsequently in its effect. Ducrot's sortie, unsupported by this diversion, proved, as we shall presently see, a failure, and with its want of success perished the last well-grounded hope of raising the siege of Paris. Moreover, the planting of the German force across the only available route to Fontainebleau blocked all movements in that direction, and rendered all efforts to reach the weakest point in the besiegers' line unsuccessful. On the 1st of December, undaunted by his repulse of the 28th of November, General d'Aurelles suddenly and vehemently attacked the German centre, under General von der Tann, while

THE SECOND BATTLE OF ORLEANS.

he was reconnoitring on the old road to Chartres, and drove him in a northwesterly direction past Lorgny. The four days which followed were days of severe and heavy fighting, though at no time, except perhaps on the 4th of December, were the greater part of the forces of either army engaged. On the 2d, General de Chanzy, who was in command of the corps making this movement, continued his advance as far as Orgeres and Bargneux; but in the afternoon of that day the Duke of Mecklenburg reenforced von der Tann, and drove de Chanzy back as far as Artenay, and a part of his force still farther, to Poupry. General d'Aurelles now found that the time for offensive action had passed, and that he must mass his troops for the defense of Orleans, which Prince Friedrich Karl was evidently bent on recapturing. He had, unwisely, made his lines too extensive; and now, so rapid were the Prince's movements, that his Eighteenth and Twentieth Army Corps, which were stationed at and near Montargis, could not be brought up for the defense of the city. Prince Friedrich Karl sent his Ninth German Corps to Toury Bazoches, his Third to Pithiviers, and his Fifteenth, with three brigades additional, to Boyne; thus interposing a force of more than three corps between the two outlying corps of d'Aurelles and the other three corps on which he was obliged to rely for the defense of Orleans. The Ninth German Corps, which the Prince joined on the morning of the 3d of December, was the centre, and marched on the road from Paris to Orleans; the Third Corps formed the left, and moved on the road from Fontainebleau to Orleans; and the Fifteenth, with the Duke of Mecklenburg's divison and the Tenth Army Corps, occupied the Chartres and other roads. The Eighteenth Division (the Duke of Mecklenburg's) advanced to Artenay, which the French had already evacuated, and at Moulin d'Anvilliers, a few miles farther on, overtook the French troops, and defeated them after some severe fighting, and continued their advance to Chevilly, which, though the key to the wood of Orleans, fell into then hands without farther fighting. On the evening of the day, the Third German Corps, after taking Sancerre, which was strongly fortified, and Chillers-aux-Bois, had advanced as far as Toury. The Ninth Corps had only reached Crottes and Aschires, as Château St. Germain-le-Grand had been strongly fortified. The Tenth Corps had taken Neuvelle-aux-Bois and driven the French back into the wood. On the 4th of December the attack was renewed. The Ninth Corps advanced, and was met by a sharp fire from the wood. General von Blumenthal took Cercottes after some very severe fighting. In the mean time, the 36th Brigade advanced about four miles beyond St. Live, where the way had been strongly barricaded. On the right wing, the Grand Duke had gradually driven the French backward toward Orleans; and on the left, the Third Corps had reached St. Loup with but little fighting. In the evening the German troops occupied the north, west, and east of Orleans. The road to the south alone remained open to the French, and by this they effected their retreat on the night of the 4th of December, the Germans reöccupying the city. In this series of battles the French lost nearly 20,000 in killed and wounded, and 14,000 prisoners taken at Orleans, 77 guns, a great number of military equipages, and four armed steamboats. A still more serious disaster was, that the Army of the Loire was cut in two, the Eighteenth and Twentieth French Corps being compelled to cross the Loire and go south toward Bourges; while the three Army Corps, which were immediately before Orleans, fled at first to Blois, and subsequently, fighting desperately, made their way toward Le Mans. On their way to Blois they were overtaken by the Germans between Meung and Beaugency; and from the 7th to the 12th of December, after severe fighting, were compelled to retreat, losing 2,000 prisoners and six guns, besides a large number of killed and wounded. The other half of the

UHLANS TRACKING A BALLOON.

French army, in their retreat toward Bourges, were pursued in the same way and with similar results. This series of disasters led the officers of the Provisional Government at Tours to determine to remove the capital to Bordeaux; but Minister Gambetta endeavored to conceal this violent disruption of his best army, by promptly issuing an order creating two armies of it, one under Bourbaki, former commander of the Imperial Guard, and the other under General Chanzy. General d'Aurelles was removed from command. This defeat was commented upon as "a blessing in disguise" by Paris papers, one of which, determined to see only the bright side of things, exultingly declared, "We have now two great armies where was only one before." Gambetta made the further great mistake of sending the escaped forces under Bourbaki on an ill-considered expedition against von Werder in the Vosges, instead of concentrating it upon Chanzy in the west.

We turn now from this disaster at Orleans, to give some account of the sortie led by Ducrot, to which we have already referred. This was by far the most important attempt made by the besieged garrison of Paris to break through the lines of the besiegers, and, though it failed to accomplish its object, partly from the contemporaneous failure of General d'Aurelles, already noticed, and partly from the extraordinary facilities possessed by the Germans for concentrating their forces on a given point, yet it was stubborn enough, and inflicted sufficiently heavy losses upon the German army to demonstrate what French troops, properly trained and skilfully led, would be capable of accomplishing.

The sortie, which had been long in contemplation by General Trochu, had for its objective the district lying on the bends of the Marne, east-southeast of Paris, beyond Vincennes. There were also feints made against the lines of the besiegers, on the south and west, to divert attention from the true point of attack.

The reasons for selecting this point were sound. Much of the tract could be rendered untenable for German troops by the fire from forts De Nogent and De Charenton, which swept a considerable portion of the two peninsulas formed by the double bend of the Marne; the investing line was weakest at this point, being held by Saxon and Wurtemburg troops—excellent soldiers, but decimated by their previous terrible fighting around Metz; they had Vincennes for a base of operations, and held already some of the small villages adjacent; and, finally, this was in a direct line toward Fontainebleau, the proposed rendezvous with the Army of the Loire. General Ducrot, who commanded this expedition, was one of the old officers of Napoleon III, who had been taken prisoner at Sedan, but, as he declared, did not accept a parole, and subsequently, in consequence of the carelessness of the guard, made his escape. He possessed considerable military ability and skill, and was regarded by General Trochu as his most trusty lieutenant. The force put under his command consisted of about 150,000 selected troops, a part of them belonging to the Garde Mobile, but all very carefully drilled. General Trochu was on the field in person, though devolving the command of the sortie entirely on General Ducrot. On the 29th of November General Vinoy led a moderate force toward L'Hay and Choisy-le-Roi, on the south of Paris; but this was merely as a feint. On the same day Generals Trochu and Ducrot addressed the army in the most energetic language, on the greatness of the issue of the intended operations, and the duty of shrinking from no sacrifice for the country.

In the night of November 29th–30th, General Ducrot issued from the Forest of Vincennes, crossed the Marne at several points with a force of about 120,000 men, and fought obstinately throughout the day (November 30th), to break through the lines held by the Wurtemburgers and Saxons. He succeeded in advancing a considerable distance, but, when night fell, had been compelled to fall back to Brie and Champigny, on the river, where, however, he remained. By a reference to our map of Paris and its vicinity, the reader will observe that the Marne runs nearly due west from Cournay for some distance, then makes a sweep south; on the eastern bank of this sweep stands the village of Brie, and then the river forms a couple of loops, within the most northerly of which are the villages of St. Maur and Champigny, and, some distance to the east of the wide neck of the loop, the larger village of Villiers-sur-Marne. It was in and around the three villages of Brie, Champigny, and Villiers, that the bloody drama of November 30th was enacted. Brie and Champigny, at nightfall, remained in the hands of the French, and Villiers was as stoutly held by the Saxons. On the next day there was no fighting, but hostilities were resumed on the 2d of December.

We have the following brief reports of the events of the sortie, from the pen of General Trochu:

"CHATEAU BETWEEN BRIE-SUR-MARNE AND CHAMPIGNY,
November 30, 3 o'clock.

"The right wing has maintained the brilliantly-taken positions. The Mobile Guard, after wavering somewhat, has carried itself bravely, and the enemy, whose losses are serious, was forced to withdraw himself behind the ridge of the hills. The situation is good. The artillery under General Frebault has fought excellently. If it had been said, a month ago, that an army would form in Paris capable of crossing a difficult stream in the face of an enemy, and of driving before it the Prussian army intrenched on the hills, no one would have believed it. General Ducrot has behaved wonderfully; and I cannot honor him here too much. Susbiele's division, which, outside of and on the right wing of the general engagement, had with great courage taken the position of Montmesly, was not able to maintain itself there against superior forces, and has returned to Creteil, but its diversion was very useful. I pass the night at the scene of the battle, which will be continued to-morrow.

"General TROCHU.

"ROSNY, 7.42 P.M.

"The end of the day has been good. A division of General d'Exea passed the Marne and resumed the offensive; we remain in the positions. The enemy has left us two cannon, and left his wounded and dead on the field.

"[These two guns were taken at Epinay, east of St. Denis.]

"December 1.

"Our troops remain this morning in the positions which they took yesterday and occupied during the night. They remove the wounded left by the enemy on the battle-field, and bury his dead. The transport of our wounded is completed with the greatest regularity. The army is full of courage and determination.

"PLATEAU BETWEEN CHAMPIGNY AND VILLIERS, December 2, 1.45 noon.

"Attacked this morning at daybreak by enormous forces. We have been more than seven hours in battle. At the moment of writing to you, the enemy gives way over the whole line, and surrenders to us again the heights. As I hastened through our tirailleurs from Champigny to Brie, I have received the honor and the inexpressible joy of the troops exposed to the heaviest fire. There will be, without doubt, offensive counter attacks, and this second battle will, like the first, last a whole day. I do not know what future awaits these proud efforts of the republican troops, but I grant them this acknowledgment, that, under tests of every kind, they have made themselves well worthy of recognition by the fatherland. 1 add to this, that to General Ducrot the honor of these two days is due.

"General TROCHU.

"Paris, Nogent, 5 30 p. m.

"I return to my quarters in the fort very tired and very contented. This second great battle is much more decisive than the previous one. The enemy attacked us at the hour of reveille with reserves and fresh troops. We could oppose to him only the combatants of the second day before, fatigued, with incomplete supplies, and stiffened by the winter nights, which they had passed without covers, since, in order to lighten us, we had been obliged to leave them behind in Paris. But the astonishing courage of the troops has replaced all. We fought three hours in order to retain our positions, and five hours to take those of the enemy, in which we remain. That is the balance of this hard and splendid day. Many will not see their hearths again; but these lamented dead have won for the young republic of the year 1870 a glorious page in the military history of the fatherland. General Trochu."

On the 3d of December the French forces recrossed the Marne, destroying the bridges, and concentrated themselves in the Forest of Vincennes, ostensibly to follow out their operations, in reality because their effort to break the German lines had proved a failure. They had taken about four hundred prisoners. The next day they returned to the fortifications. Their losses were officially stated as 1,008 killed and 5,022 wounded, prisoners and missing not given.

It must be confessed that this narrative of the three days' fighting by General Trochu is sufficiently vague. Fortunately, we have the means of knowing more fully the incidents of the three days' battle, though the narrative is from a neutral (the correspondent of the London *Daily News*) in the German camps:

"The whole Saxon forces (says this correspondent) engaged in the recent operations numbered but 10,000 men. They occupied positions at Noisy-le-Grand, Champs, Cournay, Villiers, and in their vicinity was a division of Wurtemburgers, commanded by General von Obernetz, a Prussian officer. The Wurtemburgers occupied positions at Ormesson, Chennevières, and Noiseau, and in their vicinity was a brigade of the Second Corps. This force was made up of contributions from various other portions of the same corps, and was commanded by General von Fransecky, who had nominal direction of all the operations, supervised, however, as regarded the Saxons, by Prince George in person, whose heedlessness of danger must have sorely tried the nerves of his staff.

"A contingent force supported the Wurtemburgers; the Saxons had no backing but their own valor. In all, the German troops engaged and immediately supporting amounted to 22,000 men. This force, it seems, had been detailed for an offensive movement, and the programme was greatly complicated by the unexpected counter-offensive movement of the French projected against Villiers, and with hopes of ultimately breaking through the cordon surrounding them. It thus happened that, as the Germans were pressing in to drive the French out of Brie and Champigny, the French were simultaneously pouring out to take Villiers.

"On the road that passes through Noisy, the south bank of the Marne is low, with a gradual rise, furrowed by inconsiderable rectangular depressions. As one reaches Noisy and looks southward, he sees toward Brie, and athwart the thick part of the loop of the Marne, a broad, flat space, offering a favorable scope for military evolutions. From this plain toward Villiers there rises gradually a low but shaggy elevation, covered chiefly with copse-woods and vineyards. This elevation is not continuous to Villiers. There are occasional depressions, debouchments of which cause the trivial hollows that occur on the road to Noisy. The general tendency is, nevertheless, upward, so that the table-land at the back of which Villiers lies is higher than any ground between it and the plain. The ridge, therefore, though hampered by hedges and brushwood, would form no bad position for resistance to a force which, having deployed on the plain, should attempt to carry it, if it were not swept by the direct fire from Fort Nogent at easy range, and enfiladed at longer range, but still effectively, by batteries on Mont Avron.

"When I crossed the river, at 9 o'clock, Noisy was an eligible point from which to observe operations. Shells from Mont Avron were coming very thick; now there was a shower of slates as a shell crashed through a roof, lifting the solid rafters as if they were laths; now half the side of a house went down bodily as some huge projectile struck and crushed it. Brie divided with Noisy the attentions of the French batteries, and Brie is more open to attack. The 107th Regiment had made a dash into Brie out of Rosny early in the morning, and I wondered much how it had fared with them—hard enough, no doubt —but could they hold the place under such ding-dong pelting? By 10 o'clock the question was resolved. First came a drove of French prisoners, red-breeched regulars, up toward Noisy, along the slight shelter afforded by the road; then Saxon soldiers and more prisoners; and, finally, the bulk of the 107th, in very open order, making the most of the few opportunities for cover. It was not a pleasant way to traverse. Forts fired heavily on captors and captured alike. More than one Frenchman was slain by missiles from French weapons.

"As the struggling columns came up, I learned that the 107th, in a rapid rush in the morning, had surprised the occupants of Brie, some asleep, others drinking coffee. There was a trifling resistance. Nearly 500 prisoners were taken, including eight officers. The reason for relinquishing Brie was, that the terrible, persistent fire from the forts rendered it utterly untenable.

"The prisoners looked like sturdy fellows, anything but illfed. One of them bade me good morning, and told me cheerily that, if any one indulged in the anticipation of the speedy capitulation of Paris, he was extremely out in his reckoning. Food was plentiful, he said, with a laugh, and the programme was 'sorties every day, in every direction.' The prisoners were escorted back to Chelles, where, later in the day, I saw them penned in the yard of the town-hall.

"As the Prussians from Brie finished filing through Noisy, an ominous sight met my eye in another direction as I peered through a loophole I had contrived there. On the gradual slope of the further bank of the Marne, under the wing of Fort Nogent, and extending right and left along the Chaumont railway, were dense columns of French infantry. How they came there, I know not. It was as if the spectacle had sprung up by magic. Now they stood fast, closing up as the fronts of battalions halted. Then there was a slow movement forward, as the head of the column dipped out of sight between the village of Nogent and the river. Then there seemed to be a final halt. The dense masses stood, their bayonets glittering in the sun, as if the men had come out for a spectacle.

"But little by little there was a gradual trickling off down to the bight of the river between Nogent and Brie. There was a railway-bridge (the Chaumont Railway)—a lofty viaduct—but a gap in one arch had rendered it useless. Presently, on the plain to the south of Brie, a knot of red-breeches became visible, that grew denser and denser every moment. Simultaneously, the whole sprang into life. From the farm-buildings about Le Tremblay, from St. Maur and Joinville, there poured out vast bodies of French troops, deploying at double-quick. The line seemed to extend right athwart the neck of the loop of the river.

"At Champigny, I am informed that Wurtemburgers, after desperate fighting, had driven the French out not long after 8

RUINS OF THE BURNT PALACE OF ST. CLOUD, NEAR PARIS, FIRED BY FRENCH SHELLS.

o'clock, to be in turn subjected to violent attack and partial expulsion. The sharpshooters dashed into the thicket lining the foot of the rising ground, and scrambled through. The troops behind them followed—a serried column. Whence had they come? They had crossed during the night and occupied the loop. Their bridges must have been between Joinville and Nogent; and the nullification of Brie enabled the utilization at a later hour of a bridge between Brie and the railway viaduct.

"The Bois de Grace, lying in front (south) of Champs, afforded favorable cover for a detour into the rear of Villiers, which evidently was the point for which the French advance was intended. Their force—I refer exclusively to that section of it that threatened Villiers—must have been at least 20,000. How large was the force with which the Wurtemburgers had to deal toward Champigny, I had no means of ascertaining. In those dense columns standing in support under Nogent, there could not have been less than 20,000. There were 20,000 of the left advance, with whom 10,000 Saxons had to cope—not with them alone, but with those terrible projectiles, a storm of which incessantly clashed into the upper ground where Villiers stands, and into the glades behind.

"The French skirmishers were thrown out with as much regularity as if the day's work had been but a peaceful parade. The forces were deployed with surprising rapidity and apparent discipline; but there appeared considerable looseness in their formation; a total want of intervals, and, indeed, in places an overlapping of battalions. Had there been nothing else for the Saxons to do but to repulse an assault on Villiers directed solely against it, the task would have been comparatively simple, and not very sanguinary, notwithstanding the artillery-fire by the French. But the advance, threatening, as it did, in the evolution by which it was deployed, to sweep right on, overlapping Villiers, up the space between that place and Noisy, and so to get through upon Champs, called for other tactics. Villiers could only serve as a position on which to lean the Saxon left; it became necessary to meet the French in the open space.

"From behind Villiers several (German) regiments came out to the right of the brow of the hill under the shell-fire. As the French came up the gentle acclivity, the guns of the forts continued playing without interruption. So narrow was the margin between the combatants, that I question much whether a shell or two did not fall in the French ranks. I stood by the 108th Regiment as it quitted a position in which it had found some shelter. Two lieutenants gayly shook hands with a hussar aid-de-camp who had just rode up with an order, as they passed him to go out into the battle. On went the regiment in dense columns of companies, shells now crushing into the ranks, now exploding in the intervals.

"The line was formed, rear files closing up at the double-quick, and, in a twinkling, less than fifty yards separated the combatants. Then came a volley, then sharp firing by file, and the French broke and gave ground, only to get back to the next dip of the ground, to let the guns of the fort go to work again. The Saxons had to find what cover they might. When the regiments came back—they had not been gone twenty minutes—thirty-five officers out of the forty-five had gone down. Neither of the blithe lieutenants were to the fore. Now there came a lull in the musketry-fire, as a few moments before there had been a lull in the cannon. The Saxons could not get their artillery into action with advantage. The ground itself was unfavorable, while the fire from the forts must have speedily silenced their field-guns; therefore this great advantage was lost to them.

"All this took place before noon. After a little time the artillery-fire from the forts slackened considerably. The French infantry made no demonstration. On the German left, however, about Champigny, it was evident that hard fighting was going on. About 1 o'clock the French made another advance, having received considerable reënforcements. The Saxon infantry confronted them with the old result, but a different policy was this time adopted. It was plain that the only escape from the thunderbolts of the forts lay in getting at close quarters with the French infantry, unless, indeed, a retrograde movement was to be made—and that was not to be thought of. So, when the French fell back, the Saxons followed on, as if they would settle the question with the bayonet's point. It was the old cry, "*Vorwarts, immer vorwarts!*" but the *vorwarts* was very slow.

"What happened in the next hour, I could only guess by the constant crackling of small-arms. The forts confined themselves, apparently for the chief part, to firing into and over Champigny and Villiers. At length the French were slowly and stubbornly falling back across the north side of the neck of land, the Saxons pushing them hard, the French ever and anon rallying. On this position of the plain, south of Brie, there was a prolonged struggle. The Saxons were striving to get at and cut the pontoon-bridge; but this became an impossibility when Fort Nogent went to work again with the frightful accuracy of which the short range admitted. The combatants parted about 3 o'clock, both sides falling back. The fire of the fort continued some little time longer.

"What shall I say of the result? Not much have the Saxons gained. Was there much to gain? The Wurtemburgers hold one end of Champigny. Brie stands empty and desolate; there were French in it this morning; later, there were Saxons That is all. But look at the bloody side of the picture. The number dead I cannot ascertain, but the German wounded were over 1,000. The French, if they lost fewer killed and wounded, lost 1,000 prisoners. Had it been possible for the Saxons to hold Brie, the French advance would have been impossible; its flanking fire would have prohibited breasting the slope toward

Villiers. The French had a mitrailleuse somewhere in the plain. At any rate, the day's work was the final failure of the French hopes. The German line stood everywhere unbroken. Paris was no more free than before."

In an order of the day announcing the termination of the sortie, General Ducrot said, that "if he had persevered in his plan after the resistance he had encountered, he should only have courted disasters, and imperilled the cause of the defense." This was the last important sortie made before the capitulation of Paris.

CHAPTER XII.

THE French armies had been defeated at Orleans, at Amiens, and before Paris. Aside from the temporary success of General d'Aurelles de Paladines at Orleans in 'November, and a few 'rifling engagements between small bodies of men on either side, they had been uniformly unsuccessful throughout the war; but though there was cause for grave apprehension, there was, even yet, none for discouragement. Numerically, notwithstanding the three hundred and fifty thousand or more French troops who were prisoners in Germany, the French armies outnumbered the Germans on French soil. They were, indeed, for the most part, raw recruits, innocent of any knowledge of the use of fire-arms, or of any military training or drill, and so not a match for the veteran troops of the German Emperor; but they were fast learning, and they were fighting for their homes and their country. They were badly officered; their generals and their subordinate officers knew little or nothing of the topography of the country where they were fighting, and there was no master-mind to plan engagements and combine the forces for victory, as von Moltke did for the Germans. Gambetta, who really possessed considerable organizing power, was young, impetuous, hasty in action, and seldom well-informed in regard to the localities where the German troops were, and hence made grievous blunders. His judgment of men was defective, and he repeatedly proclaimed that he had found the men who could organize victory, and, within five or six weeks, denounced the same men as traitors to France. His notorious exaggerations of trifling actions, or even serious defeats, as great victories, eventually led the people to distrust his statements. Trochu, more calm and frank in his character, seemed to lack heart in the enterprises he undertook, and, though promising constantly to make sorties or to concentrate his forces against the enemies of France, always found reasons for delay.

We should not judge these men too hardly. Their circumstances were peculiarly trying, and in these great emergencies they doubtless felt that they were unequal to the occasion. Yet there was but little more of zeal, energy, skill, and faith needed to have given them the victory on several occasions. Orleans was lost unnecessarily, by the too great expansion of the French lines. Had General d'Aurelles had his men well in hand, and manning strongly their crescent-shaped lines in front of that city, Prince Friedrich Karl, skilful general as he was, must have recoiled from a fight in which the odds would have been so great.

Still nearer to a victory did the French come under Trochu and Ducrot, in the sortie of November 30th to December 3d, which was described in the last chapter. If, instead of withdrawing across the Marne, and giving up the fight on the 3d of December, Trochu had flung his reserves against the Saxons that day, with that *elan* which used to be the characteristic of French troops, he would have broken their line, and, as the Crown-Prince of Saxony frankly admitted, have compelled the Germans to raise the siege, for the time at least.

But it was the misfortune of the French armies throughout the war to have leaders who were not thoroughly in earnest in their efforts for the preservation of the nation. So it happened that while, on the 12th of December, with suitable leaders, the cause of France would not have been wholly desperate, yet the measures which were taken before that time had rendered the overthrow of the nation, under its leaders, inevitable.

Apparently unaware that his only hope of success lay in concentrating his armies and hurling them against the weak points of that mighty cordon which surrounded Paris, and encouraging the Parisian garrison to coöperate with them by well-planned sorties, Gambetta sought rather to scatter his troops as widely as possible over France; thinking, perhaps, that it would be more difficult for the Germans to capture them. Thus, when Prince Friedrich Karl had cut his Army of the Loire in two, and Bourbaki, with his half, had gone southward to Bourges, and de Chanzy, with his *Corps d'Armée*, west-northwest to Blois, Vendome, and Le Mans, instead of bringing Bourbaki westward to Tours, where he might have been within supporting distance of de Chanzy, Gambetta sent him almost two hundred miles to the eastward, to attack General von Werder, in the vicinity of the Swiss frontier. Garibaldi, with 30,000 men, was kept in the vicinity of Dijon—nearly as far distant, and in the same direction; while General Faidherbe, with two corps, was in the extreme north of France, and General Laysel, with 30,000 more, in the vicinity of Havre. Some of these troops were indeed prevented from concentration by the interposition of moderate forces of German troops between them and Orleans; but, in most instances, a resolute will would have found a way of pushing through. The camps of instruction were said to contain 250,000 men—not well trained, it is true, but still capable of being of some service.

Yet, from the 12th of December, the outlook constantly grew darker and darker to the final surrender; while, with an infatuation which would have been ludicrous had not its consequences been so sad, Gambetta sent a despatch to Trochu, on the 14th of December, as follows:

"For four days I have been in Bourges with Bourbaki, busied in reorganizing the three corps, namely, the Fifteenth, Eighteenth, and Twentieth, of the First Army of the Loire, which, in consequence of forced marches in the most terrible rain, had been thrown into very bad condition. This work requires still four or five days. The positions occupied by Bourbaki cover at the same time Nevers and Bourges; the other part of the Loire Army retreated, after the evacuation of Orleans, toward Beaugency and Marchenoir, in which positions it has resisted all the efforts of Friedrich Karl—thanks to the unconquerable energy of General de Chanzy, who appears to be the real warrior whom recent events have brought out. That army, consisting of the Sixteenth, Seventeenth, and Twenty-first Corps, and, according to General Trochu's arrangements, supported by all the powers of the west, has accomplished a wonderful retreat, and inflicted the severest losses upon the Prussians. De Chanzy withdrew himself from a great flank march of Friedrich Karl on the left bank of the Loire. Friedrich Karl attempted in vain to cross the Loire at Amboise and Blois, and to threaten Tours. De Chanzy is to-day in the most perfect security in La Perche, ready to take the offensive in the direction of ———— as soon as his troops have rested; the latter have fought steadily and in the most extraordinary manner, against superior forces of the enemy, since November 30th and up to December 12th. You see that the Army of the Loire is far removed from being destroyed, as the Prussian falsehoods have given out. It is divided into two armies of equal strength, which are ready to take the field. Faidherbe in the north is said to have taken La Fère, with much munition, artillery, and provision. But we are very uneasy as to your fate. For nearly eight days we have no news from you, either direct or through the Prussians, or from other nations. The cable to England is interrupted. What is happening? Relieve us from our anxiety, and improve the opportunity offered by the southwest wind to send off a balloon, which will then probably fall in Belgium.

"The withdrawal of the Prussians becomes more and more

noticeable. They appear to be tired of the war. If we can keep on—and we can, if we really will it—we will triumph over them. According to trustworthy accounts which have reached me, they have already suffered immense losses. They supply themselves only with the greatest difficulty. But we must give ourselves to the greatest sacrifices, not lament much, and fight to the death. In the interior reigns everywhere the most astonishing order. The Government of the National Defense is everywhere respected, and finds obedience everywhere."

At this very time Prince Friedrich Karl was watching every movement of de Chanzy, much as a cat watches a mouse which she has already captured, but which she permits to run within certain narrow limits. Blois had already fallen, and Vendome was entered two days later; Montmedy had capitulated, and Amiens was tottering to its fall. The German forces on French soil were officially stated at 728,000, of whom more than 510,000 were effective, and the calling out of 124 battalions—equal to 62 regiments more of the Landwehr Reserves—did not strongly indicate that the Germans were withdrawing, or that they were very weary of the war. On the 20th of December, the German column on the right bank of the Loire pursued de Chanzy's army in the direction of Le Mans; while that on the left bank advanced toward Tours, finding 6,000 French wounded, abandoned without medical attendance, on the road. The next day (21st of December) an official despatch from Versailles announced:

"The Nineteenth Division reached the bridge before Tours to-day, found opposition by the inhabitants, and therefore threw thirty shells into the city. White flags were then raised, and the city begged for occupation by the Prussians. The division contented itself, however, in accordance with its instructions, with destroying the railroad, and withdrew to its appointed cantonments."

By a reference to our map of France, it will be seen that de Chanzy's army, instead of approaching toward Paris, and so being ready to second any further sorties, was being pressed gradually away from it toward the southwest. This pressure became still stronger a week or two later, a portion of Prince Friedrich Karl's army being thrown between it and the outer line of the besiegers at Nogent le Rotron and Chartres. The approach of French armies toward Paris from other points was guarded against with equal care. General Faidherbe, who had, at the head of a considerable force (60,000 or 70,000 troops), approached as near to Paris as the vicinity of Rouen (about ninety miles), when General Manteuffel, who had been detached from the army of Prince Friedrich Karl, commenced driving him northward and northwestward, causing him to retreat through Rouen, Beauconnet, Montigny, Frechencourt, Querrieux, Pont Noyelles, Brissy, Becquemont, Daours, l'Haller, and on the 23d of December, after a severe action at the last-named point, the German forces occupied Amiens, taking 1,000 prisoners, and, on the 25th, pushed on after Faidherbe toward Arras.

On the 21st and 22d of December the French garrison in Paris again made sorties against the position of the Saxon Corps, somewhat north of their previous battle-ground; but their attack was not steadily maintained by a strong force, and more than 1,000 of their troops were taken prisoners. In order to divert attention from their movements, they made two feints at the same time from Mont Valerien, on the west of Paris, toward Buzenval and Montretout, and on the north, from St. Denis, toward Pierrefitte and Stains. General Ducrot commanded the column operating against the Prussian Guards, whose position was northeast and north-northeast of Paris; and Generals Malroy and Blaise commanded the right wing in the attack upon the Saxon Corps. All told, 100 battalions were in line. The French occupied the villages Courneuve, Bobigny, and Bondy, 2,000 to

3,000 paces in advance of the forts, with their advanced posts Drancy, 2,000 paces further, being occupied only at night, as the German line was but 2,000 paces distant. The Prussian outpost line extended from Pierrefitte through Stains and Le Bourget, about 4,000 paces from the line of forts. The main body of the Guards was posted 3,000 paces to the rear in the line Garges, Dugny, Pont Iblon, Le Blanc Mesnil, Aulnay, and Sevran on the Ourcq canal, and the railroad to Soissons. Here began the Saxon (Twelfth) Corps, whose line extended to the Marne. Many points of this principal line were within range of the forts. French troops marched out of St. Denis December 20th, proceeding toward Aubervilliers, while three brigades threatened the left of the Guards, in front of Bobigny. Le Bourget was first attacked at 7 o'clock in the morning. Strong detachments moved from Courneuve toward Dugny, leading the Germans to think that the attack would be on the south and west; but, suddenly changing their direction, the French attacked at the northern gate, which, with the churchyard, was taken, and 125 men captured. The attack on the south gate failed, and, reënforcements being sent, the Germans succeeded in driving out the French after a hot fight from house to house. In storming the churchyard, the last point held by the French, the Germans took 359 prisoners. According to the reports of the latter, the relative strength of the contestants was—Germans, 2,000; French, 6,000. At Stains, on the right wing of the Prussian corps, a severe attack was repulsed without a single house of the town falling into French hands.

Elsewhere the operations of the day were begun by a tremendous fire from the forts along the whole front, and missiles of the heaviest calibre were thrown a distance of 8,000 paces; but the excessive range so interfered with the aim, that very little injury was done. Protected by the fire from the forts, the French artillery opened with two batteries before Courneuve, ten field and three mitrailleur batteries north and northeast of Drancy, near Groslay Ferme, sweeping the whole field as far as Dugny, Pont Iblon, Le Blanc Mesnil, Aulnay, and Sevran. This fire was returned by the batteries of the Second Division of Guards from positions between Le Blanc Mesnil and Aulnay. At noon, two of these batteries crossed the river at Pont Iblon and took position 2,000 paces from the French, and, being followed by two more, showed themselves superior to the French; the two batteries on the French right wing were silenced after two hours' lively work, and the fire of the others was weakened. Two other German batteries advanced, the fire of which completed the work. The French batteries gradually became silent, the infantry retired, and the sortie was repulsed. The losses of the Prussians were 14 officers and 400 men. The strength of the columns operating against them was estimated at 40,000, but only the regular troops were really in action at Le Bourget and Stains. The Mobiles and National Guards were retained at such great distance, that the reserves on the German side were not deployed.

The Twelfth, or Saxon Corps, stretching from Sevran to the Marne, had no fighting of importance until noon, when a French division advanced from Neuilly and passed the advanced posts in Maison Blanche and Ville Evrart. A freshet in the river prevented an attack upon the position at Chelles, and the Wurtemburg artillery was able to bring a flank fire to bear on the French. At five o'clock the German commander ordered the retaking of Ville Evrart and Maison Blanche. The latter was easily accomplished; but Ville Evrart is composed of strongly-built houses standing alone, and in this small labyrinth the battle continued until midnight. General Blaise, commander of a French brigade, fell here. Some of the houses remained in possession of the French until morning, when the increasing freshet in the Marne compelled the Germans to leave at three, and the

French at eight o'clock. The other sorties from Mont Valerien and from St. Denis were only demonstrations, and the fighting was nowhere severe.

On the morning of the 27th of December the Germans began a steady bombardment of Fort Avron, a large and strong work lying east of Paris and 3,000 paces beyond Fort Rosny. Thirteen batteries, mounting 76 guns, played upon it incessantly during the day from a distance of 5,000 paces; and so accurate and destructive was their fire, that the garrison abandoned it the same evening, and the Germans occupied it the next day, and, as soon as they could rearrange its guns, opened upon forts Noissy, de Rosny and de Nogent, which were silenced before the new year. The loss of Fort Avron was a very severe one for the French, as its fire had protected them in their previous sorties. On New Year's day, Mezières, a strongly-fortified town west-northwest of Sedan, after a long siege and a severe bombardment, capitulated, more than 2,000 prisoners and 106 guns being surrendered.

On the 2d of January, 1871, Count Wartensleben, commander of the Fifteenth German Division and of a cavalry detachment, both forming a portion of General Manteuffel's army, overtook General Faidherbe's troops at Salpignies, near Bapaume, in the north of France, and, after two days' fighting, the Germans were victorious, the French losing about 4,000 in killed and wounded, and 500 prisoners, and the German loss in killed, wounded, and missing being 1,066. The French retreated in the direction of Douai and Arras, on the 4th, and lost about 800 more prisoners.

The besieging army before Paris, having their heavy batteries in position, commenced, on the 5th of January, the bombardment of the southern and south-southwestern defences of the city—*i. e.*, the forts Issy, Vanvres, and Montrouge, the Pont du Jour, and the gunboats in the Seine. These points were all outside of the city walls, but formed a part of the first line of defences. It did happen occasionally, however, that the shells fired at long range fell inside of the city walls. Fort Issy was soon silenced, and the other forts not long after, as we shall see by and by. Meantime, on the 5th, Rocroy, a strongly-fortified post near Mezières, was captured, with 72 guns, 300 prisoners, and a large amount of stores.

The Army of Prince Friedrich Karl, which had been engaged since the 12th of December in a careful watch and observation of every movement of General de Chanzy's army, and had promptly followed each with a blow, discovered, on the 5th of January, by their reconnoissances, that he was again in motion near Azuy, and the Prince immediately started in pursuit. On the 6th he came up with two French army corps at Azuy, five miles northwest of Vendome, on the road to Le Mans. A heavy battle ensued, in which the French were driven out of the town and closely pursued. They retreated for the next three days, stopping every few hours to fight, and, though new troops, stood their ground well. The number of stragglers from the ranks constantly increased, however; and as they were pushed by the Germans through Nogent le Rotron, Sarge, Savigny, La Chartre, St. Calais, and Ardenay, they lost over five thousand prisoners and many guns, aside from the killed and wounded. At length the time arrived when de Chanzy felt that he could not retreat farther without destroying the *morale* of his troops; he must stand, and deliver battle. He arrived at this decision a little too late. Prince Friedrich Karl had already sent the Grand Duke of Mecklenburg-Schwerin, with a large force, to make a detour to the north and come in upon the left flank of the French, while he should attack them in front.

In the afternoon of the 10th of January the two armies converged upon the French within five miles of Le Mans. An eye-witness of the battle thus describes it:

"The French Army of the Loire, the last hope of France, has been defeated to-day in a bloody battle fought within five miles of this city (Le Mans). We heard the roar of the cannon all day, and the population crowded to the housetops and sub urbs, and through the thoroughfares, watching the progress of the fight. I have never before witnessed such intense excitement, although the French people have become accustomed to the roar of cannon.

"At nine o'clock this morning the right wing of the French army in position east of Le Mans was suddenly attacked by the vanguard of the German forces, which, emerging from the wood on the extreme right of the French, moved forward to attack. Upon the alarm being given, the advance-posts of the French infantry wheeled into line of battle, and the artillery was pushed forward, on the open ground between the severed ranks of the various commands. The cavalry took up an advantageous position on the right and left wings.

"A more perfect line of battle could not have been formed by the finest army in Europe. The artillery was well supplied with ammunition, and the infantry had 100 rounds to each man. In addition, the supply-trains were well posted, and easy of access.

"Real bloody work soon began. The field of battle was in a valley, and the two armies occupied heights opposite each other, the French line forming a semicircle extending twelve miles, overlooking the valley, which was covered by twelve inches of snow. On the opposite heights the Prussians held a somewhat similar position.

"Shortly after nine o'clock the Prussians began a furious cannonade from the wood near the extreme left. They were flanked by an immense force of cavalry partly concealed by the wood. Their position was where the German infantry massed with the evident intention of turning de Chanzy's right. The artillery-fire on both sides was continued without intermission until the ammunition was nearly exhausted. It was a fierce, well-sustained duel, the German and French artillerists displaying marked skill and courage.

"At length the Prussian commanders gave the order for an advance, and the German infantry moved forward. The French, equally rapid, advanced along their whole line, and the opposing armies met in the valley in a fair hand-to-hand fight. The musketry-fire was very severe and effective. The German troops were cool and collected, and the French impetuous and gallant. Indeed, both armies behaved with notable bravery until near noon, when the Gardes Mobiles began to waver, and, being unable to hold their position, a retreat commenced. Meantime the dead and wounded lay upon the battle-field by thousands, and the snow-fields were red with human blood.

"The carnage was fearful on both sides. Before five o'clock in the evening 15,000 French soldiers had fallen, and at this hour the whole army started in full retreat. The French and German forces were about equally matched. I should judge that they numbered 60,000 men each. Although the French have been beaten, they have not been routed."

The battle was renewed the next day with more decisive results. The Grand Duke of Mecklenburg, who had moved southward from Chartres, fighting heavily all the way, succeeded early that day in following out the strategy which had been so successful at Orleans, and isolated the French Twenty-first Corps, so that it could render no aid to de Chanzy. He reported 10,000 prisoners taken, with small loss on his side. Meantime the fighting between de Chanzy's main army and Prince Friedrich Karl was desperate, but resulted finally, as all the previous battles had done, in the defeat of the French, though more decisively than before. The same correspondent who witnessed the previous day's battle was also present at this, and thus describes it:

"After the battle of the previous day, General de Chanzy, displaying much energy, rallied his broken columns, and, having received reënforcements, determined to strike another blow to retrieve his fortunes, knowing that the whole hope of France centred upon the ability of his army to break through the strong opposition of the Red Prince, and advance to the relief of Paris. After a night of unceasing labor and anxiety, daylight found the French forces prepared for the conflict. Their army consisted of three corps, the Sixteenth, Seventeenth, and Twenty-first respectively, under the command of Admiral Jourequiberry, and Generals Colomb and Jouffroy. These corps averaged 50,000 men each, making an effective force of 150,000 men, the whole under the supreme control of General de Chanzy. By ten o'clock in the morning Jourequiberry's corps had taken up a position on the right bank of the river Huisne, General Colomb's on the plateau of Auvours, and General Jouffroy's on the right, covering the village of Brette.

"The Prussians advanced along three roads, and are said to have been under the command of Prince Friedrich Karl himself. They were apparently 100,000 strong. Soon after ten o'clock sharp firing was opened by the Prussians from well-located batteries on the left of the French. It was replied to with spirit. Very soon a large force of German infantry, flanked by cavalry, advanced under cover of a heavy artillery-fire, striking the right of Admiral Jourequiberry's position. The assaulting column was met by a fierce artillery-fire from many guns, including a number of mitrailleuses of the new pattern. The struggle now became exceedingly severe, and was well-contested. But although the Germans suffered heavy loss, they finally succeeded in driving back the French, capturing early two guns and taking and holding the important position near the river.

"General de Chanzy, perceiving the danger which threatened his position, moved forward his reserves of artillery to the support of Admiral Jourequiberry. These opened a terrific fire, which checked for awhile the further advance of the Germans in that direction. Two or three severe assaults were made by the Germans to secure further advantages, the object being to take the position held by the French at La Tillere. The French, however, were strongly posted, and fought with great courage and determination. Each assault was repulsed with serious loss to the Germans, the French also losing heavily.

"Meantime an equally fierce attack was made on the French line covering the railroad to Chartres and Paris. After two hours' desperate fighting the French centre was driven back. It retreated, however, slowly and in good order for a short distance only, to a position in rear of that first occupied, and where the rising ground afforded good facilities for the artillery. Here a heavy force of guns was parked, which, manned by the marines, opened a severe and well-directed fire upon the advancing enemy. This not only checked the Germans, but compelled them to fall back in turn. A heavy counter-fire soon opened from the German batteries, which, during the engagement, had advanced to a commanding position on the left of the railroad.

"The superiority of the German guns in firing soon became apparent. After an unequal duel the French fire slackened, the Germans causing great loss to the French lines. Still, the French infantry maintained their position heroically, and another attempt to dislodge signally failed. For some time the engagement had the character of an artillery duel; but when the German lines had taken the positions assigned them, a more active attack commenced, evidently with a desire on the part of the Germans to capture the position on the right bank of the Huisne, in order to execute a flanking movement, with the

THE BATTLE OF LE MANS.

object of cutting between the army and Le Mans, and capturing a large number of prisoners.

"At four o'clock the tactics of the Germans seemed to be changed. A heavy massing of troops took place on the French right, under cover of the wood, near the village of Brette, which was held by the French. The wood was on the extreme left of the Prussian position, stretching for miles to the southeast of the plain between the road and villages, and were commanded by the Prussian artillery, which was well-posted on the left, under cover of the wood. A sharp and precise needle-gun fire was opened on the French line and position left of the village of Brette, not more than 700 yards distant. It soon became evident that it would be impossible for them to long hold the position unless the Germans were dislodged. The heavy fire of artillery directed on the woods had apparently but little effect. A large body of French infantry advanced in good order across the plain, but were compelled to retire with heavy losses before a murderous fire from both artillery and musketry. The contest for the possession of Brette was kept up at this point till dark, when an order reached the French to fall back upon Le Mans. As the French infantry slowly fell back, the artillery was brought to the front, and it maintained a steady fire upon the German line, successfully covering the retreat. The Germans, apparently in contempt of their partial success, seemed disinclined to pursue the advantage they had gained in the day's fighting. General de Chanzy actively superintended the retreat, which was never disorderly at any time. Thus, after a bloody encounter, lasting until dark, in which the carnage had been fearful on both sides, nothing decisive had been gained by the Germans. All their successes had been negative, and the French officers and soldiers remained hopeful.

"But an event occurred which made a total change in the prospects of the French. It was an event common enough in the history of war. Had it failed, the result would have been disastrous to the Germans. It succeeded, and shattered the hopes of the French. Darkness had fallen upon the battle-field, or rather, I should say that day had gone; for the evening was not very dark. One could see the vast fields of snow, dotted here and there by dark objects—the bodies of the victims of the day's struggle—while the patches of woods rose up grimly from the midst of the white fields. Suddenly, and without their preparations attracting attention, a strong force of Germans renewed the battle. Making toward the French right at La Tillere, the most important position held by the Army of the Loire, immense masses of infantry, supported by a large force of cavalry, advanced with the utmost rapidity, scattering in all directions the French forces opposed to them.

"The attack was not anticipated by the French. The suddenness and rapidity with which the movement was executed took them completely by surprise, and but little resistance was offered. At the onset the Gardes Mobiles of Brittany were seized with panic and fled in great disorder. This completely destroyed the French line of battle, as their whole force on the right bank of the Huisne was compelled to make a rapid retreat to save itself from capture. The defeat was complete; or, if it lacked anything of being so, the movement of the next morning by General von Voights Retz, who, by a neatly-accomplished flank movement, entered Le Mans, which the French had intended to occupy, and compelled their retreat in disorder toward Alençon and Laval.

"The losses of the Germans in the pursuit of de Chanzy's army from January 6th to 12th were 177 officers and 3,203 men. They captured 22,000 unwounded prisoners, 2 eagles, 19 guns, more than a hundred loaded wagons, and great quantities of arms and war-material. General de Chanzy's effective force numbered, in the beginning, 122,000 men, so that its losses by capture amount to one-sixth its strength, while the killed and wounded were more than 8,000 more."

General de Chanzy felt this defeat very keenly, the more so as it had, aside from the actual losses, almost entirely destroyed the *morale* of his army.. In an order of the day issued on the 13th of January to the remainder of his army, he said:

" After the successful engagements in which, in the valley of the Huisne as well as on the banks of the Loire at Vendome, you gained victories over the enemy—after the success of the 11th at Le Mans, where you resisted the attacks of the hostile forces under the chief command of Prince Friedrich Karl and the Grand Duke of Mecklenburg, maintaining all the positions, a shameful weakness, an inexplicable panic, has suddenly come upon you, which partly compelled the surrender of important positions, and endangered the safety of the whole army. An energetic effort to make this good was not attempted, although the necessary orders were immediately given; and we therefore had to surrender Le Mans. France has its eye upon its second army. We must not halt. The season is severe; your fatigue is great, and you have been compelled to suffer privations of every kind; but the country suffers heavily, and when a last effort may be sufficient to rescue it, we must not refuse it. Know, too, that for yourselves safety lies in the most determined resistance, and not in retreat. The enemy will appear before our positions; we must receive him steadily, and wear away his powers. Range yourselves about your leaders, and show that you are still the same soldiers who conquered at Coulmiers and Villebon, at Jaunes and Vendome."

This studious concealment of the gravity of the situation from the army is an artifice so often adopted by military leaders, especially with a failing cause, that perhaps it calls for no remark; but we cannot conceal from ourselves the belief that de Chanzy knew that his cause was hopeless, except under some unforeseen and unexpected reverse to the Germans, from the day in which he evacuated Orleans; and that the month of fighting which followed was, so far as he was concerned, merely the grim conflict of despair.

It is certain, at all events, that he attempted no further offensive movements, but, withdrawing his troops from Alençon, which was occupied by the Prussians on the 16th, he concentrated them in the vicinity of Laval, and there awaited the not-distant end of the war.

With a brief sketch of General de Chanzy, whose merits as an officer seem to have been equal to those of any of the French leaders, notwithstanding his repeated defeats, we close this chapter.

General de Chanzy is a native of the Department of Ardennes, and was born in 1823. His early predilections were for a sailor's life, and at the age of sixteen he ran away from home and went to sea. A year of this kind of life sufficed, and in 1840 he entered the military school at St. Cyr, and, after graduating there, was ordered to duty as lieutenant in Algeria, where he remained for about fifteen years, rising by merit to the rank of major. He took part in the Italian war of 1859, where he was promoted to a lieutenant-colonelcy. In 1860 he was sent to Syria to quell the difficulties, and served with such ability as to be advanced to a colonelcy the same year. On his return to France he was, at his own request, sent again to Algeria, where he attained successively the rank of brigadier and major-general. He remained in Africa until September or October, 1870, when he was recalled by the National Government of Defense, and at first placed in command of a division. He took part in the battle of Coulmiers, on the 8th of November, and subsequently being made commander of the Sixteenth Corps, carried the strong positions held by the right wing of the German army at Patay. Of his subsequent career, both at the recapture of Orleans by the Germans, and that long, and, on the whole, disastrous retreat which terminated at Laval, we have given sufficient account in the previous pages. One radical defect seems to have been characteristic of all the French generals who had had their military training in Algeria: they regarded everything like strategy with contempt, and all topographical knowledge as useless, placing their entire reliance on the *elan*, or first impulsive movement, of their troops ; and if they failed in that, retreating somewhat dispirited, for a new attack on another day. Their tactics were those of the lion or tiger, who, regardless of all outward circumstances, makes a sudden but carefully-calculated spring, and, if he fails, slinks back to try the experiment again after considerable delay. A German general at Le Mans would have studied well his battle-ground, have guarded carefully against surprises and flank movements, and especially would not have suffered himself to be so adroitly crowded out of Le Mans, and compelled to run the gauntlet toward Alençon and Laval.

CHAPTER XIII.

THE other wing of the Army of the Loire, which, under command of General Bourbaki, had retreated to Bourges after the recapture of Orleans, and subsequently been sent by Gambetta to attack General von Werder, who was in the Vosges Department of the Haut-Saône, besieging Belfort, and keeping the newly-acquired German territories, Alsace and Lorraine, in order, comes next in place for review. We have spoken with some severity of Gambetta's want of judgment in sending Bourbaki on this expedition, instead of concentrating his troops to raise the siege of Paris. Let us, however, do justice to the fiery young War Minister. While results have demonstrated that the policy of concentration would have been the wiser one, there were still not wanting powerful arguments in favor of the course he adopted. The possession of Alsace and Lorraine was the great bone of contention between the French and Germans; Belfort, a strongly-fortified town of that region, was the only French fortress which had held out under a protracted siege, and its brave garrison deserved support. With its fall, the preservation of French territory intact would be impossible; with its preservation, and the raising of the siege so long protracted, the old French prestige might be recovered. More than this: the region beyond the Vosges was the weakest and least-protected portion of the German frontier; who could tell whether Bourbaki, who had a great reputation as a fierce fighter, might not,

GENERAL BOURBAKI.

MOVING HEAVY SIEGE GUNS AT THE SIEGE OF PARIS.

if properly supported, be able to follow the example of the Roman general, and, while the enemy were thundering at the gates of the French capital, carry the war with relentless severity into their own homes, and even cause Berlin to know the terrors it was visiting upon Paris? Gambetta was bold and daring enough to risk all upon a single chance; and, looking upon the matter in the light we have indicated, he is not to be too hastily condemned for what proved, in its results, a stupendous blunder.

Having determined to send Bourbaki on this expedition, it is but justice to him to say that he did all in his power to make the expedition successful. Recruits were gathered and armed with great promptness, till it was announced, early in January, that his force, which, when he left Bourges, was but 60,000, was increased to 200,000 men, well armed and equipped. This, like most of the French reports, was doubtless an exaggeration; but there is some evidence that he did have, for a short time, 150,000 under his command. He maintained for a time his old reputation; attacked with great rapidity and pluck first one wing and then the other of von Werder's army, which he largely outnumbered, gained some trifling successes, and, assisted by a vigorous sortie from the garrison, gave the sturdy old Teuton, for a time, a surfeit of fighting; but very soon von Werder, who had shown no disposition to raise the siege of the beleaguered fortress, was largely reënforced, and then came his turn. On the 13th of January General Bourbaki made a feint on Visoul, and, after severe fighting, was repulsed, though the action was not decisive. General von Werder the next day evacuated Visoul, and, on his way to a position before Belfort, encountered and repulsed a part of the French forces at Villerseul. On the 15th Bourbaki again assumed the offensive, attacking von Werder at Montbeliard and Chazny, six miles southwest of Belfort, but was again repulsed. On the 16th the fighting was renewed at Chazny and Bethoncourt, but with the same result. On the 17th, after a hard day's fighting, he was defeated, and began to think seriously of a retreat.

He softened this necessity, in his report to Gambetta on the 18th, under the euphemism of a "return to-morrow to the positions we occupied before the battle;" but the fact was, that the retreat had already begun. His report was as follows:

"I ordered to-day (18th) a general attack on the enemy from Montbeliard to Montvaudois, endeavoring at the same time to cross the Lisameat, Liettencourt, Busserel, and Hericourt, and to capture St. Valbert. I also gave orders that the left wing should try to turn the enemy, in order to facilitate the operation; but the troops which were destined to make this movement were threatened by an attack on their flanks, and they were obliged to maintain their positions. We had to contend against considerable forces of the enemy supported by formidable artillery, and reënforced from all sides. The enemy, in consequence of these favorable conditions, the strength of the position he occupied, and the intrenchments he had erected, was able to resist all our efforts, but suffered serious losses.

"The attack we made on the 15th was renewed on the 16th and 17th, and if it has not produced the desired effects we expected therefrom, in spite of the courage displayed by the troops, it has inspired our enemy with respect, and he has deemed it prudent to remain on the defensive.

"The weather is so bad that it renders difficult any forward movement.

"I have decided to return to-morrow to the positions we occupied before the battle."

It was time; for, although he had verified his old reputation as a brave and stubborn fighter, the odds were becoming too heavy. Von Werder's force, as now reënforced, alone was too strong for him; and two or three days later he found that Manteuffel, who had so persistently followed and so thoroughly defeated Faidherbe in the north of France, leaving von Goeben to look after the wreck of the French army, had transferred his choicest troops to the east, and was now in his rear. On the 25th, Manteuffel crossed the Doubs, and occupied St. Vit, Quingey, and Mouchard, thus crowding him toward the Swiss frontier. There was no alternative for him except capitulation, or escape into Switzerland, where his troops would be disarmed and held as prisoners. Between the 17th and the 26th of January Bourbaki had lost 20,000 of his men as prisoners, aside from the killed and wounded, and besides about 10,000 previously captured, killed, and wounded in the continuous and severe battles of January 13th–17th. Frantic with his losses, and determined not to witness the culmination of these disasters, the fierce and desperate French general attempted suicide, but, though severely wounded, he did not succeed in taking his life; and General Clinchart, who succeeded him in the command, could only march the remainder over the frontier into Switzerland, which he did on the 28th and 29th of January. Eighty thousand French troops were thus surrendered to the neutral authorities of Switzerland; but one division, under command of General Cremer, managed to escape and make their way southward.

We have already alluded to the final defeat and rout of General Faidherbe's army in the north of France. That general, after falling back to Cambrai and Arras before Manteuffel, attempted to retrace his steps in order to aid another sortie which had been determined on by the Paris garrison, and threatened the line of La Fère, Chauncy, Noyon, and Compiegne. He knew that the German force in his front had been weakened, and that General Manteuffel had left to General von Goeben the task of finishing the defeat which he had himself begun; yet, with his troops weakened by defeat and sickness, and with the knowledge that von Goeber's veterans greatly outnumbered his partially-trained troops, it was a very hazardous and unwise, though a very daring, act in him to attempt to take the offensive. General Faidherbe was really one of the ablest and best of the French generals, and the motives which he declares prompted him to this bold movement were undoubtedly the true ones, and reflect credit upon him both as a soldier and a man. The effort was, however, in every respect, unsuccessful. It accomplished nothing in aid of the Paris sortie, which, as we shall see, was, equally with this, a failure; and it only sacrificed an army which under other circumstances might have rendered some service to the French cause. On the 18th of January, when Faidherbe's command had reached the vicinity of St. Quentin, von Goeben stormed the railway station of the town, and, confronting him on that and the succeeding day in a very severe battle, defeated him and drove him out of St. Quentin, and compelled him to fall back upon Cambrai. The French loss in killed and wounded was very heavy—not less, probably, than that of the Germans, which was over 3,000; but the French lost also 7,000 unwounded and more than 2,000 wounded men as prisoners, and six guns. General Faidherbe's report is as follows:

"Sir: I have the honor to forward you a short report of the battle of St. Quentin.

"Comprehending the necessity of advancing, in order to assist the sortie of the Army of Paris, I proceeded, on the 16th instant, toward the southeast, in order to turn the army which was opposed to me, and to threaten the line of La Fère, Chauncy, Noyon, and Compiegne. I was sure I should draw upon myself a crushing force; but there are circumstances in which it is duty to sacrifice one's self.

"It was before St. Quentin that I threw myself against the main body of the Prussian troops coming from Rheims, Lahn, La Fère, Ham, Peronne, Paris, Amiens, and Normandy.

"As I informed you in my telegram of the 20th January, the Army of the North, which had given proofs of great bravery, completely maintained its positions, which were very good, until the evening; but then the continual arrival of fresh troops to the enemy, and the exhausted state of our troops, rendered it necessary that the order to retreat upon Cambrai should be given. The corps of General Lecomte was ordered to take the road by Cateau; that of General Paulz d'Ivoy, that by Castelet; while I, with the cavalry, took an intermediate road which passes by Monbrechain.

"The heads of two Prussian columns then entered St. Quentin, one by the La Fère road and the other by the Paris road.

"The enemy commenced to collect, first, the wounded; second, a large number of men who, under different pretexts, had remained in the town instead of being in their places in the battle; third, all those unfortunate men who, worn out by fatigue and suffering from hunger, after four days of forced marches and two days of fighting, were unable to effect a retreat of eleven leagues through the mud on a cold, dark night; fourth, finally, some of those brave soldiers who sacrificed themselves in the rear-guard to cover the retreat. This is the extent of their trophies. They made no prisoners on the field of battle; and we have brought back intact our twelve batteries of division and our three batteries of reserve. Our four divisions being reduced by six weeks of operation and fighting to 6,000 or 7,000 men each, we had but little more than 25,000 combatants at the battle of St. Quentin. The First German Army, having been reënforced by several corps, may be estimated as double the strength of our forces. Notwithstanding this reverse, I hope that the Army of the North will be able to prove, in a few days, that it is not yet reduced to powerlessness.

"FAIDHERBE."

The hope expressed in the closing sentences of this report was not destined to be realized. His losses in killed, wounded, and prisoners in the battles before St. Quentin, and the subsequent retreat, proved to exceed 15,000; and the retreat itself was disorderly and broken, and did not cease till a portion of the panic-stricken and wearied troops had reached Lisle. Of the 50,000 men who had taken the field in December, it would have been difficult, on the 25th of January, to have rallied 15,000.

Longwy, an important fortress near the Belgian frontier, had been summoned to surrender early in January, and refusing, the German forces had commenced bombarding it on the 18th of January, and, after seven days' endurance of a very severe fire, it capitulated on the 25th, 4,000 prisoners and 200 guns being taken. In the vicinity of Dijon, the Garibaldis, father and son, with their Italian compatriots and the force under the command of the younger Garibaldi—about 30,000 troops in all—after some trifling successes, were nearly surrounded by Prussian troops, and in two or three days more would have been compelled to surrender.

On the night of the 13th of January a series of resolute sorties, though made by an insufficient number of troops in each case, was made from Paris, toward the north, against Le Bourget and Drancy, the position of the Prussian Guards, and toward the southwest against Meudon and Clamart, the Eleventh Prussian Corps and the Second Bavarian. Each attack was promptly and fully repulsed, and the French in some parts of the line fell back in disorder.

On the 19th of January General Trochu led another and the last sortie against the Germans. His force at this time engaged was 100,000 men. The sortie was intended to keep up the courage of the people of Paris, and to assure them that the Government was doing all in its power. It was also expected to compel the Germans to relinquish for the time the bombardment of

Paris, which was beginning to be troublesome, though never pushed with any great severity, and especially to prevent their taking up any new positions for bombardment. The Germans held St. Cloud, Montretout, the heights of Buzenval, and Fort d'Issy, which they had silenced and occupied some days before. General Trochu made the strong fortress of Mont Valerien his base, and at daybreak of the 19th the three army corps under his chief command issued from the fort. The right, commanded by Ducrot, attacked in the direction of Reuil and the heights of La Jonchere. The centre, under Bellemare, took Montretout, part of St. Cloud, and the heights of Buzenval. The left, under Vinoy, went upon a reconnoissance toward the stone mill in front of Issy.

At first, as usual, the French troops met with some success. The German troops were taken by surprise and driven out of Montretout; the other two corps were repulsed from the first. But as soon as the magnitude of the sortie was discovered, the Crown-Prince Friedrich Wilhelm took command, and, the Prussian batteries being brought to bear on the French, soon checked the ardor of their advance, and presently forced them to retreat. Notwithstanding the formidable army of French troops, the attack was very feebly sustained, and in the evening Montretout was retaken by the Germans, and no resistance was made by the French. The German losses in this sortie were 39 officers and 616 men killed and wounded. The French losses were about 6,000 men, over 1,000 dead being found on the field, and almost 300 being taken prisoners. On the 20th, General Trochu sent a message to ask a forty-eight hours' truce to bury the dead, but was refused unless he would make a written application. Permission was given, however, to remove the wounded. The failure of this sortie caused great discouragement in Paris, and led to the removal of Trochu from the command of the city, which was assigned to General Le Flô.

Meantime, the bombardment of the southern portion of the city was increasing in severity, and the losses of life and the destruction of property in that section were daily becoming more serious. Several hundreds of citizens, a considerable number of them women and children, were either killed or wounded by the shells, which fell very thickly in that portion of Paris.

The outlook was becoming increasingly dark and gloomy. Nowhere on French soil were the arms of France successful; or, if there was a temporary success, it was speedily followed by a disaster so complete and overwhelming that the memory of the trifling good-fortune was obliterated from the minds of the people. The War Minister, M. Gambetta, had attempted to keep up the courage of the people by bulletins of victories whose origin was wholly in his own fertile brain, or which, at the best, were mere skirmishes; while of the heavy disasters which followed he made no report. The Army of the Loire was divided, and both sections were broken, defeated, routed, and entirely demoralized; the portion under command of General de Chanzy, though still numerically the strongest of the French armies outside of Paris, had been so thoroughly beaten and dispirited, that its commander did not dare to risk another battle with it, and it had lain at Laval for two weeks, a mob rather than an army. There could be no hope of relief to beleaguered Paris from that source, though there was said to be 100,000 men on its rolls. The other half of the Army of the Loire, subsequently the magnificent Army of the East, commanded by General Bourbaki, was in rapid and disorderly retreat, with the stern and resolute von Werder in close pursuit, and Manteuffel on its right flank, pressing it constantly nearer and nearer the Swiss border; its general sick of life, and desperate from his misfortunes, seeking an escape from his troubles by attempted suicide, and his successor completing the tragedy, by a surrender of a third of France's great armies to the neutral Swiss.

The patriot-hero Garibaldi, whose love of liberty was so intense that he worshipped even the name of a Republic, and who, despite his age, his infirmities, and his still bleeding wounds, had come with his noble sons and his trusty Italian compatriots to fight the battles of a nominally free Government, had found his way hedged up by all conceivable difficulties, and, though he persevered in his struggle against the Germans, felt that the cause for which he was contending was hopeless; and, after perilling his own life and the lives of his comrades without result, was at length compelled to withdraw to his own home.

The gallant Faidherbe, after contending for months against a greatly superior force, and undertaking, with a daring which strongly reminds us of the days of chivalry, to advance toward Paris in the face of dangers, which made the attempt the most forlorn of "forlorn hopes," was driven back in disorder and dismay almost to the shores of the Atlantic.

The schools of instruction for new soldiers had nominally 250,000 men in them—really, perhaps, half that number; but they were the rawest of raw recruits, unacquainted with the use of fire-arms, and so verdant that a dozen German Uhlans would chase a thousand of them. The conscription for 1871 could be called out, but the people were sick of war, and there was not power enough in the Government of National Defense to compel them to come into the service.

In Paris matters were approaching a crisis. The population had borne the trials and sufferings of a state of siege better than could have been expected. They were for the most part a people fruitful in resources; and so, when beef gave out and mutton was not to be had, they took to horse-steaks, mule-roasts, and asinine cutlets, without serious grumbling. When even these became too high for the consumption of the poor, the flesh of dogs and cats, and even rats, was prepared into toothsome dishes

The wild beasts of the Jardin des Plantes furnished an additional supply for their lean larders; and birds of all sorts, from the pigeons of the streets to the sparrows which abounded on the house-tops, became recognized game even on the tables of the wealthy. Bread, the great article of food with the French, had deteriorated greatly in quality, and this caused more grumbling than the meat-famine. For the bread of Paris, usually proverbial for its excellence, there had been substituted, perforce, a vile compound of wheat, rye, oatmeal, and the poorest quality of rice, the last three ingredients predominating; and the bread was black, heavy, and unwholesome.

Under this famine of bread and meat the sickness of the city had greatly increased; small-pox, typhus and typhoid fevers, and the asthenic diseases induced by famine, cold, insufficient fuel and clothing, and depression of spirits, had a notable increase. The deaths, toward the last, reached nearly or quite 3,000 per week, and, as usual under such circumstances, little children were the largest sufferers. The morals of the city, never very high, had not improved under the state of siege, yet the depreciation was rather in the general moral tone of the community than in acts of outbreaking crime and violence. There are, however, in Paris, at all times a very considerable body of lawless people who would delight in nothing so much as the reign of anarchy and terror; and there is hardly anything in this world more terrible and destructive than a Parisian mob. This class had been kept under for some months, but now there were not wanting evidences that it was likely to make itself heard and felt. The clamor which, after the failure of the sortie of the 19th of January, 1871, compelled Trochu's resignation, was largely instigated by this class; and if they once gained the ascendancy, the scenes of the French Revolution would be reenacted with all the diabolical additions of cruelty and fiendishness which their depraved imaginations could invent.

RETURN OF CARRIER PIGEON.

Throughout northern, eastern, and central France there was universal ruin and disaster. The French peasants, whose means of living are never much in advance of their actual necessities, had been unable to gather fully their crops, which this year were but scanty, and had been plundered of everything they had reserved, either by their own soldiers or by the German Uhlans, and, in the midst of an uncommonly severe winter, they were starving.

There was no room to hope for any military success which would justify any further continuance of the war.

It was probably as much from the conviction of the dangers which menaced France from within her capital, as from the consciousness of the utter hopelessness of any good result from the contiunance of the struggle, that Jules Favre, the wisest, ablest, and coolest of the members of the Government of National Defense, for the third time during the war, sought an interview with Count von Bismarck, to solicit an armistice, with a view to the organization of a Government which might be duly empowered to treat for peace.

M. Favre held a conference with Count von Bismarck on the 24th of January, before the crisis had fully come, although it was evidently fast approaching. In his previous interviews with the Prussian Premier, M. Favre had been unwilling to consider the subject of yielding any territory or surrendering any fortress; but times had changed very greatly within two or three months. In November, 1870, though somewhat crippled, the French nation was yet unconquered; its armies were strong in numbers, well-equipped, and, though not well-disciplined, they were capable of making a good fight; Paris was yet strong, and famine, though not far off, had not yet crushed the spirit of its people. Now, there was no power of further effectual resistance. Paris was subdued by famine; the armies of the provinces were defeated, routed, demoralized, and many of them prisoners; all France, in the depth of its suffering and sorrow, was praying for peace—all, except the Red Republicans, who babbled about eternal resistance, the assassination of kings and princes, and other measures of like character for maintaining the war, but who had no feasible plans to offer, and were only powerful in schemes of mischief.

There was, of course, some difficulty in arranging terms for an armistice which would be acceptable to Germany without too deeply wounding French sensitiveness. It was not in human nature to forget the cruel arrogance with which the first Napoleon, after the battle of Jena, had dictated the harshest of terms to the Prussian king at Tilsit; yet it must be acknowledged that, with France entirely at his mercy, the German statesman was quite as magnanimous as could be expected. The agreement for an armistice was signed January 28th, and we are indebted to the Emperor WILHELM for a brief but accurate summary of its terms. His telegram to the Empress was as follows:

"VERSAILLES, 2 P. M., Sunday, January 29th.

"Last night an armistice for three weeks was signed. The Regulars and Mobiles are to be confined in Paris as prisoners of war. The National Guard will undertake the maintenance of order. We occupy all the forts. Paris remains invested, but will be allowed to revictual as soon as arms are surrendered.

"The National Assembly is to be summoned to meet at Bordeaux in a fortnight. All the armies in the field will retain their respective positions, the ground between opposing lines to be neutral."

The armistice covered land and sea (excepting only the Department of the Jura, where Bourbaki then was), and was to expire at noon of February 19th. As we have already stated, Bourbaki's army within a day or two crossed the frontier into

Switzerland, and surrendered themselves as prisoners of war. The line of division between the German and French forces separated into two portions the Departments of Calvados and Orne. The Germans held the Departments of the Sarthe, Indre-et-Loire, Loire-et-Cher, Loiret, and Yonne. At Paris the Germans held all the forts, and the Parisians retained command of the city wall, but it was dismantled, the gun-carriages being taken away. At the same time, heavy guns were moved into the forts, to make sure that the Paris population did not take the law into its own hands. Within four days postal communication was opened, and the supply of food began to come into the city, the German army supplying the people and garrison for the first two or three days from its own rations. The city paid a contribution of 53,000,000 francs—equal to $10,600,000—to the conquerors.

By this armistice, and the surrenders which accompanied it, the number of French soldiers who were prisoners of war was increased to more than 700,000, aside from nearly or quite 250,000 who had died in the field of battle, or from sickness or wounds. Of these 700,000, a very large number would not live to return. When we add to these losses of fighting men the very large number of German artisans driven out of France at the beginning of the war, and the population of the ceded provinces, we shall find that France had decreased in inhabitants materially since its quinquennial census of 1866.

The meeting of the National Assembly at Bordeaux was fixed for February 15th—a date which necessitated an extension of the armistice, which was granted, eventually, to the 1st of March. At first the decree of Gambetta, which disqualified for election to the Assembly members of families reigning over France since 1789, all persons who had acted as Imperial official candidates in past elections, held office as Ministers, Senators, or Councillors of State under the Empire, and Prefects who had accepted office between the 2d of December, 1851, and the 4th of September, 1870, seemed likely to thwart the design of the armistice. It was his design, by this extremely injudicious decree, to keep out of the National Assembly all the Bourbons and Orleanists and their adherents, and every one who, by having received office from Louis Napoleon, might be supposed to sympathize with him. The effect of this decree would have been to array all classes of monarchists against the Republicans, who were not at any time a majority in the nation. Count von Bismarck at once protested against it as unjust, and preventing a free expression of the opinion of the nation, and demanded, as preferable, the re-assembling of the Corps Legislatif, which had been irregularly dissolved on the 4th of September. Jules Favre and his associates of the Paris portion of the Government of National Defense repudiated Gambetta's decree at once, and declared that the elections should be free; but Gambetta defended it very warmly, and indulged in language toward the German Premier, in relation to his supposed desire for the reinstatement of Louis Napoleon, which was, to say the least, in the worst possible taste. The power of the French War Minister was gone, however, and MM. Favre, Pelletan, Garnier, Pages, and Emmanuel Arago, repairing to Bordeaux on the 7th of February, issued immediately an order by telegraph to the Prefects of all the Departments of France, annulling Gambetta's decree as incompatible with the principle of universal suffrage. They also removed Gambetta from his position as Minister of War, though they could not turn him out of the Cabinet.

The elections proceeded with great activity from this time, and, though the effect of the first promulgation of Gambetta's decree had been unfavorable, the political complexion of the National Assembly was undecided, none of the five or six parties having a majority of the 700 votes of the Assembly. The Orleanists were somewhat the most numerous, and next, per haps, the Bonapartists; the moderate Republicans numbered about 160; and there were smaller factions of the adherents to the Bourbons of the elder branch, the Red Republicans, and the Constitutional monarchists, who had no particular fancy for any of the Imperial or Royal aspirants of Bourbon, Orleans, or Bonaparte stock.

At a preliminary session of the Assembly held on the 13th of February, for the purpose of ascertaining the probable complexion of the Assembly, and taking some measures toward an early organization, Jules Favre, for himself and his associates, resigned the powers confided to them as the Government of National Defense, the resignation to take effect as soon as a Pro visional Government could be organized.

At the first regular session of the Assembly, M. Grévy, a moderate Republican, though with some monarchical leanings but a man of high character, was elected President of the Assembly, receiving 519 out of 538 votes.

On the 17th, M. Adolphe Thiers, well known as one of the ablest of French statesmen, an earnest Royalist and adherent to the House of Orleans, and Premier of Louis Philippe, was chosen Provisional President of the Republic, with power to select his own Ministers. On the 19th, he announced as his Cabinet the following:

Jules Dufaure, Minister of Justice.
Jules Favre, Minister of Foreign Affairs.
Ernest Picard, Minister of the Interior.
Jules Simon, Minister of Public Instruction.
Felix Lambrecht, Minister of Commerce.
General Le Flô, Minister of War.
Admiral Pothuan, Minister of the Marine.
Louis Joseph Buffett, Minister of Finance, and President of the Council.

A committee of fifteen, with which President Thiers, M.

Favre, and M. Picard, of his Cabinet, were associated, was appointed by the Assembly the same day, and proceeded, on the 20th, to Versailles, and entered upon the negotiations for peace. The discussions upon this subject with the German Commissioners were very earnest, and many propositions and counter-propositions were made. The British Government used its influence to induce Germany to require a smaller amount of indemnity than was at first demanded, and it was said to have been through their influence that it was reduced from six milliards of francs, equal to $1,200,000,000, to five milliards of francs, or $1,000,000,000. Germany demanded the possession of Belfort, which had surrendered after the proclamation of the armistice; but this France was unwilling to give up. The terms finally settled upon and announced by President Thiers to the National Assembly at Bordeaux, February 28th, as having been agreed upon by the Commissioners on the 26th of that month, were as follows:

"France cedes one-fifth of Lorraine, including Metz and Thionville, and all of Alsace except Belfort, and pays an indemnity of five milliards of francs—one milliard this year, and the remainder in 1872 and 1873. The fortified cities of Lunéville, Nancy, and Belfort are left to France. Longwy, Thionville, Metz, and Saarrebourg go to Germany. The German troops will gradually withdraw from French territory as the payments are made. The armistice is prolonged to the 12th of March; and, last of all, the Germans are to enter Paris. The Champagne country will be held by 50,000 Germans, with Prince Friedrich Karl as Governor, until the indemnity is paid."

This preliminary treaty, as it was called, was ratified by the National Assembly on the 1st of March by a vote of 546 yeas against 107 nays. The Red Republicans, and some of the more

MEETING OF THE NATIONAL ASSEMBLY AT BORDEAUX.

moderate ones, voted against it, on the ground that there should be no cession of French territory.

The following detailed description of the lines laid down in this preliminary treaty was subsequently published:

"The line of demarcation between France and Germany, as at first proposed, is retained, with one exception. It commences in the northwestern frontier at the Canton of Cattenom, in the Department of the Moselle; runs thence to Thionville, Briery, and Gorze; skirts the southwestern and southern boundaries of the arrondissement of Metz; thence proceeds in a direct line to Chateau-Salins, and at Pettoncourt, in that arrondissement, turns and follows the crest of the mountains between the valleys of the rivers Seille and Vezouze, in the Department of Muerthe, to the Canton of Schirmeck, in the northwestern corner of the Department of the Vosges; thence it runs to Saales, dividing that commune, and, after that, coincides with the western frontiers of the Upper and Lower Rhine Departments, until it reaches the Canton of Belfort; thence it passes diagonally to the Canton of Delle, and then terminates by reaching the Swiss frontier.

"An alteration made at the last moment in these boundaries gives Belfort to France, and cedes additional territory around Metz to Germany.

"Germany is to possess her acquisitions from France in perpetuity.

"It is agreed that, as soon as the preliminaries are ratified, the Germans shall evacuate the Departments of Calvados, Arne, Gorthe, Eure-et-Loire, Loiret, Loire-et-Cher, Indre-et-Loir, and Yonne, and all territory on the left bank of the Seine. The French troops will retire behind the river Loire until peace is finally declared, except from Paris and other strongholds.

"After the payment of two milliards of francs the Germans

will occupy only the Departments of Marne, Ardennes, Haut-Marne, Meuse, Vosges, Meurthe, and the fortress of Belfort.

"Germany will be open to accept suitable financial instead of territorial guarantees for the payment of the war indemnity."

An attempt was made by M. Conte, a former private secretary of Louis Napoleon, who was a member of the National Assembly, on the day of the ratification of this treaty, to justify the action of the Emperor. This occasioned some commotion, but led to the introduction, by M. Targe, of a resolution decreeing the fall of the Empire, and stigmatizing Louis Napoleon as the author of the misfortunes of France. This was passed by acclamation, no voices being heard in the negative.

The Germans were very moderate in their claims in regard to entering Paris. But 30,000 troops were permitted to go within the walls, and these were ordered to confine themselves to a triangular section of the city, of which the Seine formed the east side, the *enceinte* from Point du Jour to Porte des Ternes the west side; while the Faubourg St. Honoré and the Avenue des Ternes from the Rue Royal to the *enceinte*, the north side or base. It included the *Arc de Triomphe*, in which the first Napoleon had long ago inscribed his boast, now strikingly falsified: "At the approach of the Conqueror, the German Empire has come to an end."

There were some slight disturbances, and the Paris mobs seemed determined to wreak the vengeance which they dared not visit on the German troops, upon the French police, tradesmen, and guides, who showed any civility to the Germans; but thanks to their wholesome terror of the invaders, and to the careful arrangements made by General d'Aurelles de Paladines, who commanded the National Guard of Paris, there were no serious outbreaks of violence. On the 3d of March the German troops marched quietly out of the city, and were presently on their route homeward.

The preliminary treaty was formally ratified by the Emperor Wilhelm at Versailles on the 3d of March, and was announced to the Empress in the following despatch, which was received with great demonstrations of joy in Berlin:

"VERSAILLES, March 3

"I have just ratified the conditions of peace, which the Bordeaux Assembly have accepted. Thus far the work is complete which was through seven months of battles to be achieved, thanks to the valor, devotion, and endurance of our incomparable army, and the sacrifices of the whole Fatherland. The Lord of Hosts has everywhere visibly blessed our enterprises, and by His mercy has permitted an honorable peace. To Him be the honor! to the Fatherland the thanks.

"WILHELM."

On the 4th of March the Emperor reviewed 100,000 of his troops in the Bois de Boulogne, Prince Friedrich Karl, General von Moltke, and Count von Bismarck being present. The final treaty of peace was to be negotiated at Brussels, the plenipotentiaries being M. Favre on the side of the French, and Herr von Arnim on the part of Germany. The time fixed for the commencement of negotiations was March 15th, but they would probably occupy several months. The German Emperor returned to Berlin on the 12th of March, and all the German troops, except the Army of Occupation, were on their way homeward before the 20th of that month.

Meantime, France was in a state of unrest. The departments which had been desolated by the war, except Paris, were rejoiced at the return of peace, although they were great sufferers from the privations which the war had inflicted; but the turbulent classes in Paris were disappointed that they could not have a reign of terror and bloodshed. The score of newspapers which sprang up like mushrooms at the cessation of hostilities, were loud in their denunciations of the treaty, of the Germans, and of everything like order. One of them (Rochefort's paper) openly advocated regicide; others inculcated revenge, and sought to inculcate on the people the duty of nursing their hatred of the Germans till the time came when they could take vengeance on them for their humiliation. The departments which had suffered comparatively little from the war encouraged the same sentiments, and there is reason to fear that a civil war may yet be added to the woes of the nation.

The question, What form of Government is most likely to be approved by the people? is one of great difficulty. As a permanent Government, a majority of the people evidently do not desire a republic. The French people like to be governed, and to be governed with a strong hand. A republican Government implies thoughtfulness and foresight among the people themselves, who are alike the governors and the governed; but the French people, like the other Celtic nations, do not like the trouble of doing their own thinking; they prefer that the Government shall do it for them. Thrice within the past seventy-five years have they tried a republic, and in each instance—unless the last shall prove an exception—they have lapsed from it into an absolute monarchy. For them, undoubtedly, a qualified constitutional monarchy is unquestionably the best Government. Who this constitutional monarch shall be, whether Bourbon, Orleans, or Bonaparte, or neither, is an interesting question, but one into which it is not our province to enter at this time.

We may, however, with propriety consider the burdens which the new Government, whatever it may be, will inherit. The national debt of France, on the 1st of January, 1870, was $2,852,695,870. To this was added, in the course of the year, two loans, one of $150,000,000, July 16th, 1870, and the other of $50,000,000, on the 25th of October, for the prosecution of the war. Beyond this, for military operations outside of Paris, a debt was incurred of $220,000,000, and for the defence of that city and its supplies of food, about $200,000,000 more. The indemnity to be paid to the Germans is $1,000,000,000 more, making a total of $4,472,695,870, or about twice the amount of our national debt; while her population is less, and her national wealth materially less than ours. Her annual current expenditure for interest on debt and Government expenditure in 1869 was $425,000,000; and there will be an addition of nearly, or quite, a hundred millions a year for interest, giving her an annual expenditure of $525,000,000—a very heavy load for her already over-taxed people to bear. She is, indeed, under bonds to keep the peace for a generation to come, at least.

The advice given to the nation by the veteran Thiers, on accepting the Provisional Presidency on the 19th of February, 1871, was eminently sensible, and indicated a far higher statesmanship than most of the French leaders have manifested. The first duty of the nation was, most certainly, to endeavor to repair her losses, restore her national credit and her commercial prosperity, and keep her people well and profitably employed. The discussion of political questions and constitutionl provisions could in their case be profitably postponed to a more favorable period. These are the words of the venerable statesman. Will France heed his counsel?

" Without placing before you a plan of government, which is always somewhat vague, I shall present you with some views on the thought of union which governs me, and on which I would base the reconstruction of our country. In a state of society that is prosperous, regularly constituted, and yields gently to the progress of opinion, each party represents a political system.

To combine all in the same administration, would be placing there opposing forces which would either neutralize each other, or, in the event of dissensions, end in inertia or conflict.

"But, alas! does our present situation show society regularly constituted, yielding gently to the progress of opinion? France, precipitated without serious reasons or sufficient preparation into war, has seen one-half of her soil invaded, her army destroyed, her fine organization disrupted, her old and powerful unity compromised, her finances embarrassed, the greater part of her sons withdrawn from labor to die on the battle-fields, order profoundly disturbed by the apparition of anarchy, and, after the enforced surrender of Paris, war suspended only for some days, and ready to recommence if a Government esteemed by Europe, courageously accepting the authority and assuming the responsibility of doleful negotiations, fails to put an end to appalling calamities.

"In presence of this state of things, are there, can there be, two policies? But must there not be only one, strong, expedient, consistent, and urgent, in order to make peace as promptly as possible under the evils which overwhelm us?

"Who will not maintain that we must, as soon and as completely as possible, terminate the foreign occupation by means of a peace courageously negotiated, and which will not be accepted unless it is honorable; relieve our fields of the enemy which tramples and destroys them; recall from foreign prisons our captured soldiers, officers, and generals; reconstruct of them a disciplined and valiant army; reform by election our Councils-General and our dissolved Municipal Councils; reorganize our disorganized Administration; terminate ruinous expenses; re-establish, if not our finances, which would not be the work of a day, at least our credit—the only means of meeting our pressing engagements; return to the fields and workshops our Mobiles; open obstructed roads; rebuild destroyed bridges, and thus create employment—the only means by which our artisans and peasants can live?

"Is there any one who can say that there is anything more pressing than all this? And is there here one, for example, who would gravely discuss articles of the Constitution, while our people, dying of hunger, are obliged to give foreign soldiers the last morsel of bread that remains?

"No, no, gentlemen! Tranquillize; reorganize; revive credit; reanimate industry; behold the only policy possible, or even conceivable, at this moment. In all this, every sensible, honest, enlightened man, be he for a monarchy or a republic, can work usefully, and, if he works only for a year or six months, he may return with a high head and satisfied conscience into the ranks of his countrymen.

"Ah, no doubt, when we shall have rendered our country the pressing services I have enumerated—when we shall have raised from the soil where she lies prostrate that noble being called France—when we shall have stanched her wounds, restored her strength, she will return to consciousness; and then, reanimated, and in full freedom of mind, she will say how she wishes to live.

"When this work of reparation shall be over—and it may not be very long—the time of discussion and of considering the theories of government will have come, and, having accomplished our reconstruction under a republic, we can determine with discernment our destinies; and this judgment will be pronounced, not by a minority, but by a majority of our fellow-citizens—that is, by the national will itself.

"Such is the only policy possible, expedient, and adapted to the unhappy circumstances we are in. It is to it my honorable colleagues are ready to devote their experienced faculties; it is to it that, for my part, despite age and the fatigues of a long life, I am ready to consecrate all the strength that remains to me, without any design or any other ambition, I swear to you, than to attach to my last days the regrets of my fellow-citizens, and, permit me to add, without even being assured of it, after the most intense devotion, to obtain justice for my efforts. But, no matter; in presence of our suffering and perishing country, all personal considerations would be unpardonable. Let us be united, and, by showing that we are capable of concord and wisdom, we shall obtain the esteem of Europe, and, with her esteem, her support, and, further, the respect of the enemy himself; and all this will be the strongest support you can give to your negotiators, when defending the interests of France in the negotiations that are about to open. Defer, then, to a period which cannot be far, the political dissensions which have divided us, and may divide us still more; and let difference of opinion, which I know is the result of sincere convictions, only return when it shall no longer be an attack upon the existence and safety of the country."

CHAPTER XIV.

WITH a brief review of the leading incidents of this great war, we take our leave of our readers.

When, on the 15th of July, 1870, Louis Napoleon Bonaparte declared war with Prussia, the numerous vicissitudes of his eventful life may have suggested to him the possibility that the war, if long protracted, might prove unfavorable to his hopes; but no seer could have predicted to him that, in seven weeks from that day, he would be defeated, dethroned, and a prisoner to the one man among all the crowned heads of Europe whom he most hated; and that all the hopes and dreams in which he had indulged of the perpetuation of a Bonaparte dynasty in France would be utterly dissipated.

And yet, as we look upon the matter now, it seems the most natural thing in the world that just this thing should have happened. He knew that he was unprepared for the war he had most wantonly provoked; but he did not know that the frauds and moral corruption of which he had been guilty had permeated the entire body politic; that all his subordinates, finding their chief defrauding the nation, had undertaken the same game for themselves.

He knew that Prussia was strong in her armies, her finances, her resources; but he did not know her condition of preparation for war, her complete military organization, the genius of her great strategist, nor the enthusiasm which would be awakened throughout Germany by her going to war in a just cause.

And, after the declaration of war, in the three weeks which followed before a blow was struck, amid all his boastings and declarations of the necessity by which he was driven unwillingly into war, was there no fear of a retribution for his numerous crimes against the nation, and against the God who rules over the nations; no misgiving that the time was approaching when his conduct as a ruler should be judged impartially by the nations whom he had attempted to dupe? Whether this was so or not, there was a marked and manifest difference between his manner and proclamations and those of the Prussian King. The one was boastful, defiant, and appealed to the passion of his nation for glory; the other, quiet, and confident of the justice of his cause, looked to Heaven for aid and success.

The slight affair at Saarbruck on the 4th of August possessed no significance or importance in itself, but was made the occasion of a vainglorious despatch by the Emperor, and the announcement of the weeping of his veterans over the tranquillity of his wonderful boy. The more serious battles of Forbach and Spicheren Heights, and of Weissenburg on the 6th of August, showed the boastful Emperor that victory would not always perch upon his banners; and when this was followed, on the 8th, by the decisive battle of Woerth and the precipitate retreat of MacMahon, it was almost pitiable to see how quickly his tone was changed from vaunting to terror. "Frossard has lost a battle," he telegraphs. "MacMahon has been defeated, with heavy loss, at Woerth. All can yet be reëstablished." Bad news followed fast and faster. Strasbourg, Pfalzburg, and Toul were besieged. MacMahon, while doing his best to collect reënforcements, was pursued pitilessly and relentlessly by the Crown-Prince. Bazaine's army, with which his headquarters were, and which had thrown out its advance toward Saarbruck and Forbach, was compelled to fall back in hot haste to its fortifications at Metz, and, pressed by the greatly superior force of the German King and his trusty Lieutenants von Steinmetz and Prince Friedrich Karl, found itself compelled to attempt to gain the open country and the highways leading from Metz to Paris, to avoid being shut up in the fortifications of Metz.

The attempt was made too late. The battle of Courcelles, fought on Sunday, August 14th, detained Bazaine in Metz to save the city, which was threatened with instant capture if he left it. The delay of the 15th to bury the dead gave time to the army of Prince Friedrich Karl to cross the Moselle and plant themselves strongly across the lower road to Verdun and Paris, at Mars-la-Tour, while a sufficient number of Steinmetz's veterans threatened the upper or Conflans road, to make a passage by that difficult, if not impossible.

Bazaine had waited too long; but, convinced more fully than before of the absolute necessity of his controlling one or both these roads, he made, on the 18th, his final effort to obtain possession of the lower, and, failing in that, of the upper road. But he had by this time more than 250,000 troops opposed to him; and, though the fighting on the French side was more gallant, earnest, and obstinate than in any other battle of the war, and they returned to the charge again and again with an energy and resolution worthy a better cause, yet, at 9 P. M., they were thoroughly beaten, and driven into the fortifications of Metz, from which most of them only emerged as prisoners.

Thus far the Germans had been uniformly successful, rather from their ability to endure "hard pounding," their persistence and determination, than from any remarkable displays of skill on the part of their leaders. Their losses had been heavy—heavier, somewhat, probably, than those of the French; but their superior size, weight, endurance, and intelligence had given them the advantage even over the vaunted and really deadly mitrailleuse.

From this time forward the victories of the Prussians were

as much the result of strategic skill as of hard fighting. Bazaine being shut up, or, to use an expressive phrase of General Grant's, "bottled up" in Metz, a large army of observation was required to hold him in check; for this purpose the Landwehr, or reserves, were ordered up, and, meanwhile, the greater part of the First Army (Steinmetz) was put in marching order for Paris. At Chalons it formed a junction with the Third Army (that of the Crown-Prince), and a Fourth Army, made up from the Saxon troops, the Royal Guard, and a corps from Prince Friedrich Karl's army, joined the two.

MacMahon, who had been marching swiftly on Paris, had, on reaching Chalons, been ordered by the Emperor, now at Rheims, to turn northward and make a détour by Rheims, Rethel, Sedan, and Montmedy, in the hope of relieving Bazaine and raising the siege of Metz.

The movement was a stupendous blunder, and the great strategist von Moltke saw it, and at once improved his opportunity. No sooner had MacMahon fairly turned northward, than von Moltke commenced pushing his troops toward the north between the Aisne and the Meuse, through a difficult country, the forest of Argonnes and the Ardennes mountains, and, in spite of the difficulties of the route, was soon on the flank of MacMahon's advance-guard. True to his strategical principles, he struck a heavy blow just as they were attempting to cross a river—the Meuse; and, meanwhile, he was sending over the Fourth Army, under the Crown-Prince of Saxony, at a higher point, while he obstructed the passage of the French. The next day, the eventful 1st of September, the battle began early. Pressed in rear and on either flank, the French army could only fall back upon the fortified town of Sedan. MacMahon was dangerously wounded early in the day, and the command devolved upon General de Wimpffen, though Napoleon III was present and directed in part. It was about 3 P. M. when the jaded and beaten French corps attempted to enter Sedan. All order was lost; it was more a mob than an army, and part of the town was already in possession of the Germans, who had entered with the French. There was no alternative but surrender. German troops occupied every height, and were in such position that, while they could soon make the town untenable, there was no way of escape. Under these circumstances, the Emperor, General de Wimpffen, and the entire army, 127,000 strong, including sick and wounded, were surrendered. This event precipitated the revolution already imminent in Paris. The overthrow of the Napoleonic dynasty was demanded by the people and accorded by the authorities; the *Corps Législatif* perished with it; the Empress took her flight to England; the Tuileries was taken possession of by the people, and a self-elected Provisional Government, professedly in the interests of the Republic, but composed of men of all shades of opinion, took control of the national affairs.

"The Government of National Defense," as this new and almost self-constituted body was called, while denouncing in the strongest terms the deposed Emperor for bringing the nation into such great and sore troubles, yet was equally vindictive with him toward the Germans, and hurled its anathemas against them, while it frantically implored other nations to intervene to procure for them a peace. At this juncture, peace might have been made with Germany on comparatively favorable terms. The line of the Saar might have been prolonged through the Vosges so as to include Belfort and Strasbourg, and some moderate indemnity demanded; and this would then have fully satisfied Germany; for neither Strasbourg, Pfalzburg, nor Metz had yet capitulated, nor was Paris besieged. But, with a most unwise determination to tickle the ears of the mob, the new Government raised the cry, "Not a foot of territory nor a stone of a fortress shall ever be surrendered!" And, though they sent Favre to negotiate for peace with the German statesman Bismarck, they had so hampered him by these war-cries, that he was unable to effect any arrangement looking toward peace; and an angry correspondence followed, in which the cool and diplomatic German had greatly the advantage.

It was at first proposed to hold elections for a Constituent Assembly; but the War Minister, Gambetta, opposed it, because it was decidedly uncertain whether such an Assembly would allow them to retain their power.

Meantime, the Germans prosecuted the war relentlessly. Paris was reached by their troops on the 15th of September, and its investment commenced on the 20th; and though the circuit of their lines around it was almost ninety miles, and they had not for some time more than 200,000 troops which they could employ for this siege, their cordon, once formed, was never broken. The railroads leading into the city were severed, and its supplies cut off; the Government divided—Gambetta, Crémieux, Glais-Bizoin, and Fourichon going to Tours, while Favre, Trochu, Emmanuel Arago, Garnier, Pages, and Pelletan, remained in Paris. During the month of September the new French Government contented itself with abortive negotiations for peace, missions to neutral powers, and somewhat high-sounding proclamations; but when, on the 27th of that month, Strasbourg, with 17,000 men, capitulated unconditionally to the German forces, and Orleans was bombarded and occupied by von der Tann's army on the 11th of October, the French War Minister was roused to almost superhuman exertions; and, while occasionally sending out absurdly exaggerated proclamations of French successes which proved to have been French defeats, he certainly deserved credit for the energy and executive ability with which he gathered armies from all parts of France, organized, armed, supplied, and put them in the field. He formed, in the vicinity of Orleans, a great army of over 200,000 men, most of whom, indeed, had never borne arms, but, under skilful officers, could soon be made serviceable troops. The skilful officers were, to be sure, not readily to be obtained, for most of those who had seen service were prisoners. But it was not alone this Army of the Loire which was to be organized and officered. Another of equal numbers was formed in the north of France, and placed under the command of General Faidherbe. Still another, though of less extent, was organized in the east in the vicinity of Dijon, and Garibaldi's Italian Legion was made its nucleus. Schools of instruction for troops were established at all the military dépôts, and within two months he had gathered in these over 250,000 troops, independent of the conscription of 1871, which was being called out as rapidly as possible. In addition to these great assemblages of regular soldiers, a considerable force of irregular troops, to perform the duties of scouts, rangers, and guerillas, were organized under the names of *Franc-tireurs*, *Partisans de Gers*, &c., &c., which were intended to render similar service to the French army with that performed by the Uhlans for the Germans. In thus reorganizing the French army from the population which for twenty years had not borne arms, M. Gambetta certainly displayed great executive ability; and though there were, every now and then, examples of his impulsive nature, such as that proclamation in which he declared that Bazaine was a traitor, and outlawed and put a price upon his head; or those in which he announced successive victories, whose details he had manufactured to encourage the French troops; or those in which, with fiery indignation, he denounced the Germans and their king as foes to universal humanity, because they would not grant an armistice on the terms he desired; or vented his wrath on generals whom he had a week or two before exalted as almost demigods, when their successes turned to failures; yet much can be pardoned in a man who, with all his failings, showed a truly patriotic spirit, and who, in the midst of a corrupt and demoralized nation, was thoroughly and unimpeachably honest.

But these great executive abilities were not sufficient to save France, or to drive out the German force which had planted itself so strongly upon her soil. The work of conquest went steadily forward. Closer and closer were drawn the lines around Paris, and nearer and nearer approached the grim spectre of famine; and the feeble sorties made from time to time could not sever the cordon which bound the beleaguered city. Outside of Paris, after the fall of Strasbourg and the capture of Orleans, which we have already chronicled, there was such a succession of disasters as never before befell a brave and warlike nation. Metz capitulated on the 27th of October, together with Bazaine's army, consisting of 3 marshals, 66 generals, 6,000 officers, and 173,000 privates. Dijon surrendered on the 30th of October, New Breisach on the 6th of November, and Verdun on the 9th. Thionville, after obstinate and protracted resistance, capitulated on the 25th; and the sorties from Paris, from Mezieres, from Belfort, Montmedy, and La Fère, were promptly repulsed, with heavy loss on the part of the besieged. There was, indeed, a temporary relief from these great disasters in the repulse of the Prussians at Coulmiers and Patay; and the recapture of Orleans by the Army of the Loire, under General d'Aurelles de Paladines; but it was only temporary. The German General von der Tann, soon after his evacuation of Orleans, was reenforced from the army of Prince Friedrich Karl, and soon began to make demonstrations looking to the recovery of his lost ground. The most formidable sortie from Paris made during the war, under Trochu and Ducrot, from the 29th of November to the 2d of December, proved a failure after two or three days of hard fighting, though another day's conflict would probably have resulted in success. A succession of severe battles around Orleans, in which Prince Friedrich Karl managed to separate and isolate two corps of the French army, resulted, on the 4th of December, in the surrender of Orleans, and the retreat of the sundered French Army of the Loire, one portion toward Tours, Blois, and Le Mans, and the other toward Bourges. The retreat was attended with considerable losses. M. Gambetta, with ready tact, organized the two divisions into two armies, one under General de Chanzy, the other under General Bourbaki; the former commander, General d'Aurelles de Paladines, being under a cloud for his want of success.

The tide of disaster continued to swell. Rouen was occupied by the Germans on the 5th of December; Beaugency on the 8th; Dieppe on the 9th; Pfalzburg, a strong fortress and bravely defended, capitulated on the 12th; and Montmedy, almost as strong, on the 14th. The French were driven from Vendome on the 16th, and from Nuits on the 18th. Tours capitulated on the 20th; Sangre, Blois, and Bapaume were captured on the 25th and 26th; and Fort Avron, the strongest of the defences of Paris on the east, bombarded and occupied on the 29th; and Forts Rosny, Noissy, Nogent, d'Issy, and Vanvres, on the east and south of Paris, bombarded and silenced.

General Manteuffel had had, during the month of December, numerous conflicts, generally but partial ones, with General Faidherbe's army in the north of France, and had pushed it back through Rouen, Amiens, and Bapaume, to Arras; but early in January, Faidherbe, under instructions from Paris, began to move southward again; and General Manteuffel and his trusty lieutenant, General von Goeben, moved against him as speedily as possible. This was part of a concerted movement of Gambetta's, in which General de Chanzy, who was not far from Le Mans, General Faidherbe, who was to move southward in the line of Rouen, and the Parisian garrison, who were to make a sortie to the southwest and west of Paris, were to coöperate. It proved a failure in all its parts. Faidherbe found himself resisted by a superior, or at least a more resolute force, under General von Goeben, and was driven back with heavy losses, and his army demoralized, through St. Quentin to Arras and Lille. General de Chanzy, who had been followed closely and watched carefully in all his movements from the time he left Orleans, on the 4th of December, found that he must fight Prince Friedrich Karl's entire army before he could approach any nearer to Paris; and, after four days of severe fighting (December 9th-13th), being twice flanked by the Grand Duke of Mecklenburg-Schwerin, was thoroughly defeated and routed, losing about 15,000 in killed and wounded and 22,000 unwounded prisoners, and compelled to retreat to Laval, with his troops almost disorganized. Through some misunderstanding, the sortie from Paris was not rightly timed, and, being feebly made, only resulted in heavy loss of prisoners.

. In the east of France, Garibaldi had had some trifling successes over the Germans in the vicinity of Dijon; but when the siege of Belfort by von Werder, and the movements of Bourbaki with his Army of the East, had led to the reënforcement of the German forces from Manteuffel's army and a portion of Prince Friedrich Karl's, Garibaldi's little army of about 30,000 men was in great peril, and only escaped capture by reason of the armistice.

Bourbaki undertook to raise the siege of Belfort, and to drive von Werder's army across the Rhine; but after four days of hard fighting (January 13th–17th), repulsed each day but returning to the attack, he was compelled to commence a retreat, in which he lost heavily both in killed and wounded and in prisoners, and finally, outflanked by Manteuffel and crowded upon the Swiss frontier, he attempted suicide; and his successor, General Clinchart, about the 1st of February, surrendered to the Swiss the remainder of his army, said to number over 80,000 men. Meanwhile, Abbevilliers, Longwy, and finally Belfort, surrendered.

On the 24th of January, 1871, M. Jules Favre, the ablest diplomatist of the French Cabinet, commenced his third effort to arrange with the German Premier, Count von Bismarck, for an armistice of sufficient duration to permit the negotiation of a treaty of peace which would be binding. In his previous attempts M. Favre had been greatly hampered by the refusal of his colleagues to submit to any cession of territory, or anything less than the whole of their demands, some of which were utterly untenable, and hence both the former attempts at negotiating an armistice had failed. Now, however, their pride was humbled, and they began to comprehend how fatal would be any further resistance if peace was attainable, and hence did not put him under such limitations as they had done previously. The discussion of the points involved in the armistice occupied three days; and on the 27th M. Favre returned to Paris, and an armistice was agreed upon, which was to commence on the 29th of January and last twenty-one days. It was subsequently extended to the 26th of February, to the 1st, and, finally, to the 6th of March.

This armistice provided for the surrender of the fortifications of Paris, for the laying down of the arms of its garrison, except a division of 12,000 men, to whom was assigned the duty of keeping order in Paris during the armistice. It also prescribed the lines which should bound the captured territory, required an indemnity of $40,000,000 from the captured city, and permitted its revictualling, and the exchange of prisoners. Provision was made, further, for the election and assembling in Bordeaux, on the 15th of February, of a National Assembly, who might authorize the negotiation of a treaty of peace, and who should be qualified to ratify it.

Some obstructions were thrown in the way of the carrying

out of the measures agreed upon by the contracting parties to this armistice, by Gambetta and Trochu; but they were speedily repudiated by the other Members of the Government of National Defense, and their authors were removed from office.

The National Assembly met, elected M. Grevy its presiding officer, and, receiving the resignations of M. Favre and his colleagues, chose M. Adolphe Thiers President of the Provisional Government; and he appointed M. Favre his Premier. The preliminary treaty of peace, whose provisions we have already cited, was negotiated by MM. Favre and Thiers on the French side, and Count von Bismarck and Herr von Arnim on the German, and ratified by the National Assembly on the 3d of March, and by King Wilhelm (who had been crowned, on the 19th of January, by vote of the Confederated States of Germany, Emperor of Germany) on the 5th of that month. On the 1st of March 30,000 German troops entered Paris, and marched out on the 3d; and within the following ten days all except the Army of Occupation returned to Germany.

Thus ended the most remarkable war of modern times—remarkable alike for its rapidity of movement, the vast masses of men put in the field, its terrific slaughter, its stupendous surrenders—for the Germans had, on the 10th of February, in their hands and in the hands of neutrals, over 900,000 prisoners of war; four of the largest armies of modern times, viz., McMahon's at Sedan, Bazaine's at Metz, Trochu's at Paris, and Bourbaki's in Switzerland, having surrendered within five months, besides more than a hundred and fifty thousand prisoners taken in the various engagements of the war. It was remarkable, too, for the new weapons brought into use, and the extent to which modern appliances in chemistry and the arts were made subservient to military purposes. The *mitrailleur* and the various breech-loading rifles were tested far more thoroughly than ever before, some of them, indeed, for the first time in actual warfare.

The superiority of the rifled steel cannon of Krupp over the French bronze guns was conclusively shown; and the folly of dependence upon a navy, however perfectly constructed, armed, or manned, in a war between two powers whose lands are contiguous.

Terrible and destructive as this war has been both to human life (for it is estimated that, from wounds and sickness bred in the camps, and from death on the battle-field, more than six hundred thousand men to-day lie dead because of this war, and perhaps two-thirds as many are hopelessly crippled and maimed) and to property ($2,500,000,000 will not cover the losses of France alone, including the indemnity), it is yet destined, we firmly believe, to prove beneficial to civilization, and for the ultimate advantage of both nations, in the political changes which will ensue from it. In France, it has broken forever the power of one of the least progressive and the most mischievous and belligerent people of Europe, and the one which has most disturbed the general peace for ages. In Germany it has suddenly elevated to the position of arbiter of Europe the most peaceful and domestic of races. It has reduced from the first position that one of the great powers most positively committed to the false policy that its national prosperity depended on the misfortunes of its neighbors, and that to embarrass other powers and to contract other influences was the surest way of extending its own importance. It has elevated to the first rank that nation which, of all others in Europe, believes that individual and national greatness depend on the general prosperity. It has destroyed an Empire whose policy was War, while its cry was Peace; but it has at the same time created a greater and a better one, whose undoubted policy must be Peace. In France it has pricked and instantly exploded a despotism, which might have continued for a generation of peace to enervate the people it tyrannized over. In Germany it has not less suddenly aroused a spirit of nationality, which renders at once possible that long-coveted unity of the German race which an age of peace might not have consolidated. While the French Empire existed, there could be no real peace in Europe. While the German Empire remains, there can be no war without its consent; and the past policy, the fixed principles, the natural sympathies of her people, not the mere written records of her Government, violable at the will of one man, are pledges of her peaceful purposes. Let us sympathize with the race which has been so painfully humiliated; but let us also rejoice with that larger civilization of all Europe which gains by what the French have lost. The war is yet to find its most important result, its chief apology, and its greatest blessing, in the increased impulse it will give to a higher and better civilization in Europe. It is in their enlarged liberty that the French are yet to see themselves blessed by their own overthrow. France has not merely been relieved of the cancer of the Empire that ate its heart out, but her people have been liberated from false and enervating direction, and are free to enter upon a sounder and truer education than that which has heretofore made them a race of polished but frivolous people—smooth and elegant of exterior, but too deficient in the great impulses which belong to more earnest and progressive races. We shall not be many years—the French will not be a generation—in recognizing that the war has been one of the mysterious agencies of civilization, spreading knowledge, which is the only true source of power; the unsuspected means of developing industry, which creates wealth. By the war, France is relieved of a ruler, an army, a system of government which absorbed and wasted her prosperity; and not only she and Germany, but all Europe, will be saved henceforth much of that cost in wealth and loss in national spirit which follows the maintenance of large standing armies. Relieved of these dread incubi, France may become the rival of England and Germany in manufactures; for the delicate taste, the natural appreciation of the beautiful in art and mechanism, and the deftness and skill of her operatives in all the finer manufactures, assure her a ready preëminence in this direction; and, once educated beyond the belief that the glory of a nation is found in its prowess in war, not its peaceful prosperity, she may become, as a manufacturing state, more prosperous and truly influential than at any period of her former existence.

The influence of the war, also, in favor of religious liberty, and the progress of that freedom of religious worship which has so long been withheld in France, cannot but be beneficial. The war had its origin in part, and in great part, in the machinations of Jesuit managers to humble Prussia as the great Protestant power of the Continent, and to place upon the throne of France a ruler fully committed to reaction, to religious persecution, and to the enforcement of the Roman *Concordat*. It closes with Prussia at the head of the German Confederation, more powerful and influential than ever before, and France humbled, but more hostile than ever she was in the past to the sway of a despot, or the intolerance of Rome. The war has shown France the evils of fraud, corruption, and deception. It has made her citizens a sadder but a wiser people; and with the disappearance of their former frivolity and thoughtlessness, and the inordinate conceit which has marred their character, we may well hope there will come a disposition to profounder and more serious thought, a greater earnestness of purpose, and a higher moral principle. If this result shall follow, we may rejoice in the belief that the present misfortunes of that fair land have worked out for her greater blessings than any material prosperity could have done, and that all Europe, and the world, will participate with her in the benefits which have come to her from adversity.

To nations, as to individuals, there should, and generally does come, in seasons of disaster, that penitence for past errors and that desire to begin a new and better national life, which causes these afflictions to be subsequently recognized as "blessings in disguise," and as having wrought out a higher and nobler national destiny.

But if, alas! these bitter lessons should all be lost, and France, despite her heavy burdens and her sad experiences, become again what she was under the Empire—vain, thoughtless, frivolous, and corrupt——

No! no! we have not the heart to portray, or the words to describe, the ruin which must come upon a nation so often and so terribly admonished, if it does not heed the warnings it has received.

APPENDIX.

PHILANTHROPY OF THE WAR.

IT is not so widely known as it should be, that, at the close of our war, and before the short war of 1866 between Prussia and Austria, an International Sanitary Commission was organized in Central Europe, mainly through the efforts of Rev. Dr. Bellows and some other members of the United States Sanitary Commission, M. Aug. Laugel, of Paris, and some prominent and philanthropic citizens of Switzerland and Prussia.

This organization bore good fruit in the war of 1866, and secured from France, Prussia, Austria, Switzerland, and Italy, a pledge that the badge and flag of its members—a red cross on a white ground—should be protected at all times on the field.

No sooner was war declared, in the summer of 1870, than the Commission organized its branches and Ambulance Corps in both countries, and made large preparation for the fierce battles which were soon to come. In France, the Empress patronized and aided the Commission in their work; but the most efficient assistance they received was from American and British citizens, who organized Ambulance Corps, and contributed largely to the fund for supplies. Dr. Evans, who had rendered good service to our Sanitary Commission during our war, was at the head of the American movement. In Germany, the Queen and Princesses were all active in the promotion of this good work, and the King and Crown-Prince aided it by their influence and authority. Queen Augusta took charge of the hospitals at Berlin; the Crown-

Princess Victoria of those at Frankfort; Princess Alice of Hesse of those at Darmstadt; the Grand Duchess Louise of Baden of those at Carlsruhe; and the Crown-Princess Caroline of Saxony of those at Homburg.

The Grand Duchess of Mecklenburg-Schwerin, a sister of the German Emperor, was not behind her royal sisters and cousins in her devotion to the wounded. She had a large hospital for them under her own special charge, and was ably assisted in its care, as well as in its organization, by an American lady, Miss Clara Barton, whose services to the sick and wounded, and to the dead soldiers of our own civil war, will ever be held in grateful remembrance. Other American ladies who had been active and useful in our war, also lent a helping hand in this good work; among the number, Miss Safford, so well remembered by our soldiers as the "Cairo Angel," Mrs. Evans, &c., &c.

There was need of their best efforts: for, before the close of the war, there were of the two armies almost half a million sick and wounded. Ambulance Corps were organized, with their superintendents and attendants, in both France and Germany; and in both countries many English and German gentlemen and ladies enlisted, and the large sums contributed from America and England were faithfully and carefully expended, and the supplies distributed. Rev. Dr. Bellows gave to the French Sanitary Corps the benefit of his large experience and great administrative ability, and was ably seconded by Dr. Evans, of Paris, Messrs. Sykes, Swinburne, Johnstone, and other American gentlemen and ladies who had been for some time residents of that city. These generous philanthropists continued their devotion to their work till the close of the war, and many of them endured great hardship and suffering, and, as was often the case in our war, the overtasked body, when the terrible strain was over, sank from exhaustion.

Many of the wealthy citizens of France vied with the German princes in the largeness of their gifts to the suffering soldiers, not only offering large sums of money, but giving up their chateaus and castles for hospitals for the sick and wounded. Notable among these was the Count Henri de Chambord, the representative of the elder Bourbon line, and a claimant for the French throne. His extensive chateau,

AUGUSTA
EUGENIE
VICTORIA v. PREUSSEN
ALICE v. HESSEN
CAROLINE v. SACHSEN
LOUISE v. BADEN

amply furnished, and provided with several hundred beds, was placed at the service of the Government for the wounded French soldiers.

Large contributions were made to the sanitary funds of both countries by the people of the United States and of Great Britain. It was estimated that nearly $1,500,000 was sent from the United States to Germany, a considerable portion of it, of course, from citizens of German birth or family. To France the amount was not so large, but was estimated at $500,000 before the close of the war; and subsequently, on the representation of the famine and suffering in those portions of France which had been traversed by the armies of the two nations, a sum of more than $200,000 was made up and sent to relieve the suffering.

In consequence of the surrenders at Sedan, Strasbourg, and Metz, and those of the smaller fortified towns, as well as the great number of prisoners, wounded and unwounded, taken in the frequent engagements and retreats of the French armies, many thousands of the French sick and wounded fell into German hands; and the testimony of these to the tender care of their captors for their needs is almost uniform, the few exceptions being due either to ignorance or the misconduct of the patients themselves. The Zouaves and Turcos in some instances manifested a brutal and cruel temper, and returned injuries and violence for the kindness they received. Of the few wounded Germans who fell into the hands of the French, some complained of harsh treatment and cruelty; but this was, doubtless, generally the result of ignorance or penury, rather than of intentional malice, though some of the cases required a broad mantle of charity to cover them.

The record of the International Sanitary Commission and its branches during this war is the one bright spot in the midst of the horrors of war. There was also an impromptu organization, something like the Christian Commission in our war, which did a vast deal of good in the distribution of portions of the Scriptures, and moral and religious periodicals, tracts, and books among the soldiers. It was not so thoroughly organized, or prepared for so extensive and general a work, as the Christian Commission, but it supplied to the soldiers who could read, much literature which was both instructive and profitable.

APPENDIX II.

M. LOUIS ADOLPHE THIERS,

President of the French Provisional Government of February, 1871.

THE venerable statesman who was chosen in February, 1871, to guide the helm of State in France, at a time when she was in the condition of greatest peril, has been the subject of more vicissitudes and changes, and has kept up a stouter heart and a more constant faith in the future, than any other public man in France.

LOUIS ADOLPHE THIERS was born in Marseilles, April 16th, 1797. His father was a large manufacturer of cloths, and was ruined by the Revolution. His mother was from the illustrious family of Chénier, and her brothers undertook the education of the young Louis Adolphe, who early manifested remarkable abilities. He entered the Lyceum (collegiate school) of Marseilles at the early age of nine years, and at eighteen graduated with the highest distinction. He studied law at Aix, and was admitted to the bar in 1820, but soon became convinced that, for him, the path to distinction lay in politics and literature rather than in the practice of the law. The year of his admission to the bar he contended for a prize offered by the Academy of Aix for the best memoir of the Marquis de Vauvenargues, a French moral philosopher and author, who had been a native and citizen of Aix. His memoir was found to be the best; but the judges, being Royalists, and regarding young Thiers as a Jacobin, postponed their decision to the next year, to give opportunity for further competition, making the same topic the subject for the next annual prize also. M. Thiers revenged himself for this injustice in a characteristic way. He sent in his manuscript the next year without change, but wrote another memoir of Vauvenargues in different style, which he dated and mailed from Paris, for the new prize; and, when the decision was made, received both prizes.

In September, 1821, he went with his faithful friend and classmate, M. Mignet, to Paris, to seek his fortune. Both were poor and without powerful friends, and it was at the most reactionary period of the Bourbon Restoration. They worked hard for a bare subsistence, and at first found but slight encouragement. At length, just at the close of the year, Thiers, through the influence of the great Liberal orator, Manuel, obtained a subordinate situation on the staff of the *Constitutionnel*, where his brilliant talents soon secured his advancement. His skill in political discussion, his wide range of general knowledge, his extraordinary memory, and his complete fearlessness, made him invaluable to the paper, which was the principal organ of the Liberal party. He was not less brilliant as an art-critic than as a political writer, and his dramatic criticisms attracted attention in all quarters. A narrative of a short tour in the Pyrenees and the south of France, published in the columns of the *Constitutionnel* in 1824, and subsequently issued in a volume, gave him some additional reputation. It is not surprising, then, that, before the close of 1823, he was in receipt of a liberal share of the profits of the paper which he had already so greatly benefited by his ability as a writer. His literary activity was even beyond the needs of the *Constitutionnel*, and he added to his labors there the editing of *The Historic Tablets*, a magazine of great merit, in which Mignet and some of his other friends were his collaborators.

He went into society considerably at this time, and one of his friends thus describes his personal appearance: "The smallness of his stature, the extreme plainness of his features, which were half hidden under an enormous pair of spectacles, his peculiar pronunciation, and his singular habit of constantly shrugging his shoulders, and dancing (or, as a New Englander would say, *tetering*) at every word, and an absolute lack of the ordinary graces of manner, made him appear a being apart from all others. But when he spoke, you could not refrain from admiring his wit and vivacity, the glow of his Oriental imagination, and the vastness of his attainments. Nothing seemed to be foreign to him; he was equally at home in science, literature, and art; and, turning from the most brilliant literary improvisation, he would discuss, the next moment, with equal fulness of knowledge and soundness of judgment, questions of finance, political economy, war, or political action. He was a great favorite, at this period, with Talleyrand, and the other eminent men of the Opposition."

Young as he was, he had already commenced the great literary labor of his life, his " History of the French Revolution," the plan of which he subsequently expanded to include the history of the Consulate and the Empire, the Restoration, and the Monarchy of July (the reign of Louis Philippe). The "History of the French Revolution" appeared complete in 1827, in ten octavo volumes; and though, in subsequent editions, some crudities were removed, and there was occasionally a substitution of a maturer style of thought and a sounder judgment, yet it was, in its first edition, one of the most remarkable works of the century. We miss the stateliness of style of Chateaubriand, Lamartine, and Martin; but in its profound knowledge and comprehension of the whole subject, the rapid march of the narrative, its intensely dramatic character, its admirable clearness, and its evident sympathy with Republican freedom—a sympathy which it required some courage to avow under the administration of a Government so despotic as that of the Restoration—it has not been surpassed in modern times.

After its publication, M. Thiers entertained a project for writing a general history, and resolved to prepare himself for it by an extensive tour of travel. He had made all his arrangements, even to securing a passage for a voyage round the world, in August, 1829, when the Polignac Ministry was organized, and he resolved to remain at home to do battle against that Cabinet, which daily advanced toward an absolute despotism.

Feeling that the old methods and weapons of warfare of the *Constitutionnel* were not sufficient for a strife which had for its ultimate purpose the establishment of liberal opinions and government, M. Thiers founded, with his friends Mignet and Armand Carrel, the *National*, of which each in turn, for a year, was to be editor-in-chief. M. Thiers's turn came first, and then began a struggle in which he put himself at once at the head of the Liberal party, or Young France, as it was called.

The Polignac Ministry had for its object the subversion of the

French charter; the *National* was devoted to its maintenance, even at the cost of the overthrow of the Bourbon dynasty. Nothing could exceed its fearlessness; and when, after a succession of bold and uncompromising articles, one of them bearing the title "The King reigns, but he does not govern," the *National* announced the candidature of the Duke of Orleans (Louis Philippe) for the throne, the Bourbon Government, exasperated beyond measure, prosecuted the paper, and condemned it to pay a heavy fine. Thiers had so fully won the confidence of the people, that a subscription was promptly started, which soon raised the amount of the fine, and letters of sympathy poured in upon him by thousands. From this time forward the paper assumed a defiant attitude, and day after day demanded of the Government why it did not consummate its *coup d'état*. The Government, aware that it was treading on dangerous ground, and fearing a revolution, hesitated long, but finally, on the 20th of July, issued its decrees, one of which suppressed the *National*. A protest was at once drawn up and signed by all the Liberal leaders and journalists; and when the police officers came to take possession of the office of the paper and prevent its further publication, M. Thiers answered that he should yield only to violence. The Bourbons were too late; the Revolution of July had already begun, and on the 31st of July the Bourbon King and his Ministry were in exile, and Louis Philippe Lieutenant-General of the kingdom, and, ten days later, proclaimed King of the French. The active part which M. Thiers had taken in accomplishing this revolution indicated the propriety of making him a member of the Government. He was assigned to a position in connection with the finances. He was promoted in this department four months later, under the Lafitte Ministry. He was at the same time a member of the Chamber of Deputies from the College of Aix, and Counsellor of State. The next four months he was really, though not nominally, Financial Minister, and showed remarkable aptitude for the position.

On the fall of the Lafitte Ministry he withdrew from office, and made a visit to the south of France. In 1832 he was called into the Cabinet as Minister of the Interior, and three months later was transferred to the post of Minister of Commerce and Public Works. In this position he did much to beautify and adorn Paris, and to promote a harmony of feeling throughout the nation. At his direction the statue of Napoleon was replaced upon his column. The *Arc de l'Étoile* and the palace of the quay d'Orsay were erected, the Madeleine restored, and new fountains, boulevards, and canals were constructed. In 1834 he was again Minister of the Interior, and remained in power, though with occasional attempts at withdrawal, in consequence of the rivalry between M. Guizot and himself, until January, 1836, when he resigned. In February, 1836, he was made Premier of a new Cabinet, and Minister of Foreign Affairs, but resigned in August following. In 1834 he had been elected a Member of the French Academy. A year of travel in Italy and two years of opposition in the Chamber of Deputies followed, and in March, 1840, he was again Premier, and Minister of Foreign Affairs; but, owing to disagreement with the King on some matters of policy, and the rivalry of Guizot, he resigned in October following. For the following seven years, though in the Opposition, M. Thiers did not devote so much time as previously to politics, but set himself diligently to the work of preparing his great history of the "Consulate and Empire." He travelled extensively over the ground of Napoleon's triumphs and defeats, and collected material from all sources in great abundance. The first two volumes appeared in 1845, and the others (there are twenty in all) at occasional intervals up to 1862. The work was crowned by the French Academy in 1861, and received the prize of 20,000 francs ($4,000); but the prize was returned to the Academy by M. Thiers, who made it the foundation of a new prize to be called by his name. On the approach of the Revolution of February, 1848, M. Thiers avowed himself in favor of it. He reproached the Government of Louis Philippe with its weakness and cowardice, and its lack of a definite policy, and acknowledged his conviction that another revolution was needful, and that the career of royalty was completed. Just at the crisis, the King sent for him to form a new Ministry with Odillon Barrot, but it was too late to accomplish anything. Though distrusted by the more radical Republican leaders, he soon conquered for himself a position, and, as the advocate of the great middle class in the Constituent Assembly and the National Assembly, he became alike the foe of radical measures and of all reactionary tendencies. He sustained Cavaignac, acquiesced in the election of Louis Napoleon as Prince-President, though he had at first opposed it, predicted the *coup d'état* long before its occurrence, was arrested at the time (December 2d, 1851), banished to Frankfort, but in the following August was, without any application on his part, notified that he would be permitted to return to Paris. He did return, and for eleven years lived in retirement, occasionally travelling in other countries, and devoting himself sedulously to literary and art studies. In 1863 he was elected to the *Corps Législatif* from one of the districts of Paris, notwithstanding the strenuous opposition of the Government, and took a decided position in opposition to the Government. In 1866, after the Austro-Prussian war, he reviewed the course of the French Government in a speech replete with his old fire, closing with the memorable words, "There remain no more errors to be committed." His thorough knowledge of the administration of Government, his fearlessness, and the fierceness of his invective, rendered him a terror to the imperial Government; and when he was again a candidate for election to the *Corps Législatif*, in May, 1867, they made great efforts to defeat him, but in vain.

The Ollivier Ministry of January 2d, 1870, was composed mainly of his personal friends, and at first he seemed disposed to treat it with some kindness, interposing in its behalf when it was too severely harassed by the radical Republicans; but when Ollivier became merely the mouth-piece of Napoleonic ideas, Thiers applied the lash of his invective unsparingly. When the war was announced, he opposed it vehemently, and at no inconsiderable personal peril; predicted disaster to France from it, and refused to vote aid for it. After Sedan, he was one of the most active of the Opposition in aiding in arrangement for a Provisional Government, and visited most of the courts of Europe to interest them in intervening for a peace; and though his mission had not the success he must have hoped for, yet it undoubtedly had some influence in modifying the terms of the final treaty. The National Assembly, which met at Bordeaux according to the armistice, elected him, on the 19th of February, Provisional President of France, with power to select his own Cabinet. In the negotiation of the treaty which followed, as well as in his counsels to the Assembly and to the French people, he manifested that strong, clear common sense which has ever been one of his most marked characteristics.

While not devoid of faults, M. Thiers is eminently a patriot. He believes in France, and seeks her interests first and last. He has been charged with fickleness, but his modifications of his views, when there are changed conditions of affairs, is rather an indication of sound judgment than of fickleness. As statesman, historian, legislator, diplomatist, and patriot, M. Adolphe Thiers has few equals, and no superiors, in France to-day.